GURDJIEFF

GURDJIEFF

*An Introduction to
His Life and Ideas*

John Shirley

JEREMY P. TARCHER / PENGUIN

A MEMBER OF PENGUIN GROUP (USA) INC.

NEW YORK

The Way of Hermes: New Translations of The Corpus Hermeticum and The Definitions of Hermes Trismegistus to Asclepius, translated by Clement Salaman, Dorine van Oyen, William D. Wharton, and Jean-Pierre Mahé, is quoted by permission of Inner Traditions, Bear and Company. Translations copyright © 2000 by Inner Traditions.

Permission to quote from Jeanne de Salzmann granted by Stephen Grant, for the heirs of Jeanne de Salzmann.

Bibliographic material for sources quoted can be found in Appendix A.

Most Tarcher/Penguin books are available at special quantity discounts for bulk purchase for sales promotions, premiums, fund-raising, and educational needs. Special books or book excerpts also can be created to fit specific needs. For details, write Penguin Group (USA) Inc. Special Markets, 375 Hudson Street, New York, NY 10014.

Jeremy P. Tarcher/Penguin
a member of
Penguin Group (USA) Inc.
375 Hudson Street
New York, NY 10014
www.penguin.com

Library of Congress Cataloging-in-Publication Data

Shirley, John, date.
Gurdjieff : an introduction to his life and ideas / John Shirley.
p.   cm.
Includes bibliographical references and index.
ISBN 1-58542-287-8
1. Gurdjieff, Georges Ivanovitch, 1872–1949.   I. Title.
BP605.G94G877   2004   2003061375
197—dc22
[B]

Printed in the United States of America
1   3   5   7   9   10   8   6   4   2

This book is printed on acid-free paper. ∞

Book design by Lovedog Studio

Very special thanks to Jacob Needleman

Very distinctive thanks to Mitch Horowitz

Lots of large thanks to Daniel Duncan

Unique thanks to Richard Smoley

*Very particular gratitude to Chuck St. John
for help on several levels*

*Vast gratitude also to Walter Driscoll, Micky Shirley,
Richard Sandor, and Mitch Ryan*

Thanks to Barry Schoor

AND

*Special thanks and credit to Paula Guran for
digital rendering of diagrams*

There is a thousand times more value even in polishing the floor as it should be done than in writing twenty books.

—G. I. GURDJIEFF

This book is dedicated to the memory of those who have now passed on, who inspired this book either directly or through their pupils. I met only a few of them, and only briefly, but somehow I feel all these people were part of the current of inspiration that energized this book.

Jeanne de Salzmann

John Pentland

William Segal

Michel de Salzmann

A. L. Staveley

David Langmuir

CONTENTS

Foreword   1

ONE   Where We're At and Where We Wish to Be   11

TWO   Meeting a Remarkable Man   41

THREE   The Search Begun   67

FOUR   In Search of the Miraculous   111

FIVE   Three Mirages: Progress, Evolution, and Unity   139

SIX   Finland and the Miraculous; The Caucasus
         and Revolutionary Psychosis   167

SEVEN   Beelzebub in France and America;
         G. I. Gurdjieff Beyond   205

EIGHT   "Gurdjieff, *Not* Will Die!"   271

APPENDIX A   Farther up the Octave:
              Bibliographical Suggestions   277

APPENDIX B   Are We "Food for the Moon"?   287

APPENDIX C   The Octave and the Ray of Creation—
              and Theoretical Physics   289

Index   293

GURDJIEFF

FOREWORD

WHY THIS BOOK, PARTICULARLY, EH?

First, why this book at all? Besides the usual scruffy personal reasons an author writes a book, why write an introductory volume on G. I. Gurdjieff now?

There is, it seems to me, a certain urgency, at least a need, for an updated, compact, straightforward book on Gurdjieff for the general public. The "terror of the situation," in Gurdjieff's phrase, is with us intensely in the twenty-first century. We feel real fear when we contemplate humanity's unconsciousness of its own violence, the brutality it enacts while sleepwalking. This has always been with us, of course—every generation has its own crises—but some feel we're reaching a kind of social critical mass. It may indeed be only the latest of many social flashpoints; but it's not impossible that the fatal chain reaction has already begun. The human world always has been in danger; it might be in greater danger now than ever before, due to the various risks accompanying globalization, and the ever-increasing technology of war. If the danger is greater now, then the need for people to understand themselves is greater, too—on every level.

The lifestyle of the twenty-first century is like a powerful giant who won't be denied: the laser-sharp efficiency of the entertainment media and modern demands on our time make it harder than ever to find the real meaning at the core of life. As Professor Jacob Needleman has it, in his book *Time and the Soul*:

> In fact, everything we call "progress" is actually measured by the degree to which it enables us to conduct ourselves without the need to bring thought into conscious relationship with movement or feeling. We measure progress by the automaticity by which we are enabled to conduct our lives. Even thinking, or what is called "thinking," is being performed more and more by machines. These machines are supposed to liberate us—but for what?

Are machines liberating us only so we can retreat into the lethargy of digital entertainment, within a technological womb?

It doesn't matter *when* you're reading this, since the "terror of the situation" is perennial. Gurdjieff's teaching, showing humanity how it is asleep—trapped in interlocking patterns of individual neurosis and collective psychosis—is always a teaching urgently needed.

G. I. Gurdjieff's intention, after all, was to begin something truly new (at least, new to modern man), to ring a bell whose tolling would wake others. Such people would then take up the same reverberation, conduct the same current, eventually waking up enough people to change the course of history. But the process comes about through individuals, and most people are struggling to awaken for their own sakes first. They struggle to awaken for the benefit of their souls. The need to waken, the serious hunger to waken, is vital.

Certainly there exist more substantive, knowledgeable books on Gurdjieff's ideas than this could ever be: apart from Gurdjieff's own works, there is, for example, *In Search of the Miraculous: Frag-*

ments of an Unknown Teaching by P. D. Ouspensky. But it seems to me that in this harried, media-saturated age, an introductory book is called for, a straightforward book that speaks with at least a respectable accuracy on the subject; a book that might open a door, for some readers, to a deeper study, and even real hope.

AND WHAT OF MR. GURDJIEFF HIMSELF . . . ?

Born in Russian Armenia, probably in 1866 (conflicting dates have been offered), his father Greek, his mother Armenian, the young man later known as George Ivanovich Gurdjieff set out to bring to light the secrets of life and death.

Some say he succeeded, by the time of his death in Paris in 1949. Certainly he searched for decades through the most resistant topography of the Middle East and Asia; from Afghanistan to Tibet and India; from Turkey to Africa. He found his way to remote monasteries others had written off as mere legend; to secretive spiritual masters and to the mastery of spiritual secrets.

To pay for his quest he found it necessary to be variously an impromptu entrepreneur, a professional hypnotist, an importer of exotic rugs, even, at least once, a performing "fakir"; he endured a host of exotic diseases, returning home to recover from illnesses that felled many another man and discouraged even more. Yet his will to find out the truth, his *wish,* carried him through these rigors, past "power-possessing men" bristling with weapons, through civil wars, and eventually through the chaos of the Russian Revolution. He was shot, he tells us, three times—and saw significance in the fact that all were stray bullets.

Many of the details of his early history and his quest are difficult to document, and thus arguable. What is certain is that Gurdjieff and his philosophy hit the inquirer like an unexpected icy shower, at the very least leaving an unforgettable impression: a welcome shock of wakefulness.

When Gurdjieff set out to teach what he had learned, he laid out a system that reinterpreted man's most fundamental dilemmas. He stunned the mathematician and metaphysical philosopher P. D. Ouspensky, among others, with a host of revelations, including: a detailed cosmology; a depth psychology; a new understanding of the nature of consciousness; a historical revisionism that includes a radical and unprecedented approach to understanding human history and the annals of metaphysics; a specialized music integrated with a theory of the relationship of octaves to man and the cosmos; an intricate choreography of spiritually instructive dance; specific methodologies for increasing consciousness and harmonizing inner disunity; and a breathlessly timely fusion of Western scientific method with the "wisdom of the East." Here is Ouspensky's *In Search of the Miraculous*: "I was most of all interested in the *connectedness* of everything he said. I already felt that his ideas were not detached from one another, as all philosophical and scientific ideas are, but made one whole, of which, as yet, I saw only some of the pieces."

Gurdjieff said that there were basically three Ways for the growth and maintenance of a soul: the *way of the yogi,* that of the mind; the *way of the monk,* that of the heart; and the *way of the fakir,* emphasizing the body. Gurdjieff offered another way he sometimes called "a fourth way," encompassing a version of the three other ways and new methods as well.

And as we will see, Gurdjieff was also the master of a teaching praxis that incorporated satire and an unnerving exposure of everything false in his students. He could camouflage himself as an ordinary man, when he chose, exchanging the usual pleasantries, playing the expected social games, acting a part. In one case a notorious charlatan came nosing around a place where Gurdjieff sold carpets, the charlatan claiming he wanted to be a student, but Gurdjieff, knowing the man for a rascal, played the part of a muddled, vapid shopkeeper, continuously trying to sell the man a carpet; the man went away assuming that the person who had sent him there had been playing a joke on him. With students, one of Gurdjieff's methods was to refuse, at times, to acknowledge the usual set of preprogrammed reactions, to discard niceties, superficial amenities, responding instead with a kind of lucid, watchful silence, or a piercing question that made irrelevant all the automatic reactions the student would normally use: for we each of us have a store of these mindless responses that help keep us comfortably asleep in our dealings with others. Students would then find themselves entering a place where automatic and false responses were meaningless—as one had no other responses to hand, all that was left was a feeling of falling into the void of one's own nonbeing, the insight into one's own falseness. And perhaps, out of that initial disorientation, the student caught a glimpse of freedom. Variations of this method have been picked up on by others—one of many areas in which Gurdjieff had been enormously influential.

Indeed, few teachers of the esoteric, in modern times, have influenced so many so deeply and so broadly as G. I. Gurdjieff. One thinks of such seminal figures as the critic, editor, and essayist A. R. Orage, the novelist Henry Miller, the architect Frank Lloyd Wright, the playwright J. B. Priestley, the author Jean Toomer, the composer Thomas de Hartmann, the author Katherine Mansfield, the spiritual teacher Ram Dass, the author Kathryn Hulme, the theatrical innovators Alexandre de Salzmann and Peter Brook, the Sufi teacher Idries Shah, the scientific theorist P. D. Ouspensky, and such figures as Gorham Munson, René Daumal, and Timothy Leary; and of contemporary authors such as Colin Wilson, Charles Tart, Ravi Ravindra, Michael Murphy, Jacob Needleman, and

Robert Anton Wilson. All have acknowledged Gurdjieff. Leary, for example (in a letter to Robert Anton Wilson), said of Gurdjieff: "I resonate to his wisdom more than anyone else's."★ Leary's interest in Gurdjieff is perhaps ironic, since Gurdjieff did not recommend drugs as a path to spiritual growth—quite the contrary.

In his preface to Fritz Peters's memoir *My Journey with a Mystic,* Henry Miller called Gurdjieff "a perpetual surprise . . . a most unusual human being, a man who has been called a Master, a Guru, a Teacher, everything but a Saint. . . . At times he reached sublime heights."

Gurdjieff influenced a generation of seekers and, sometimes, "spiritual" impresarios who have utilized—and often distorted—aspects of his teaching. Confused, almost unrecognizable dilutions of Gurdjieff's teaching have been concocted by various "self-help" groups, purveyors of seminars, certain modern heavily franchised "religions," and even cults. Oddball interpretations of his nine-pointed enneagram find their way into books on "personality analysis."

More congenially, Gurdjieff's teaching influenced the pop singers Peter Murphy and Kate Bush, King Crimson composer Robert Fripp, and modern jazz legend Keith Jarrett. The movie *Groundhog Day* seems a whimsical parable about Gurdjieffian self-observation and Ouspenskyan "eternal recurrence." There is even a musical about Gurdjieff: John Maxwell Taylor's *Crazy Wisdom: the Life and Legend of Gurdjieff.* Many manifestations of Gurdjieff's presence are but distant echoes.

As for Gurdjieff online, I'm aware of exactly *one* really well-informed Gurdjieff website, www.gurdjieff.org.

The primary school that Gurdjieff inaugurated, now called the

★*Cosmic Trigger* by Robert Anton Wilson.

Gurdjieff Foundation, walks the line between openness and the traditional inconspicuity of an esoteric school. On the openness side, Jeanne de Salzmann collaborated with the influential film and stage director Peter Brook on a movie of Gurdjieff's early life, adapting Gurdjieff's own semiautobiography, *Meetings with Remarkable Men.* The Gurdjieff Foundation occasionally publishes or otherwise promulgates books that examine Gurdjieff's life, ideas, and methods.

It should be noted that some of the most vital Gurdjieffian teachings are given only orally, through the Gurdjieff Foundation or in the better spinoff groups, like the late A. L. Staveley's Two Rivers Farm, in Aurora, Oregon, or the Nyland groups, which are scattered around the U.S.

I won't be giving out much about the methods taught at such places. I will be speaking in general terms, checked in part by the sharp limitation of my own understanding. It is a teaching that is easily misunderstood and misused—hence those who cherish it also protect it.

If anything is called for, in discussing G. I. Gurdjieff, it is a kind of *soundness*. His ideas have powerful effects on people; his wake through the world sent out powerful ripples. Glib constructions crumble before this conceptual tsunami.

Understanding and conveying metaphysical ideas of any real power is always a daunting task. It may be that the more difficult a teaching is, the more one suspects one is close to authenticity. Facile "truth" deserves its quotation marks. Still, I hope to do an honorable job of it.

On one level, Gurdjieff's teaching is conceptually fairly straightforward, even unsentimentally methodical—but there is no such thing as "on one level" with Gurdjieff. Every particular Gurdjieffian idea seems to resonate with the whole of his ideas—and with the whole of esoteric and spiritual philosophy, from Kaballah to Hermeticism to Vedanta; even those Gurdjieffian notions that come to us fragmentarily are, as Ouspensky noticed, self-evidently part of something larger, as a note implies a scale.

I have just used the term "Gurdjieff's teaching," but this book is subtitled *An Introduction to His Life and Ideas.* It would have been more usual, in any other tradition, to use the term *Teaching* instead of *Ideas,* in that title, but in the Gurdjieff Work the tendency is to use the term *ideas* in referring to what he brought us, and for good reason. A *teaching,* too often, is presented as being something one must mindlessly, passively ingest. *Ideas,* on the other hand, has a provisional, skeptical sound to it—it implies that these are concepts that will be *tested.* They will be *explored* by those who use them, and—as Gurdjieff himself insisted—can be subjected to rigorous confirmatory experiment to see if they are true. Most of them, anyway, can be investigated, in this way—as ideas.

Gurdjieff's ideas are arguably the esoteric of the esoteric. I don't mean they're very obscure—they're not esoteric in the sense of "obscure." I am suggesting that they may provide something of the more deeply concealed actuality underlying what is usually sold to us as "esoteric" or "spiritual."

Michel de Salzmann warns us that the capacity to understand esoteric ideas "involves an experiential and practical work which, little by little, gives knowledge the taste of *wisdom.* . . . From a certain point of view, esotericism has never really been hidden; it is simply invisible. It is self protected by nature, since it cannot be truly grasped without an adequate inner preparation."✲

Hence, books like this one can offer only a distant approach to

---

✲"Footnote to the Gurdjieff Literature," by Michel de Salzmann. In *Gurdjieff: An Annotated Bibliography,* edited by Walter Driscoll.

some esoteric truths. I do hope to convey, in outline, the critical points of what is publicly known of G. I. Gurdjieff's life; to provide at least some fresh perspective on Gurdjieff as a man and as a teacher; to collate together, in the service of that perspective, the insights of a few of the commentators who worked with him that have not before been organized into one book; and to offer a glimpse of his ideas—perhaps, now and then, even a taste of them. Within those parameters, I hope to write about G. I. Gurdjieff with authenticity, and to do so requires sincerity.

Webster's New World Dictionary defines *sincere,* first, as honest and trustworthy; second it offers "being the same in actual character as in outward appearance." Interestingly, the third, "archaic" definition is "not adulterated"; hence the intriguing old phrase "sincere wine." This is suggestive of unity, of completeness—which further suggests connectivity with something greater that confirms its relative "rightness."

A man or woman struggling for authenticity opens one shutter of a multishuttered lantern. The small light from that lantern provides some measure of insight.

What little light I have, I will share, because I'm frightened by the gathering darkness.

ONE

WHERE WE'RE AT
AND WHERE
WE WISH TO BE

Thus, the everyday life of man goes by with his real *I* asleep, and the first obstacle to the awakening of this real *I*, which is the beginning of his possible evolution, is that he does not see this sleep.

—Jean Vaysse, *Toward Awakening:*
An Approach to the Teaching Left by Gurdjieff

I remember it vividly . . .

When I was a rather lonely boy living in a rural area, I could usually count on Nature to lift me from my self-pity and sadness. On certain rare occasions, the experience was especially powerful.

I would set out into the fields, conscious that if I was willing to climb pasture fences I could go pretty much any way I wanted until my energy or courage failed me. The sheer *openness* of the world, then, was intoxicating. I felt freed, for a while; I was an explorer, in such moments, and the world seemed charged with possibilities. It was as if in moving through the world, in active participation with it, I was like a magnet turning in a motor: electricity passed through me and I generated more in my turn. Something flowed from the world to me and back again. And at such times there was nothing more than *now*, the eternal present, so long as I remained in that state. Even my senses were more acute than normal. I can still smell those bracing autumn fields now, and feel the rising mist on my cheeks and hands . . .

Yet there is so very much that has happened to me in life since that I do not remember as well as those moments in the pastures. Memories that should be consequential are now recalled only blurrily—yet they happened far more recently.

I believe that I remember those vivid boyhood moments because I was a little more conscious on those occasions than I was, later, on those half-remembered adult occasions. My boyhood experience of "awake-ness" was only a little of what is possible, but once one has had such an experience, one finds oneself wondering why it doesn't happen more often.

And the questions follow: How awake *are* we, really? Is consciousness relative?

Carl Jung once said he suspected that we exist after death as much as we were truly conscious in life. I suspect that in any afterlife I might experience, those moments in childhood will go with me, will be part of my being, if any experience is, while the blurry moments of an unconscious adulthood will not survive.

Not long ago, driving to San Francisco, I was stuck in traffic on the Bay Bridge with nothing better to do than listen to someone on the radio: there was an NPR interview with a fellow who'd been in prison for some time in South Africa. He said that for some years he'd been in a part of the prison where he couldn't see out a window, couldn't see more than 20 feet in any direction. Every-

thing there was either gray or dull brown, including clothing. Day
after day, month after month, there were no colors but those two.
Bright colors were so rare that after two years, if a brightly colored
thread was blown in on the wind to fall, say, onto a guard's uniform,
the sight of it struck like a thunderbolt. A mere thread was almost
overwhelming—because of its color alone. He said that for relatively sensitive people, prison changed one's perspective on the outside world in many ways. After a while, in prison, one becomes a
kind of zombie to survive. But once released, he said, the riot of
colors and the sudden freedoms are startling, and the world seems
overwhelming in its profusion of shapes and possibilities—you are
shocked by this searing variety, shocked into waking up, into *seeing
things you didn't see prior to prison.* Ordinary people of the outside
world now seemed, he said, like zombies themselves. All this richness was around them that they didn't see. They were also asleep,
said the ex-prisoner, with respect to what he called the "moral
atmosphere" of life outside prison. I think he meant the richness of
moral possibility, the awakening to the sense that one could go this
way, one could go that way—like the boy I was in that wide-open
field—one could do so many things. That is, there are so many
choices in the nonimprisoned world. And these choices all have
moral implications that we ordinarily never think about.

Sudden shocking release after a long term in prison made him
glimpse, for a time, human life as it typically is: mechanical,
asleep, blinded.

We're all aware that there are times when we're much more
here, when things are more vivid, when we feel more in place,
within ourselves and within the world. At such times we are literally more awake. These moments may come when we first see
our newly born baby; when we've survived some great danger;
or, more rarely, they may come inexplicably, "out of the blue"—
like a gift from above.

But such moments are fleeting. They leave us longing for more, and their absence brings about an intuition of *incompleteness* in our lives, and in our selves. Something doesn't measure up. It's a feeling that goes beyond general anxiety, beyond the worry that we could be more successful, "happier," smarter, more loved: some nameless recognition that we're called to something finer, to a way of living that could be—above all—more *meaningful*.

Oh yes! Meaning! Life doesn't quite seem meaningful, in the absence of that mysterious something. Yet in our hearts we know that meaning can't be merely a phantasm conjured up by the human imagination. When we hear music or take in fine art, or in moments of real connection to those we love, we intuit that there is a meaning to life. We can't articulate that meaning; we're not sure what it is. But we know it exists.

This perception of something missing extends to all of life, and is underscored by life's inequities, life's cruelties. A man paralyzed by a drunk driver is quite sure that something is missing from life— something more than just his mobility. There's no sense, no justice to what happened to him. Everything may now seem pointlessly accidental to him. People afflicted by wars and famines and diseases and persecution wonder what the meaning of it all is—they wonder if there isn't something more, something that could lift them up above the harsh, apparent randomness of existence.

Then there are those people who don't wait for life's difficulties— they create their own. They're self-destructive people, caught up, say, in gambling, drugs, sex addiction, alcoholism; or they're monomaniacally in pursuit of the shiny gimcracks of contemporary life, of sportscars and designer clothes and trophy mates to the exclusion of all else. Such people may trample marriages and their own lives. Another class of people looks for prestige in their professions to the exclusion of other experiences, until they become workaholics, just fancy beasts of burden. All of these people sense they're going in the wrong direction—but they can't seem to stop, though they're wracked with regrets. And they ask themselves *Why? Why* can't I control what I do?

But the case need not be so extreme. Everyone has probably had moments when they realized they were not really in control of their lives, when they saw themselves being mindlessly habitual, shouting at their children for no good reason; in a bad, selfish mood and not knowing why. "The good that I would do, I do not," said Saint Paul. And why, though we may have everything we need materially, do we all too often still feel empty, incomplete?

All people—and these examples represent, in some respect, all people—sense that something is missing, that there is a meaning that eludes them, a larger truth that would free them, if only they knew what it was.

Such musings are not new. The Old Testament's Job demands to know why so much suffering has been heaped on him. God eventually tells him that there is a vast scale of being between Job and the throne of heaven, and at Job's end of the scale, his place is acceptance and duty, and not defiance. God has his reasons, which are incomprehensible to Job.

But there were some in ancient times who held out for another order of insight into the nature of things. And they were deeply alienated from things as they are in this harsh world—they were practically obsessed with that feeling of discontinuity, of having been disinherited; of being Fallen.

They were called Gnostics. Some Gnostic sects denounced the "creator God," the "jealous God" of the Old Testament, the demiurge whom they called Ialdabaoth. These Gnostics believed it was this Old Testament tyrant who, in vanity and blindness, created the flawed world, somewhere "beneath" the notice of the Absolute, the highest Godhead. Seeing the consequent mess, the Sophia, the feminine principle of wisdom, struck sparks off the Higher and sent them into humanity, so that we might fan these sparks, so to say, into something like real spiritual flame; we might use their light to find our way past the Archons, the dark spiritual despots placed over us by grim old Ialdabaoth, back up to reunion with the Absolute. The process for returning to the Higher was the cultivation of *gnosis*: a combination of turning away from the false self—from egocentrism—with a special sort of *seeing* with all of one's being. That process opened up our receptivity, eliminated our perceptual dualism—"making the male female, the female male," as the Gnostic Gospel of Thomas has it—and eventually made us whole again. In our fragmentary states, the Gnostics taught, we're trapped in the fallen world; but whole and refined, we're capable of ascension and joyful reunion with the Absolute.

Egyptian myths speak of the shattered God who had to be restored to unity by a cosmic intermediary before he could return to the stars. Judaic Kabbalistic mysticism also speaks of "sparks," or subtle spiritual lights, that must be "harvested" by holy men so as to be restored to the great light that is God. This is "yechidut"—the unification of the higher and lower, a reconnecting of the material world and God, that only awakened human beings can hope to bring about.

Sometime between 400 and 600 B.C., a young prince named Gautama stole out of his father's palace, surveyed the world of men, and found it pervaded by nightmarish suffering. Struggling to understand how this came to be, he became known as the Buddha, the Awakened One. In a nutshell—or a curled bodhi leaf—he said human suffering was caused by uncontrolled desire; the burdensome weight of our desires causes us to be fallen from the bliss that is all around us yet somehow just beyond reach. He said that a kind of waking sleep keeps men from seeing the futility of desire, hides from them their real identity, keeps them from returning home to Nirvana, to their rightful place in a higher, finer, all-pervasive mind from which all originally sprang, a place where peace is finally found.

In Christian tradition, humanity is fallen from grace—driven from the garden of Eden—and returns to grace only through active surrender to an intermediary force, which in Christianity is represented by Jesus the Christ, the anointed of God, who acts as a kind of living bridge over which we can cross to the kingdom of heaven. Christian mystics like Origen (third century A.D.) perceived the tale of the fall of man in Genesis as an allegory of man's identification with desire, with his animal nature, or ego, distracting him from the freedom of *real I,* the higher, nonidentified self.

In the mysterious mystical classic the Corpus Hermeticum (or the Hermetica), written between the first and third centuries A.D., probably by Greco-Egyptian initiates in Alexandria, we are told that "all souls which wander around the whole cosmos, as if separate, are from a single soul, the soul of all . . . the [trapped] spirit, ignorant of itself, becomes a slave to monstrous and miserable bodies. It carries its body as a burden and does not command but is commanded."*

Similar patterns recur in legends and spiritual traditions from around the world. In every case there is a perception, expressed through the unique symbols of each tradition, that we're not where we should be—but that there is a Way to get where we ought to be. We feel that we're separated from a birthright, from another, grander home that, all along, has been rightly ours—if only we knew how to find it. We sometimes sense someone is reaching out to us from that higher place, trying to lift us up to it but requiring us to do our part in the ascension. God provides the wind, Augustine said, but man must raise the sails.

The Way of Hermes, translated by Clement Salaman, Dorine Van Oyen, William D. Wharton, and Jean-Pierre Mahé.

For many people, simply trying to behave according to the strict dictates of a conventional religion, along with the appropriate rituals and prayers, may be enough to set their minds at rest about "getting back" to God.

But others are called to something more. Others are inwardly stirred, tantalized, by some half-heard summons—like Gurdjieff, who said that even as a boy he was "gnawed by the worm of curiosity" and was later driven by this "gnawing worm" to a series of odysseys in order to find out: "What is true? [Is it] what is written in books and taught by my teachers, or the facts I am always running up against?"*

Like Gurdjieff, some of us must ask: what exactly do the ancient myths of creation and separation *mean*? What exactly is missing in us and what can we do to become complete, to reconnect, to penetrate that mystery that enfolds our vanished birthright?

What do we need to do to really understand our place in the cosmos? And what is required to become conscious and whole?

Great teachers, over the centuries, have offered their answers. They have provided particular paths; special Ways. But each era seems to require its own kind of spiritual teacher. Man in the modern era, simultaneously overconfident and utterly baffled, at least has developed one side of himself that has some practical value: scientific inquiry—the willingness to put the fog of superstition and mere imagination aside and, if there's a higher reality, to look for it unflinchingly through pure reason. Scientific reasoning is "Western" science and philosophy's means of inquiry into ultimate reality. But this approach seems incomplete. There is a kind of understanding that science can contribute to but not complete—we come to an abyss that calls for another kind of bridge, the kind of intuitive, inward-turned seeking characteristic of "Eastern" spiritual inquiry.

Meetings with Remarkable Men by Gurdjieff.

The modern era demands some teacher who can straddle the two hemispheres of inquiry; a teacher who encompasses both the analytic and intuitive, both the quantitative and qualitative.

G. I. Gurdjieff is the ideal candidate. He seems almost to have been sent—he may well have been sent—to provide just the requisite all-inclusive teaching.

Certainly, his teaching acknowledges who we are. He demands that we look squarely at what and where mankind is, before we go on to the means with which mankind can be more.

It's no secret that there is a connection between self-knowledge and the ability to grow as a person. Psychotherapy is, at least in principle, about discovering what makes you tick; about understanding your inward self. We've all heard stories of people who got some therapeutic insight into themselves that changed their lives. It doesn't happen often enough.

But if it can happen, if self-knowledge can change people, then isn't it a vibrant ray of light in a dark, brutal world? Suppose that there was a method that made it truly practicable, a Way that could be extended to a much deeper kind of self-knowledge? Couldn't it, eventually, change the whole world? If people are conscious enough to really see themselves, really understand themselves, they bring a finer, deeper state of mind to decision-making. They're less likely to act out of prejudice and less likely to act out on violent impulses.

To that end, the first thing we need to understand is the relativity, indeed the partial *absence,* of human consciousness.

JUST LOOK AT YOURSELF!

Before sketching G. I. Gurdjieff's early life, I'll look briefly at two of Gurdjieff's ideas about who we are—and who we aren't—to set the stage. Here's the Buddha, from the Dhammapada:

Among those unaware, comes the one aware;
Among the sleepers you'll also find the wakeful;
The one with great wisdom simply moves on.

Among the sleepers—as if the "one with great wisdom" is all alone in the world, one man awake, surrounded by sleepers. Calling Gautama the Awakened One suggests he is very nearly the *only* one awake. The idea that we're insufficiently awake is fairly commonplace, especially among people with some interest in spirituality. Those who've experimented with psychedelic drugs claim to have witnessed the relativity of consciousness firsthand. But Gurdjieff's notion of what constitutes man's sleep is far more challenging.

As Gurdjieff blithely informed P. D. Ouspensky, people are asleep when they think they're awake. They sleepwalk through life. They live and die for the most part asleep, at best half-waking in fitful starts. If they think they're more awake than the next person, most of the time they're probably at least as deeply asleep.

Gurdjieff was quite blunt:

The most characteristic feature of a modern man is the *absence of unity in him* and, further, the absence in him of even traces of those properties which he most likes to ascribe to himself, that is, "lucid consciousness," "free will," a "permanent ego or I," and the "ability to do." It may surprise you if I say that the chief feature of a modern man's being which explains everything else that is lacking in him is *sleep.* A modern man lives in sleep, in sleep he is born and in sleep he dies. . . . But at present just think of one thing, what *knowledge* can a sleeping man have? And if you think about it and at the same time remember that *sleep* is the chief feature of our being, it will at once become clear to you that if a man really wants knowledge, he must first think about how to wake. (From *In Search of the Miraculous.*)

We can see our daytime, workaday sleep at one level if we consider that when we take a walk, setting out on an errand on some familiar route, we typically notice setting out and notice when we arrive, but we often don't remember much of the intervening walk. We were on "automatic pilot" during that walk—we go into "automatic pilot" in walking, driving, cleaning the house. Our attention was being used up in mental rumination; we were chewing the cud of some vague personal fantasy as we went about our errands.

But just suppose . . .

Suppose that "automatic pilot" state is simply more noticeable in those contexts—and suppose that, in fact, we're actually on "automatic pilot" *most of the time*? Even now—as I write this, and as you read this. Suppose that sleep, that numbness, that buffering from one's real self, is far more extensive than we can easily imagine?

If what Gurdjieff says is true, then in this waking sleep, a man may plan to build a shining steel bridge over a roaring river; may draw up the plans, obtain the funding, hire the workers, carefully supervise the whole business for two years and do a pretty decent, craftsmanlike job—and still be *asleep* the entire time. He is not at the same level of sleep as he is at night in bed, to be sure. Consciousness, Gurdjieff notes, comes in levels. The *sleep* that commands our lives extends to aspects of ourselves we're scarcely aware of.

What is our real condition? Picture a man whose limbs have gone numb, with most of his remaining sensation in his head. And perhaps this peculiar man has had his body hidden from him since birth; he cannot look down and his limbs are numb so *he doesn't know his arms and legs are there.* In addition, he's been blind from birth. So he can hear, he can smell and feel and taste, he can communicate, but he cannot feel most of himself. Yet if he is never informed that he has limbs he can't feel, that there is a vista he should be able to see and can't—he may assume that all he has is all there is.

He may even loudly declare that is the case, that what he can access is all there is, if anyone casts doubt on it, because anything else is too frightening to consider. Yet he must, somewhere within, have a nagging intuition of frustrated potential; that there is vastly more to him if only he could break through to it somehow.

We all have that nagging intuition. Is there a reason, besides psychological makeup, that induces a person to take up flying a fighter jet, or climbing cliffs? And why are we attracted to novelty, to roaming, or to the "latest" fad; why do advertisers like to let us know when a product is "New!" Perhaps because risk and novelty offer the same thing—a little *frisson* that feebly simulates that which we subconsciously sense we're missing: The vividness, the *real*ness, of being awake, truly present in the moment. Perhaps daredevil pursuits or novelties are our futile ways of trying to reclaim a little of our lost heritage.

When people get older, it often seems to them as if time is "passing faster." They become alarmed by how rapidly the years seem to flash by; how old age seems to rush toward them. How different our relationship to time was, when we were children! Gurdjieff said that when we are young we are more our "essence" and are not so imprinted with automatic responses to input. Some automatic responses are good—they're skills, and we need them for life and labor. But the tendency to accumulate programming tends to have a life of its own—or more accurately, to steal the life that belongs to us. We go on "automatic pilot" in a thousand different ways—and while we're on it, we're not really present, we're drifting along in a sort of daydream, vaguely present, or we're chewing over anxieties. The more we're on automatic pilot, the "faster" that time seems to go, because we weren't present to take a conscious part in the flow of time. And thus we waste our lives away, letting ourselves be carried along on a conveyor belt of automatic reactions—and at the end of the conveyor belt is a furnace.

One day, not so long ago, I was walking in my yard on some household errand, thinking of my career, and generally free-associating. Then suddenly something recalled me to myself—this recollection to myself was the product of past attempts at such remembrance—and I made an effort, forcing myself to step back from my free association; to stop dreaming, and look around. As I did this, I tried to see my sleepwalking state of a moment before, and did indeed glimpse it. So there was a moment of contrast between my earlier state and this fresher, slightly more awake state: my previous state seemed like a *tunnel* to me now. It was like a dim burrow, with only a few blurs of color, and twined in the shadow walls were the people I'd been thinking about and the desires I'd been anxious to satisfy: these had been a kind of shifting, nauseating wallpaper for my perceptual tunnel. As if I'd been, up till that moment, what the Tibetans call a "hungry ghost" in my own personal bardo state—for surely I had not been truly alive. I had been sleepwalking through this tunnel; now I was out of the tunnel and able to look around—and simply see where I was. I was in my yard, on a fine early autumn day, its details springing at me with a new three-dimensionality: with dappled sunlight and vivid oleander blossoms and ribbon-shaped crackling leaves underfoot and an astonishingly engineered spider web to one side catching the light; bees drumming the air, birds calling with intricate repetitiveness, the fragrance and gentle pressure of the air, the feel of my body, sensations alive in the midst of all this—and a great deal more. All of this was around me, within me—and I'd been completely unaware of it. I'd been walking through a living, sumptuous garden, a feast for the senses, but unable to take it in, until I'd taken a moment to step out of the stream of my free associations to turn my attention to what *was,* then; to simply what is.

Before I'd made this effort to come to myself, I'd been walking along, carried about by my body—but I hadn't been *inhabiting* it. I felt that, at least for that living moment, *I was actually inhabiting my body.*

The effect, too, was not only vivid—it was liberating. I felt, for a little while, like a man who's been trapped in a caved-in mine, emerging into the open air. I felt like a newly released prisoner. Suddenly there was freedom, there were wide-open spaces. And there was amazement that this liberation, this enormity, *had been there all along.*

Then—my wife called me to the phone. I answered the phone, was instantly caught up in the business of the phone call . . . and quickly went back to sleep. I was walking around the house, working at my computer, talking on the phone—

But sound asleep.

An Initial Exercise in Scale

The psychologist and philosopher William James said: "One conclusion was forced upon my mind. . . . It is that our normal waking consciousness, rational consciousness as we call it, is but one type of consciousness, whilst all about it, parted by the flimsiest of screens, there lie potential forms of consciousness entirely different."★

Gurdjieff gives us a simple outline of the basic levels of consciousness.

First, there's slumber, the sleep we enter into at night, the lowest state of consciousness. It is a passive state, in which dreams work according to their own logic, without our control. Man

★ *The Varieties of Religious Experience* by William James. Lecture XVI, "Mysticism."

spends much of his time in this healthy state of sleep, and he needs it to restore his energies, and to cleanse his body of fatigue poisons. In its deepest form we're nestled in some essential, primordial state of being.

The second state of consciousness, the next important one up from slumber, is the ordinary "waking" state. This is the state in which we spend our ambulatory days, going about our business. We respond to stimuli with a fair briskness, as we've learned to, and as we are instinctively programmed to, but we're only "awake" relative to slumbering abed. It's difficult, at first, to clearly see this state as being one of only relative wakefulness, until we actively set out to observe our state, to observe when we're more and less conscious—and then we're startled by what we observe.

If a man wanders the streets drunk and falls into a stupor in a locked and wintry doorway, he may be convinced he's already home. Before he can actually get to his real home, he must sober up and convince himself he's not yet there. Until then he will sit on the cold stone stoop, with his feet in the rain. Similarly, before we can reach a state of even relative wakefulness, we have to decide we're not yet there.

"The third state of consciousness," Gurdjieff tells us in *In Search of the Miraculous*, "is *self-remembering* or self-consciousness, or consciousness of one's being."

Being wrongly convinced that we're already self-conscious, Gurdjieff said, is *the first great obstacle to self-consciousness.*

And let's be clear: Self-consciousness is a level higher than our ordinary, typical waking state.

This state of consciousness is nothing like mere introspection, or being nervously "aware" of oneself. Instead, it involves an attention to the self that is constantly refined, compassionate, nonjudgmental, and nearly unblinking. It is ideally a constant honest self-appraisal, much of it directed internally, and involving the higher functions of the emotional center—a process I'll talk about further on. As the Gnostics have it in the Gospel of Thomas, "Jesus said, 'When you come to know yourselves, then you will become known, and you will realize that it is you who are sons of the living Father. But if you will not know yourselves, then you will dwell in poverty, and it is you who are that poverty.'"

"Self-remembering" is a critically important idea in the Gurdjieff Work—but the term takes on different shades of meaning as used by various people, rather like the variability one finds in the use of the term "dharma" in other traditions. Most basically, as used by Ouspensky in his book *In Search of the Miraculous,* "self-remembering" seems to mean simply being present to oneself, in a way that excludes daydreaming, rumination, vagueness; in addition, one observes oneself, senses oneself—and tries to bring conscious decision-making to whatever arises. This is a process of *remembering* your true self, so that you can strive to rise above your automatic self. There appear to be degrees of self-remembering, as different teachers use the term—from ordinary mindfulness to a profound inner unification.

One tool for self-remembering is "divided attention"—which Ouspensky diagrammed with a doubleheaded arrow, showing some attention turned inward, in a quiet way, while we continue simultaneous attention to the outer world (See figure 1).

The fourth and highest state is *objective consciousness.* In this state we see things unfiltered, as they truly are, and including a much broader spectrum of the energies of life. This state, we're told, "cannot be described in words" but has various names in various places, most famously "enlightenment." Most of us do not experience this state, except passingly. When we do catch a flash of it, we don't understand it—we are not in it enough to

FIGURE I

Normally, our active attention goes primarily toward the outer world . . .

But with self-observation, attention is double-arrowed, pointing outwardly—and to ourselves, objectively, at once . . .

understand it. Unless we've developed it in ourselves, we lack the spiritual substance that would help us sustain our understanding at that level.

"The fourth state of consciousness in man," Gurdjieff says, "means an altogether different state of being; it is the result of inner growth and long and difficult work on oneself."

There it is, a term we will revisit many times: "work on oneself." Or "inner work." From whence comes the expression "the Work" to denote the actual praxis, the application, of Gurdjieff's teaching.

If the fourth, highest state comes only through much work on oneself, the third *should* be the natural state in which we live. A person should not be a closed book to himself or herself. A person's being should be transparent to his or her attention. But it is not so, because we are caught up in the habit of an inner fogginess, and a fragmentariness, a subjectivity reinforced by childhood conditioning we receive partly from parents, and partly by that great hypnotist the human world.

What are we, after all? A teacher in the Gurdjieff work liked to say, "Where my attention is, there 'I' am." If my attention is solely identified with daydreaming, anxiety, anger, vanity, ambition, and so forth—our usual state—then *that's what we are*. We are ambition-drunk daydreamers, or perhaps angry worriers, to name two "I's" that might be uppermost. But if I choose to reserve some attention for self-observation, ultimately for self-transformation—then I *am* that attention.

Then, while I'm working within myself, I am that conscious self-observer, that garden for self-transformation.

What do we find out about ourselves, if we engage in self-observation? We'll see patterns of behavior that surprise us—we'll see ourselves without the "buffers," the blinders that hide our mechanicality, our sleep, and our selfishness from us. We may see our *identification*—identification in this sense is not referring to our identity. Quite the contrary. *Identification* means getting caught up in an emotional reaction, especially negative feelings like anger or resentment or fear, so that we *become* what we're identified with. We lose all objectivity. It may be very extreme, as in fanaticism, or it may be something as ordinary as self-pity. Identification is often fear based—we are scared of rejection, or failure, or suffering, so we bury ourselves in identifying with some feeling or notion that keeps us "safely" occupied.

Seeing ourselves as we are, with cool detachment, it becomes possible to see also what else we might become. Real freedom becomes a possibility.

Moments of seeing ourselves as we are—of self-observation—are called *impressions,* in the Gurdjieff lexicon. An impression is not necessarily of something negative—it's just as we are, good, bad, indifferent. It's like a snapshot we take with our attention. And it's also . . . food! Gurdjieff taught that the soul that develops within us needs several special foods for the "crystalization of its being." And one of these foods is impressions—these moments of objective self-knowledge literally feed one's soul.

SOME GOOD TASTES ARE BITTER

According to the Gospel of Thomas, "Jesus said, 'Let him who seeks continue seeking, until he finds. When he finds, he will become troubled. When he becomes troubled, he will be astonished, and he will rule over all.'" Truth, then, is often troubling.

My experience has been that if some generalization about the nature of life is very agreeable to hear, if it's very sweet to the psychological palate, then it's probably not true. This is not to say that everything true is grim and hopeless—or that there isn't honest joy, that there aren't genuine glad tidings, in life as it stands. Of course there is and of course there are. But if a statement about life has the cheap perfume, the sickly sweetness of sentiment about it, then it's usually either untrue or at least vague or simplistic.

It's at first dismaying to consider the challenges we face—to accept that we're all sleepwalking through life. But the fact of sleep carries the implicit possibility of awakening from it, and that possibility is exhilarating.

Many of Gurdjieff's ideas are shocking to people, especially when they realize how definite, how *unmitigating* he is about them. But consider the texture of life. Real life is wondrous, seamed with miracles—but also complex, challenging, dangerous, sometimes harsh, and always lawfully unrelenting. The Grand Canyon is gorgeous to see—and deadly if you step into it blunderingly. Indeed, some of its austere beauty is in the perilousness of it.

Perilous, too, is the second idea we'll touch on in this chapter: *Man is a machine.*

Gurdjieff taught that human beings are completely mechanistic in their responses, their thinking, their activities. Ouspensky's book *In Search of the Miraculous* cites Gurdjieff in a Russian café, pointing at the crowd in the street and saying, "Look, all those people you see are simply machines, nothing more."

Hearing this, Ouspensky was at first shocked. But we're not entirely machines, he protested. Art, poetry, philosophy—in this people are more than mechanical, surely.

No, said Gurdjieff emphatically. All that is mechanicality too. And so are the "great deeds" of history. "Man is a machine. All his deeds, actions, words, thoughts, feelings, convictions, opinions, and habits are the results of external influences, external impressions. Out of himself a man cannot produce a single thought, a single action."

If that's true, then it's terrible to consider that most of human history is the history of *re*action and not action, of response and not *doing*. Human history is a comedy—and a tragedy—of errors, with only spates of inspired activity and bursts of ingenuity to relieve it. In our individual lives, what we suppose we've decided to do, we've actually *reacted into doing,* despite some moments of thoughtful planning. (I told you it was a dismaying concept!) Man can rise above his machinelike programming—but for that "it is necessary to know the machine."

Of course everyone has some obvious machinelike functions: the autonomic systems of the body, which keep the heart beating, keep us breathing; reflexes, the biomolecular activity of the nervous system. But Gurdjieff was saying that everything that humanity regards as *above* the machine level is yet only mechanical. He insisted that we're kidding ourselves, most of us, about being other than machines. People are locked into mechanical behavior, down to the last detail. Men and women are in large part not responsible for their actions, because they are machines. We must nevertheless hold them accountable, but in what Gurdjieff called "the real world" they cannot be really responsible—or real Christians—until they become *actual* men and women. Right now most of us are "men" and "women" only in quotation marks.

From the point of view of Gurdjieff's ideas, there is a sense in which we don't fully exist. What is missing in mechanical man, Gurdjieff tells us, is *real I,* a right relationship to the biblical "I am" within each of us. This "I am" *is* there in a nascent form—tiny as a mustard seed, it is what experiences the world, the pristine nub of our consciousness, that which sees without reaction, without subjective judgment. And for each of us, this "I am" is like a wave on the sea of consciousness that is God; it is what connects us, both innately and potential, to the Higher. But we are not profoundly connected to this Inner Eye—we don't have the connective *being* that would make it possible to be guided by *real I.* We suffer from an insufficiency of sheer *being.* Real *being,* said Gurdjieff, is fed, and grows, each time we are sufficiently conscious; each time we're genuinely present to ourselves. This presence in turn brings about internal unity.

Most of us, however, are nonunified, fragmentary. We have many "little I's"—fragmentary subsets of ourselves that take over automatically. For example, when we have good luck we're cheerful; when we have bad luck we're grouchy. But a man or woman with enough being to realize *real I*—a person capable of *objective reason*—accepts everything that arises, good and bad, with authentic equanimity, with inner freedom and understanding.

Most of us just aren't that present. We are not sufficiently here—we have not awakened the capacity for inner and outer attention that makes that *here*ness fully possible, and so we're clunkily interacting fragments of people. We *aren't.*

Consider these remarks by the great seventeenth-century philosopher Baruch Spinoza:

We are tossed about by external causes in many ways, and like waves driven by contrary winds, we waver and are unconscious. . . . For an ignorant man, besides being agitated in many ways by external causes, never enjoys one true satisfaction of the mind: he lives, moreover, almost unconscious of himself, God, and things . . . the wise man . . . is scarcely moved in spirit; he is conscious of himself, of God, and things by a certain eternal necessity, and never ceases to be.*

Spinoza was well versed in the writings of the mystics Moses of Cordova and Moses Maimonides—thinkers paralleling Gurdjieff in some respects.

Our usual reactions to events seem to us like very genuine expressions of what we think of as our Self—but this is only because we're caught up in those reactions. If someone holds a Fourth of July sparkler up near a drunk, his gaze will tend to fixate on it. Our attention is habitually focused—squandered, really—on the sparks flying from our personality's interaction with the world, on the needs of our superficial self, on satisfying the appetites and urges of the body.

The sister of a man accomplished in business comes over and irritates him by boasting of her new job, preening herself. He doesn't stop to think that she's only boasting because she's always felt overshadowed by him, and all Sis wants is a little recognition that she can be successful too. He's simply annoyed. "She's so vain about her accomplishments . . ." He himself is as vain as they come, as he would know if he'd observed himself—self-observation is fraught with these ironies. His buffers—his numbness and denial—prevent him from seeing his own pettiness. He presumes that his reaction is the way he "really feels." But it's only the superficial reaction of his

*The Story of Philosophy by Will Durant. Chapter IV.

defensive personality. His "emotions" in the matter are a kind of sparkler fizzle—not the actual feeling inside. His essence self, with an awakened emotional center, would feel compassion for her.

If we had a glimpse of the Whole of ourselves—our possibilities, our essence, our psychological mechanism—then what we take to be our usual selves, the rotating slide show of "I's," would seem, well, like a mere rotating slide show by comparison; we would no longer be certain that the little reactions and pettinesses of the personality represent our real self. We might turn and have a look at the person standing behind the projector.

Gurdjieff liked to compare the primary aspects of man to a horse, carriage, and driver. Usually the driver is asleep, or drunk—so either the horse goes where it wants, or every passenger who likes can misappropriate the carriage, sending it this way or that way according to his temporary whim.

One of the tragedies of our internal absence from real decision-making is that any "little I" may "run up a bill," as Gurdjieff put it, signing "promissory notes" that another "I" has to pay later, usually shaking his head and wondering how he came to incur this bill. Gurdjieff was using a figure of speech—but sometimes promissory notes and running up a bill is literally the way of it: A man goes to Las Vegas and runs out of cash; caught up in gambling fever, his temporary "I" goes to a machine that gives out casino chips for a credit card swipe. In this way he runs up tens of thousands of dollars in debt and loses his house. It happens all the time. Later he wonders how he could have done it. He says, "I was out of my head." He was just that—out of his head, more literally than he realizes.

A woman may get swept away by the honeyed words of some Lothario while her essential self tries to warn her that this charmer cannot be trusted and he's not really suited for her anyway. Deep inside herself, she feels a *wrongness* about him—but she suppresses that feeling because superficially he's making her feel good. She marries him—signing, so to speak, a promissory note—and he makes her life miserable when it turns out he's a domineering, loafing, wife-beating cad. If she had been present, really present to herself, she'd never have married this oaf.

"Whole lives often consist in paying promissory notes of small accidental I's," Gurdjieff said. Too true! But the evolution of real individuality provides more than just better decision-making. It provides the possibility of real awakening.

When we hear that we're asleep, we may try to become aware of it; we try to *see this sleep.* Until we've seen it, we can't hope to awaken from it. In corollary, when we observe our machinelike behavior, actually turn the light of conscious attention on the mechanicality in our reactions—perceiving the mechanisms of emotional, intellectual, instinctual automata, both useful and wasteful—only then can we hope to effect the changes in ourselves that will someday free us of the negative aspects of our automatic behavior.

But something is working dynamically against our awakening. Sleep protects our machinelike programming, keeps us from taking conscious control. If for a time we awaken, our machinelike programming stuns us back down into sleepwalking once again, as if this mindlessly mechanistic "it" is fighting for its survival, using sleep as its weapon.

Gurdjieff went on to suggest to Ouspensky that people who are more than machines exist but are quite rare. "All the people you see," he told Ouspensky, "all the people you know, all the people *you may get to know,* are machines, actual machines working solely under the power of external influences. . . . Machines they are born and machines they die. . . . Even now, at this very moment, while we are talking, several millions of machines are trying to annihilate one another. What is the difference between them?"

In our mechanicality, we start wars; in our sleep, we sleepwalk through them—and do terrible things . . .

One day I noticed a TV show on cable, in which contestants send small homemade remote-controlled "killbots" to fight it out in a little robot gladiator ring. I changed the channel and came immediately to CNN's latest news on the current real-life human war; armies programmed to obediently fight against armies. Sometimes the spirit of irony seems to be in charge of television scheduling.

We are to some extent comfortable in our sleep, our mechanicality. "Waking is bitter," Gurdjieff once said. Despite some delightful vividness, some greater capacity to take part in energies previously denied to us, *real* waking up is a difficult process, in its early stages. It's no wonder we usually choose to sleep.

Something else self-observation may bring us is confirmation of Gurdjieff's claim that we have localized mechanisms within us, for the exchange of energy, one part to the next, and for transforming energy. That is, we are *three-centered beings*—the three centers are the *intellectual, the emotional,* and the *instinctive-moving (bodily)*—with our different centers working with different degrees and qualities of energy. Each center has its own "food," and each has been programmed with a certain amount of automatic behavior. And each is divided into higher and lower functions.

We may observe behavior that is typical of one or another center, and we may see that if we bring more of ourselves into observation, and active participation, we begin to harmonize our centers, with dramatic results. I'll discuss this more in chapter 5.

IN DREAMS WE STRUGGLE TO WAKE

It's important to emphasize that Gurdjieff did not mean that we are asleep and mechanical in some vague metaphorical sense. He meant it literally. But there are *degrees* of sleep and of wakefulness. Normally, we're caught up in dreams. As Ouspensky put it in *The Psychology of Man's Possible Evolution,* "dreams become invisible exactly as the stars and moon become invisible in the glare of the sun. But they are all there, and they often influence all our thoughts, feelings and actions—sometimes even more than the actual perceptions of the moment." Despite our straitjacketed condition, something in us senses that we're asleep and struggles, at times, to wake up. Even when we haven't encountered this teaching, we know something's wrong: that the light is too dim; that we are driven by drivers we cannot see. This unconscious, uneasy half-comprehension of our condition finds expression in art—especially in theater and film.

Think of the plays of Samuel Beckett. In his unnerving, austere productions, people walk about in "purgatorial loops," repeating nightmarish scenarios, seeming caught up in entrapping states of mind. They battle for dignity, for some eking out of individuality. In Beckett's short play *Catastrophe,* two ruthlessly officious, controlling individuals, a "director" and his secretary, set about arranging every last detail of "the Catastrophe," a miserable-looking, ragged old man frozen on a stage. At the end, the old man, *against directions,* lifts his head, and looks up at the audience— a tiny act of defiance, all he can manage, so controlled is he by outside forces. Beckett spoke of his plays as "objects" and probably wasn't making a spiritual statement. But again and again he poignantly expressed man's condition: trapped, mechanical, struggling to emerge from a purgatory he doesn't understand.

Popular film resonates with Gurdjieffian themes. *The Matrix* is about a man who discovers that the whole human world is asleep and dreaming, with mankind enslaved by machines, and ultimately indistinguishable from machines themselves. Numerous films—most coming in recent years, as if people now are especially restless in their sleep—point to the same truths with a timeliness and convergence of intent that seem to make them part of an inadvertent "movement" in cinema. I'm thinking particularly of *American Beauty, Fight Club, Dark City, eXistenZ, Mulholland Drive, The Truman Show, Vanilla Sky, Waking Life,* and *Simone.*

American Beauty, written by Alan Ball, is the story of a dysfunctional family paralyzed by resentment, by alienation, and by simply being lost in the centerless maze of modern life. Kevin Spacey's character can't touch his wife in any way that matters; he can't reach his daughter though she's right in the same house with him. He has an encounter with a pot-dealing young bohemian who moves in next door—whose obsession with the innate visual beauty of the ordinary world seems an adventure in perception—and is inspired to wrestle his way free of his middle-class funk. The overall impression is of a man recognizing that he's been asleep, dreaming his way through an air-conditioned, wall-to-wall-carpeted misery—who had forgotten the choices, the almost infinite ways out, that life offers to the wakeful in every single second of existence.

In David Fincher's *Fight Club,* characters desperate for connection to something real go to twelve-step groups for problems they don't have just to feel emotions by proxy; they are so numb that they start a Fight Club, where ordinary people meet in secret to beat the crap out of each other with their fists, merely to experience the *realness* that confrontation brings. They allude to a society caught up in consumerism and corporate striving, dumbfounded by masks and media-star worship and empty recreation—and they recognize that it's all a kind of sleepwalking, a hypnotic state that must be struggled with, even battered with bare fists.

Alex Proyas's *Dark City* is a noir fantasy, a Gnostic fable (I asked the director if it was a Gnostic fable, and he confirmed it was), about a man who finds himself on a search for truth and identity in a shape-shifting city that turns out to be a sort of living urban stage designed for sinister, arcane purposes by malignant entities— all may be a dream, or may not.

David Cronenberg's *eXistenZ* involves a virtual-reality videogame that—like so many Philip Dick–influenced tales—makes us wonder where reality ends and the game begins. Fantasy and reality inevitably overlap in this film. There are cultlike antigame revolutionaries in the background, and the game's player wonders what's real, and if the game could be a game within a game . . .

In David Lynch's *Mulholland Drive* a young actress seems to have her soul, or identity, stolen by evil forces embedded in the city of Los Angeles (no one who's worked in The Business there needs much convincing), as she goes through an enigmatic quest to find her real nature—in what turns out to be, apparently, a dream.

In *The Truman Show*, Jim Carrey discovers he's in a false reality, literally staged by people who are using him as an entertainment and have done so for a generation. He must find the confines of the staging area and break out into the real world, to find actual love, an unscripted destiny.

Cameron Crowe's *Vanilla Sky* is inspired by a Spanish thriller; this Tom Cruise vehicle once again gives us a hero who by degrees realizes that his nightmarish reality is fabricated—is intricately computer-animated and transmitted into his brain, which is in modified cryogenic freeze. He chooses to wake up, and face the real world of a dark future, rather than centuries of the improved dreams the cryogenics company offers him.

Richard Linklater's *Waking Life*—a brilliant innovation that perfectly fuses conventional movie photography and animation—gives us a hero who keeps waking up from a complex dream that seems to push him into profound social and philosophical dialogues with the sundry intellectual outlaws he encounters; only each time he's sure he's awakened, he finds once more he's only dreaming.

Andrew Niccol's *Simone* is a comedy about a movie director who's so disgusted with actors that he computer-generates Simone, a beautiful actress programmed with the best of all the great female movie stars. The audience falls in love with her, and people refuse to accept she's not real, even when he tries to tell them so. Niccol sends up the public's willingness to collaborate with illusion on a global scale.

The emergence of a remarkable number of films questioning reality itself—each suggesting a sinister puppeteer and pointing to a kind of dreamy disorientation prevailing in the median consciousness of the industrialized world—seems a defined cultural current, however unplanned, emerging from a consensus about our condition. What is it we're trying to tell ourselves, with *The Matrix* and so many other films on the same theme?

These filmmakers are not deliberately making reference to Gurdjieff—they may well be unaware of him—but on some level they seem to confirm some of Gurdjieff's ideas. Artists express their perception of the human condition. And a perceptual consensus is beginning to emerge: mankind is asleep, mechanical, strictured, fragmented.

But unlike Beckett—and unlike many of these filmmakers—Gurdjieff offered hope. He offered the possibility of a way out . . .

Before he could offer that Way, however, he had to find it himself.

TWO

MEETING A
REMARKABLE MAN

Only he will deserve the name of man and can count upon anything prepared for him from Above, who has already acquired corresponding data for being able to preserve intact both the wolf and the sheep confided to his care.

—ancient saying, quoted in
G. I. Gurdjieff, *Meetings with Remarkable Men*

Ouspensky in *In Search of the Miraculous*:

I saw a man of an Oriental type, no longer young, with a black mustache and piercing eyes, who astonished me first of all, because he seemed to be disguised and completely out of keeping with the place and its atmosphere . . . this man with the face of an Indian raja or an Arab sheik seated here in this little café . . . in a black overcoat and a velvet collar and a black bowler hat produced this strange, unexpected and almost alarming impression of a man poorly disguised.

Kathryn Hulme, in her book *Undiscovered Country*: "We stood before his table waiting for him to look up. He made us wait for an interval that felt like eons, then slowly raised his head and gazed at me with the most beautiful eyes I had ever looked into—even slightly angry as they were, scowling. *"Excusez-moi, Monsieur . . . etes-vous Monsieur Gurdjieff?"*

Solita Solano, quoted in W. P. Patterson's book *Ladies of the Rope*: "I hoped for a demigod . . . not this 'strange' ecru man about whom I could see nothing extraordinary except the size and power of his eyes. . . . He seated me next to him and for two hours muttered in broken English . . . I decided that I rather disliked him. Years passed. In the autumn of 1934, in a crisis of misery, I suddenly knew that I had long been waiting to go see him and he was expecting me."

A. L. Staveley, in *Memories of Gurdjieff*: "You could say his regard rested on us—upon each one of us, and in that regard was the merciless compassion that never missed anything. . . . We sat in a circle around him, attentive and in that strange state of heightened awareness. . . . Something in one was free, even light, and something else seemed to be squirming and twisting to get back to what was familiar, known, secure. It was very disturbing. Everything was unpredictable."

John Bennett, in his autobiography, *Witness*:

It must have been half-past nine before Gurdjieff appeared. He came in without a trace of embarrassment, greeting the Prince in Turkish with an accent that was a strange mixture of cultured Osmanli and some uncouth Eastern dialect. When we were introduced, I met the strangest eyes I have ever seen. The two eyes were so different that I wondered if the light had played some trick on me. . . . He had long, black mustaches fiercely curled upwards . . . his head was shaved. He was short, but very powerfully built. . . . I discovered that Gurdjieff had the peculiar property of appearing to be a different man to everyone who met him.

Who was he really?

He was a startlingly rare bird. He was like no other. His methods were unsettling, sometimes shocking. He was in all probability a spiritual master—though one of unusual stripe even for that unusual attainment. His sense of humor and his capacity for satire were exquisitely refined, and, though not unknown, the frequent use of humor is uncommon in a master—biting irony like Gurdjieff's even rarer. By some accounts he could be exasperating, infuriating, upsetting; but there is good reason to believe he was usually that way on purpose and with reason: he was a true "trickster," in the higher sense. (Of course, being human, he was capable of making mistakes with people, too.) He encompassed contradictions: he was sly, unstintingly generous, ruthlessly practical, vulgar when he chose to be—and at the same time an intellectual powerhouse. He could often appear to be bullying, liking to tell people they were *merde*—that is, that they were as low as shit because they were living in dreams, just sort of mindlessly oozing, reeking through life—and all the while he could be kind beyond tenderness. He was deeply reverent and almost toxically irreverent all at once. He was capable of a compassion so powerful it could, by some accounts, literally be seen to *emanate*. He was a world traveler, a composer, a choreographer, a successful businessman (when he needed to be), and a healer. He was also a writer, author of *Meetings with Remarkable Men* and the incomparable *Beelzebub's Tales to His Grandson,* the latter a vast allegorical myth structure in a literary form all its own (no one else would dare such a book!). Gurdjieff had his own definition of *food*—and as regards the food we consume in the usual sense, he was very interested in it as a way of consciously participating in the cosmos and the world, and had an almost occult expertise in its preparations; he was fond of dining, perhaps overfond of it. He was also fond of drinking armagnac and peppered vodka, and, as the great but apparently snobbish sage Krishnamurti sniffed, after meeting him, "He smoked *cigarettes!*"

All these contrasts were somehow harmonized in his highly individualized person.

Gurdjieff is a Russian variant of the Greek *Giorgiades,* his actual surname at birth. His full Russian name was Georgei Ivanovich Gurdjieff. His follower Thomas de Hartmann said that the Russians in his circle called Gurdjieff by the familiar *Georgeivanich.*

Biographers differ as to Georgei Ivanovich Gurdjieff's birthdate, but he himself gave January 13, 1866, confirmed by at least one passport (he had numerous conflicting passports!) and given weight by his accounts of historic events taking place in his youth. Other sources have indicated later dates—the question of birth year is exemplary of many biographical uncertainties.

Still, his semiautobiographical work *Meetings with Remarkable Men,* despite probably being a mix of fact and parable, has the ring of truth. The description of his early life certainly rings true, and I shall draw on it here, as well as on the research of people who have worked harder than myself, his biographers, and accounts by his students.

Gurdjieff was born in the small Russian-Armenian city of Alexandropol, son of a well-to-do owner of extensive herds of cattle and sheep, Ioannas Giorgiades, a Greek. Gurdjieff's mother was Armenian. He was the eldest—his younger sisters were Anna Ivanovna and Sophie Ivanovna; his younger brother was Dmitri.

Alexandropol was a garrison town that, the biographer James Moore tells us in his *Gurdjieff: Anatomy of Myth,* "defended Russia's border with Turkey, and its heaped-up walls, bastions, and gun-emplacements conveyed a sense of immemorial disputes, wars and forced migrations."

The garrisoning and movements of troops in Alexandropol and Kars, the struggle between Turks and the Russians, must have made an impression on the young Gurdjieff. The world must have seemed "under siege"—and this impression was only to be strengthened by the conflicts he witnessed firsthand in adulthood.

The Giorgiades' was a patriarchal household, probably traditional in many respects for that part of the world, but Gurdjieff's father was more than a herdsman: his avocation was the art of the *ashokhs*, the traditional reciters of memorized epics and legends in verse. Gurdjieff made many references to the *One Thousand and One Nights*, Scheherazade's tales, and he probably heard some of them first from his father, as well as the Gilgamesh epic, stories of the mythic mullah Nassr Eddin—Gurdjieff later made up his own Nassr Eddin material—and especially the resourceful inventor Mustapha the Lame Carpenter. The tales of Mustapha implanted in the young Gurdjieff the notion that there's always a way to actively solve a problem, if one is sufficiently ingenious—something that became a hallmark of Gurdjieff the peripatetic seeker.

Gurdjieff's *Meetings with Remarkable Men* tells us that when he was a small boy his father compelled him to handle creatures he felt an aversion for, even putting worms and other crawly fauna in his bed to "immunize" the boy against any distaste for nature. Perhaps because Georgei was the eldest, and therefore expected to be the heir, he must be strongest; to the distress of the women in the household, Gurdjieff's father would often drive his beloved son from his bed at first light, "when a child's sleep is particularly sweet," and in the remorseless winter of the Caucasus the young Gurdjieff was commanded to go outside, strip himself bare, go to the fountain and there splash himself with cold water, then run around naked and barefoot in the frosty air. And if he resisted? In that case, Gurdjieff tells us, in *Meetings with Remarkable Men,* "my father, though he was very kind and loved me, would punish me without mercy. I often remembered him for this in later years and in these moments thanked him with all my being. If it had not been for this, I would never have been able to overcome all the obstacles and difficulties that I had to encounter later during my travels."

The boy soon had in his father an exemplar of the right way to face greater difficulties than bare skin on frosty mornings. The rug, however ornate, was pulled out from under the Giorgiades family when Georgei was seven. A cattle plague destroyed the Giorgiades herds, to the last ruminant. Since Gurdjieff's father was responsible for his countrymen's smaller herds, which by traditional arrangement ran with his, he was expected to reimburse them for their dead cattle. As he was a scrupulous man, he did so—with his savings and by the liquidation of his property. The Giorgiades estate was reduced to penury.

Thereupon Ioannas Giorgiades shook his head, drew a deep breath, sold what little was left to him, and opened a lumber yard.

The family moved from what had been a fine house to something far humbler. The elder Giorgiades was generous to a fault and not a sharp businessman; the lumber yard did not thrive and devolved into a workshop for carvings and odd carpentry jobs.

Georgei Giorgiades—Gurdjieff the boy—was as impish and mischievous as any other lad. But he was close to his family and was acutely affected—and perhaps truly influenced—when his grandmother gave him this advice on her deathbed: "In life never do as others do. Either do nothing—just go to school—or do something nobody else does."

At her funeral, in honor of her advice, the young Gurdjieff danced around her grave singing an irreverent song. This could not have gone over well with the other mourners, but it might have been his first step into the unorthodoxy that would culminate in a kind of spiritual radicalism—and in his naming the hero of his great symbolic novel Beelzebub. No diabolist was Gurdjieff, but he was to swim contrary to the usual currents, making his way to "another river" that flowed impossibly upward, almost against gravity: Gurdjieff drove himself with a will that, if not devilish, seemed anyway to embody the energy of "the wolf" that human beings have in them, as the saying goes, along with the lamb.

In 1877 Tsar Nicholas II sent the Christian Armenian general Loris-Melikov against the forces of the notorious Sultan Abdul "the Damned." After a six-month campaign, Alexandropol's churchbells tolled in celebration when news came that the Turk had been driven back, the tsar's forces taking the ancient mountain town of Kars, claiming it for the Russian empire.

Gurdjieff's uncle had a business in Kars, and things were only getting worse in Alexandropol, so the Giorgiades household joined a polyglot parade of impoverished hopefuls seeking a new beginning in the reclaimed Kars—which was suddenly predominantly Christian.

The eleven-year-old Gurdjieff was fascinated by the riot of races in this high, bleak, chilly mountain crossroad. But materially things were only nominally better there. A third sister had been born, another mouth to feed, and business competition in Kars was formidable.

The young Gurdjieff went to a Russian municipal school, but his powerful mind made short work of his studies, and he had free time to help his father earn money for the family in the woodshop and, quite independently, to make pencil boxes and toys to sell to other students, the money going into the family coffer.

. . .

Gurdjieff's *Meetings with Remarkable Men* (which was actually the "Second Series" in a trio of works entitled *ALL AND EVERY-THING*) is indeed formulated around remarkable men; it lacks any other coherent organization, being only intermittently linear. Each of Gurdjieff's remarkable men had something special, or found something special, which in turn crystallized in Gurdjieff a facet of the truth he would come to actively seek out as part of that group of friends and colleagues he called the Seekers of Truth—a loose organization of aspirants after hidden knowledge who pooled their resources and discoveries and sometimes undertook expeditions together.

He read many books, ancient and contemporary, and he visited many sacred places, but he turned to personal contact with men who had "this certain property"—men with aspects of their being developed—to get the real understanding he needed. It was as if, finally, books or no, something must be passed on in person, something that made the knowledge given more than just knowledge. Gurdjieff's father, for example, though unschooled in the conventional sense, had a wisdom culled partly from the primal, sometimes even antediluvian chants of the ashokh, but also a "something more" that shone in times of difficulties: "there stands out in my memory all the grandeur of my father's calm and the detachment of his inner state in all his external manifestations, throughout the misfortunes that befell him . . . he did not lose heart, never identified with anything, and remained inwardly free and always himself."

This inner state, this way of being present but free before whatever arose, was characteristic of his father's individuality, which Gurdjieff could feel for himself, somehow. It entered into Gurdjieff's own being, and ultimately into his teaching.

Gurdjieff himself used the word *individuality,* in a particular way, in speaking of his father. Individuality is a special quality with Gurdjieff. It does not mean the selfish individualism of Ayn Rand but an individuality in cosmic context, and the definite fulfillment of oneself as one was always intended to be: the spiritual fleshing-out of what—untrained—tends to remain emaciated. This process calls for the removal of masks—except those consciously used for a mindfully appropriate purpose—leaving the actuality of *essence.* Gurdjieff was very impressed with his father's essence, with his inborn, fully developed individuality, just as he was touched by the individualities of each of the remarkable men he met.

But Gurdjieff was drawn to more mysterious qualities of humanity, too. Somewhere around the time of their move to Kars, the lad was punished for running away for nearly a week with a family of Carpathian gypsies; he'd gone with them partly because of their wild, free life with their fine horses, and partly because of their ability "to *see,*" for they had developed something that made them psychic. Already the boyish Gurdjieff was drawn to the mysterious, to what people called "the supernatural."

According to *Meetings,* young Georgei sometimes accompanied his father to competitions among the ashokhs; these bards came from as far away as distant parts of Turkey, Persia, the remoter Caucasus and Turkestan to demonstrate their skills in composing and reciting poems, folktales, and legends. Like Gurdjieff's father these ashokhs "possessed such a memory and such alertness of mind as would now be considered remarkable and even phenomenal." A participant would literally *sing* a question on spiritual or philosophical matters, or on the symbolism of ancient legends, and another would reply in kind, with improvised song in the common tongue Turko-Tatar. The contests could go on for days, weeks, with prizes of cattle, or rugs, or other valuables. The Peter

Brook film hauntingly dramatizes one such contest, a scene in which we see the young Gurdjieff almost awestruck, sensing a connection with something ancient through an art form that is now nearly extinct.

Closer to home, Gurdjieff's father was invited to gatherings around Kars to tell his folktales and to recite ancient legends, including the epic of Gilgamesh.

> *I will tell thee, Gilgamesh,*
> *Of a mournful mystery of the Gods:*
> *How once, having met together,*
> *They resolved to flood the land of Shuruppak . . .* ★

The recitation goes on to speak of Ubara-Tut, who was commanded: "Build thyself a ship, take with thee thy near ones, and what birds and beasts thou wilt . . ."

Gurdjieff's father believed this legend came from the Sumerians and was probably the origin of the tale of the Flood in the Old Testament, and that Ubara-Tut was the basis of Noah.

Hearing from his own father the assertion that this story from the Old Testament was something far more ancient than the Bible; hearing from him tales of Atlantis, of the Imastun Brotherhood, of sages and astrologers who traveled the Earth "observing celestial phenomena from different places," maintaining telepathic contact with home through entranced "pythonesses," . . . from just such colorful hints, Gurdjieff had a foreshadowing of his later conviction that certain of the ancients possessed a secret knowledge, a greatness since lost to conventional history. And perhaps at such times the ghostly beginnings of his first grand aim manifested somewhere within him: that it might be possible to find

★Quoted in *Meetings with Remarkable Men.*

what remains of those mislaid secrets, of that grand knowledge drowned in the Flood and lost in "the fall of man"—to piece it together into a unity, ferreting out the secrets behind the secrets, the esoteric of the esoteric.

Many modern scholars would agree with Gurdjieff's father, the un-lettered cattle herder and carpenter, that the Gilgamesh legend was the kernel of the biblical Flood story. But a certain Dean Borsh did not agree—naturally not, since this good friend of Ioannas Gior-giades was a priest; he was in fact dean of the Kars military cathe-dral and the highest official of the local Russian Orthodoxy.

At seventy, Father Borsh was a lean, frail man, which only masked his considerable spiritual force. As dean he was well rec-ompensed and could have lived in lavish, comfortable quarters, but—unlike the priests under him—he chose a Spartan room in the cathedral. All his free time was spent in science, astronomy, chemistry, and medicine—and in music, especially the compo-sition of sacred canticles, which Gurdjieff said became Russian classics.

Dean Borsh would come to the humble Giorgiades residence to enjoy hours of debate and speculation with his friend. Borsh seemed to see a spark worth fanning in the eldest child, Georgei, and he became one of Gurdjieff's personal tutors. Borsh may also have noticed that young Gurdjieff, long before the first of millions of cigarettes, had a fine singing voice, for Georgei Giorgiades was soon privileged to sing at the cathedral in the boy's choir.

Though sometimes in philosophical disagreement, Dean Borsh and Gurdjieff's father were friends—which is interesting, consider-ing that Gurdjieff's father was so convinced of the worthlessness of most priests that he used to say "The cassock is to hide a fool." And even "If you wish to lose your faith, make friends with a priest."

What would lead the headman of all local priests to spend hours in the woodshop of this skeptical poet of the mountains? Surely there was something extraordinary about Gurdjieff's father to keep Borsh coming back to him.

And to recognize that something extraordinary, to transcend what must have been the prejudices of his calling, Borsh too must have been a remarkable man himself. And so he was—so much so that one wonders if the cosmos had not contrived to put him in place to help the young Gurdjieff "acquire the necessary data" for the task that was one day to be his.

Father Borsh believed that a priest should care for both the body and soul of his flock—a priest should also be a physician. A physician, he pointed out, needs to have access to the soul of the patient to truly help him; a priest needs to know the physical ills of his parishioners. In Gurdjieff he saw the opportunity to create the perfect priest—he seemed to perceive a young man who mingled scientific analytic capability and spiritual sensitivity. In this he had an insight into Gurdjieff, who indeed was to treat both body and soul. Gurdjieff, on his own, perhaps, added a third concern: the mind. For as we shall see, Gurdjieff saw man as a "three-brained being," a creature of *three centers:* the intellectual center, the instinctive-moving (bodily) center, and the emotional center. Each of these categories is divided into other definite functions, but without their harmonious interplay man is incomplete and incapable of the development that should be his birthright. Like Father Borsh, Gurdjieff's emphasis was on the *completeness* of the approach to the development of man.

Strangely for an Orthodox priest, Borsh apparently also revered ancient, pre-Christian "'Great Laws' . . . as elucidated by the wise men of past epochs." There was, for example, a science for divining the corresponding "types" for each person, among the opposite sex, to determine who exactly was right for each marriageable individual. And if marriage prospects were not matched according to this arcane system, everything would thereafter go badly wrong.

Gurdjieff does not say if Dean Borsh taught him the traditional mysticism of the Orthodox. This mysticism centers on the prayer of the heart, the "hesychasm," in which a prayer is spoken silently, deep within, with mantra-like repetition, together with an openness of feeling in the heart center, a special *receptivity* there to divine impulses. It's probable that Gurdjieff learned of this process from Father Borsh and from other mystics. He would later refer knowledgeably to the teachings of the Eastern Orthodox monasteries of Mount Athos, where such methods were taught.

It was Dean Borsh who decided that his "young garlic-head," as he fondly called Georgei, would be taken from school and personally tutored, by himself and select priests, to prepare him for a possibly unique destiny. This was an unusual step to take—Borsh must have seen something correspondingly extraordinary in Gurdjieff.

GLIMPSES OF THE MIRACULOUS

As a teenager, Gurdjieff became almost obsessed with the dichotomy that continued to reveal itself wherever he looked. He was told by some that Orthodox Christianity had the final truth—but here were Muslims, and other faiths, just down the way, and each had their own "final truths" at cross-purposes with the Orthodox. Was he to believe his own people right—merely because they were his own people?

As for what it all means, he had received the usual explanations about the world, and nature, the meaning of life—and he had also been handed contradictions of the usual explanations from his own father, from Dean Borsh, and from his own observations.

So there was much contradictory testimony with regard to

God, and the meaning of life; and there was the testimony of life that seemed to contradict almost everyone. For example, if you asked the priests, the spirits of the dead were consigned to heaven or hell; if you asked the scientists, there were no spirits at all—but Gurdjieff had seen mediumistic demonstrations that fit neither explanation. (Gurdjieff, however, was not a believer in mediumistic spiritualism per se, and he later ridiculed it in *Beelzebub's Tales to His Grandson*.) Gurdjieff's beloved grandmother passed on, then his favorite sister died, and the great question posed by the fact of death was prominent in his mind.

One occasion in 1882, recorded in *Meetings with Remarkable Men*, brought him so close to that snuffling predator, Chaos, he nearly had his questions about death answered prematurely. He and a group of friends met in a bell tower to eat sweets and share the banter of youth: talk at once airy with meaninglessness and heavy with meaning. Among these was one Karpenko, who, it turned out, was in love with the young lady that the boyish Gurdjieff also fancied. She coyly encouraged both boys, enjoying fanning the sparks of their competition. This flared into confrontation, and, with the absurd romantic solemnity of such boys, they decided that only a duel to the death would settle the matter. But how to duel? A comrade suggested that the matter be resolved by bravery and risk: there was an artillery practice range nearby, where the boys sometimes went to gather spent shells that could be resold to scrap dealers. The rivals would go there and lie down near one another, concealed in the cratered range, and whoever survived the bombardment—if either did—would get the girl. Fate would decide.

The boys agreed. In the predawn grayness, young Karpenko and Gurdjieff laid themselves down in shell craters, on the banks of the river Chai, and waited. The firing began. Shells fell short of targets and burst all around them.

Imagine it—a boy, barely a teenager, forcing himself to remain on an artillery range, as the earth shook around him, over and over again, burst after burst, each one, should it hit close to him, capable of shattering him into bloody wreckage. The flaming shell-bursts, the thunderous shaking, the acrid reek of powder and smoke—it went on and on, consuming the world, and at any given moment that certain shell might pick him out . . .

After an initial stupefaction, the young Gurdjieff experienced an intensity of feeling that arose from a "logical confrontation" between terror and the desire to remain where he was and prove himself. These two forces seemed to oppose and then blend in him, to produce, he tells us, what seemed more than a year's worth of thought and experience in a few minutes' time. Correspondingly accompanying this confrontation within himself there came "the whole sensation of myself." And then came a realization that this suddenly sharply experienced selfhood was in jeopardy, was about to be annihilated.

In time the exhaustion of his overtaxed nerves became resignation—and then sleep. When he woke, he found the bombardment ended, and himself all but untouched. His young rival, however, lay still. After a breathless time, Gurdjieff discovered that Karpenko was injured but still lived. He and his comrades carried the wounded boy to a surgeon and then home.

When Karpenko awoke in bed, he looked around—and smiled on seeing that Gurdjieff was alive too. "Something moved in me," says Gurdjieff, "and I was overcome with remorse and pity. From that moment I began to feel towards him as a brother."

And the girl? Their love for her had "suddenly evaporated." Something more important than what usually passes for "love" had revealed itself.

Although some episodes in *Meetings with Remarkable Men* seem to be amalgamations of events, or invented allegories, the majority have the ring of historicity. Gurdjieff's artillery-range duel has the flavor of truth.

That morning on the artillery range, Gurdjieff had glimpsed some of the hidden possibilities in himself. He saw that it was possible to be more alive, more present, and that there was much more going on within oneself than he'd imagined. Gurdjieff also credited the experience with creating in him an objectivity about life's difficulties; he had, thereafter, a sense of the absurdity of expending energy on anxiety over small problems as if they were life-and-death issues. He had, after all, met life and death and had them within him, as guests, on this occasion—as a boy cowering on an artillery range with shells bursting around him.

He was also, thereafter, capable of a greater compassion for those who live in fear. And he had gained another order of objectivity, a sense of the power of detachment over identification. For complete identification with his terror would have propelled him into panic and exposure and death—he was saved only through his *reason,* perhaps to some extent awakened by these extreme conditions. He learned, then, that it was possible to bear any amount of fear and still remain intact: and that was the seed of a finer, fully flowered detachment to come much later.

Again the Dhammapada of Buddha seems in agreement:

With sustained trying and sincerity
Will power and self-control
Wise men happily become like islands
Above all the floodwaters.

But no one can for long forget the question of death and what, if anything, comes after. Much later, as a seeker of Truth, Gurdjieff carried with him "stereotyped questions" that he asked everyone, so as to methodically obtain a consensus. Almost as an afterthought, as a grown man on a visit home, he asked his father these questions, especially about life after death. His father (cited in *Meetings with Remarkable Men*) said: "In that soul which . . . exists independently after death and transmigrates, I do not believe; and yet . . ." And yet, he added, "something" can be formed—especially in certain men who have "certain experiencings"—and this "something" does not disintegrate at death. Formed in a kind of collaboration between psychic, cosmic, and bodily processes, this other body has a "much finer materiality," with properties that are influenced—before and after death—by "certain surrounding actions."

The elder Giorgiades did not believe in "a soul *which exists independently* after death"—perhaps implying that one's soul disintegrates (or rather, integrates?) into some oversoul, losing its individuality. This is not the same as believing in *no* soul.

But Ioannas Giorgiades also believed that a soul that wishes to be truly individual in the afterlife, a discrete self in harmony with the Higher but relatively independent, will seek out those "certain experiencings"—that is, "work on oneself"—that create this more lasting body. Certain esoteric Buddhist traditions—and Sufi traditions—speak of a "body of light" that is created by this conscious work and that may survive death with, so to speak, special privileges of freedom. The medieval philosopher Moses Maimonides and other sages also suggest that a soul that can survive death more or less independently must first be consciously created in life.

Similarly, Baruch Spinoza said of the human mind after death: "There is some part of it which remains eternal." Spinoza hinted that something more than "some part" might be possible if a man were sufficiently perfected in "reason."

It's unlikely that Gurdjieff's father merely stumbled on this doctrine entirely through his own cognizing—it may be that the elder Giorgiades had subtly derived it from the ancient legends he'd recited in epic form, or from some lore passed down to him by other ashokhs, originating, ultimately, from the primordial teaching Gurdjieff would seek out.

Sometimes the discrepancies between conventional wisdom and the reality that the young Gurdjieff encountered were simply a matter of what people pretended to believe and what they really believed, as in the case of a young priest sent to tutor Gurdjieff, whom he calls Bogachevsky. Father Bogachevsky confessed to Gurdjieff that there are two moralities: an *objective* morality, "established by life in the course of thousands of years," and a *subjective* morality. Objective morality is rare to encounter; subjective morality is everywhere but is characterized, ironically, by its variability. For example, in much of Utah, Mormons are strictly monogamous; in certain other parts of that state they are haughtily polygamous. In Berkeley, California, in many households, you were a cowardly dupe of the imperialists if you let yourself be drafted; in other nearby communities you were a coward if you avoided the draft. It is all relative to where you were raised, and by whom. But, Bogachevsky said, there is an objective morality, which arises from conscience. Real conscience, he said, is everywhere the same, if only people knew.

When Gurdjieff speaks of conscience, through Bogachevsky or through *Beelzebub's Tales to His Grandson,* he doesn't mean merely a little prod of guilt that warns us, now and then, but a state of being, a function of higher consciousness—a connectedness to something higher within oneself that, once firmly established by work, is an infallible guide in any situation. Conscience, Gurdjieff taught, was also the fulcrum on which man can lever his way out of the prison of sleep.

This teaching of Father Evlissi—as Bogachevsky was to be called later—implies that the usual Christian morality is as subjective as any other. Bogachevsky was assigned to Gurdjieff by Dean

Borsh . . . perhaps knowing that this teaching would be passed on to the young man. Father Evlissi, Gurdjieff tells us, eventually left the church and became assistant to the abbot of "the Essene Brotherhood," an esoteric school situated "not far from the shores of the Dead Sea." It may have been related to that school where some speculate that Jesus studied before coming into his own—and which Gurdjieff, in *Beelzebub's Tales*, mentions as offering a profound proto-Christian teaching.

It's notable that according to Gurdjieff, this Father Evlissi was one of the few people who "has been able to live as our Divine Teacher Jesus Christ wished for us all." He seems to suggest by this that Bogachesky/Evlissi was still Christian, even while being an Essene (which is usually thought of as mystical Judaism); that is, he was a Christian as Christianity was originally intended. And it's clear from this short passage that Gurdjieff had a profound reverence for Jesus—whom he calls "our Divine Teacher."

THE INDICATIONS THAT ARE ALSO CONTRADICTIONS

Again and again the young Gurdjieff came upon indications that seemed to contradict the usual set of "facts," and the dichotomy was etched ever deeper. For example, science labeled clairvoyants fraudulent, religion was prone to labeling them sorcerers, and the common people believed in them fervently as helpmeets—each point of view contradicting the others. Most fortune tellers and "psychics," of course, *are* fraudulent, but Gurdjieff seems to have encountered some authentic clairvoyants. A twitchy half-mad psychic called Eoung-Ashokh Mardiross sat for Gurdjieff's aunt; staring into his thumbnail between two candle flames the tranced clairvoyant saw that her nephew was to be injured on a certain day. In due course, young Georgei was indeed wounded in a hunting accident.

Gurdjieff encountered many such troubling anomalies: a case in which a man seemed to rise from the dead and walk; several occasions of miraculous healings from sacred icons and springs; a miraculous rainstorm called down by prayer. How were these events to be understood?

One day, sitting under a tree in a grove of poplars, working on some commissioned craftwork, Georgei heard a shriek. A short distance away he found a Yezidi boy sobbing in the center of a circle drawn on the ground; other children, who were not Yezidis, were standing to one side laughing at him. The boy in the circle made odd movements as he struggled to leave it—but seemed trapped. The other children had drawn the circle in the dirt around him and they explained that because he was a Yezidi, the boy could not leave it until the circle was rubbed away. The young Gurdjieff rubbed out the circle and, set free, the Yezidi boy ran off.

The Yezidi are a sect of certain tribes living in the shadow of Mount Ararat. It was, Gurdjieff learned, apparently true of all of them: that if a circle is drawn around a Yezidi, "he cannot of his own volition escape from it."

No one else, that day among the poplars, showed an interest in discovering why the Yezidi boy reacted this way. Only the young Gurdjieff made it his aim to find out what he could. And in this we see again a fundamental fact of his nature: a dislike of accepting flawed explanations for any mystery, and the dogged pursuit of answers.

He asked all the adults of his acquaintance who might know anything: officers and priests and doctors. The best answer he got was "hysteria." Gurdjieff had read widely in the field of neuropathology already, he knew what hysteria was—but he doubted that this dismissive word "hysteria" completely explained the Yezidi circle phenomenon. What was the actual mechanism of this hysteria?

Gurdjieff kept this inquiry in his vest pocket, as it were, and pursued it when he could: In an experiment carried out in later years he learned that it takes two strong men to drag an old Yezidi woman from an unbroken circle drawn on the ground; she then falls into a cataleptic state that may last up to a day—from which she can be roused only by her own priests speaking certain incantations.

Eventually, in studies like this one, from instruction in certain monasteries, and through an unfaltering attention to the activity of his own inner nature, Gurdjieff formed his convictions about man's psychological nature. He confirmed man's mechanicality, making clear our tendency to follow dictates *imprinted* on us, much as, in a metaphor he favored, sonic information was imprinted on old-fashioned phonograph rolls. By an analogous means our programmed sets of reactions are imprinted by experience and childhood conditioning. The stymied Yezidi boy may have been an early clue to that system of psychology.

But Gurdjieff would not be content with psychology, and— whether through his own efforts or through studies he made in combination with esoteric initiations—he was to connect psychology with metaphysics and these with the study of energy movement in the body.

How to Begin to Search?

The young man Gurdjieff was ever more driven, goaded by the anomalies he'd seen—and also by the fundamental questions that arise in any thinking person: Is there a meaning to life? Why are we alive at all? Is there a Creator? Why do we suffer? Why are there wars? What is man's real purpose and destiny, and what happens after death?

Gurdjieff made it his innate wish—his living purpose—to answer these questions. Since modern men seemed unable to provide satisfactory explanations, he cast about for other ways to answer them, and he hit on two main approaches. First, there must have been men who, in the past, had asked the same questions and found real answers. Surely in all of human history some had succeeded. And if they'd succeeded in finding the answers, some of them must have left traces, messages, even "legominisms"—encrypted messages from the past. Some would have founded schools, and some of those schools might still exist. He suspected that there might be an ur-revelation, a kind of pleroma of knowledge from which religion as it is now known would be just a fragmentary, murky declension. And presumably that original prototeaching included a science of human development that the contemporary world had not yet touched. Might it be possible to reconstruct that prototeaching? He made up his mind: he would seek out that vanished knowledge— and the hidden people who protected it, if they existed.

There was another way to get at least some of the answers— experimentation, the scientific method. He and his companions carried out many experiments, and by all accounts Gurdjieff never ceased to experiment.

George Ivanovitch Gurdjieff was uniquely prepared for this great, dual undertaking. In a spontaneous talk in New York City, in 1924, Gurdjieff elucidated "The Material Question" (which appears as a postcript to *Meetings with Remarkable Men*), and how he had raised money for his researches and ultimately for his Institute. As a boy and a young man, he said, his father had forged in him, partly with tales of Mustapha the Lame Carpenter and "by means of other 'persistent procedures' . . . the irresistible urge always to be making something new." He was taught various manual skills and crafts by his father and other tutors, but as soon as his father noticed that he was becoming reasonably adept at any skill, and beginning to like it, he immediately forced the boy to turn to another craft entirely. Besides familiarity with many crafts, the point was to be ready to tackle any new difficulty presented by any challenge that arose. This engendered in Gurdjieff "a certain subjective property which . . . finally became fixed in the form of an urge frequently to change my occupation." He became vocationally eclectic, and always eager to penetrate the mysteries of craft. Because of this, he "was able to grasp . . . the very essence of each branch of learning, instead of being left with merely an accumulation of empty rubbish, which is the inevitable result among contemporary people of the general use of their famous educational method called learning by heart."

There one gets a bit of typical Gurdjieff cantankerousness—he offhandedly dismisses the whole of the educational system as leaving one with an accumulation of rubbish. Few are the human institutions that Gurdjieff does not disdain. He was always the critical outsider—though he maintained that dogmatic religious institutions, the ordinary scientific establishment, and so on, were the real "outside." *They* were the abnormality. He insisted that a "normal" man was educated according to the primordial and more authentic process he was *reintroducing*. Indeed, Gurdjieff was fond of talking of the *real world*—something austere, where sharply defined, unrelenting cosmic laws held absolute dominion; a place that gave the lie to a man's fantastic vanities about himself. He did not paint the rainbow-shimmery spirituality of "higher planes" that the purveyors of theosophy and so-called new age wares so often peddle. Men as they stood, in the modern world, were not only abnormal, they were wandering aimlessly in a daydreaming, mechanistic *unreality*. He only wished to return them to something as manifestly real as "the rain making the pavement wet." The esoteric side of the "real world" was paradoxically both a study of "material" and a work with energy; it was both about our mechanistic nature and about accessing currents making their way to us from that apex of being we call God.

More to the point, Gurdjieff's account in "The Material Question" sketches his approach to the necessaries of life in his adult years. If he ran out of money, he improvised something, often quite ingeniously—always then using the money to fund his search for truth. For example, as an adult searching through the Middle East for esoteric truth, he found himself low on funds. Before he could continue the search, he had to replenish his resources. In a bazaar he found a used Edison phonograph, along with a simple recording apparatus, and rolls, which most of the people in that area had never seen and didn't know how to use. He recorded songs and spicy anecdotes on the "Edison rolls," then went to a town where such contraptions were even more unknown and set up a booth where he sold short earphone-listenings on the device for one or two of the local "bucks" and had a long line of people supplying him money, for almost no work, all day long. When he replenished his funds, he moved on to something else.

He entered into a wager with a friend: Which of them could first find a way to generate the large amount of money they needed to continue their search? With the very skills inculcated in him by his father, he set up another booth—designing the hand-bills himself—for "The Universal Traveling Workshop," which repaired anything at all, especially whatever was supposedly irreparable. People brought him things that, very often, they only *thought* were broken—they simply didn't know how to use them properly—or that were scarcely broken. At a glance he took in the soul of the thing and set it right—and if the customer seemed like someone who could afford it and who deserved it, he sometimes charged a disproportionately large fee.

His father's approach to acquiring skills was to be applied to Gurdjieff's spiritual seeking too: he was able to enter and probe many spiritual schools (and spiritual books) in a concerted way that allowed him to glean *essentially* what they taught—something he was uniquely fitted to do—without being caught up in the kind of identification with the school that traps a man in rote dogma. Gurdjieff was then free to choose aspects from one or another teaching, to link them up and fill in the missing blanks of that hidden Way and thus reconstruct the missing prototeaching that reconciled all the apparent contradictions.

In 1915 he told Ouspensky that most esoteric schools specialize: some in philosophy, some in theory; that they're located in widely distributed geographical locations; and that there remain no general schools. One must collate information from one school and then another to get the total picture. He was helped in this by his fellow members of the Seekers of Truth, who brought information back from specific sources and shared it. Nevertheless, eventually he evidently found a greater school, one that, if not "a general school," nevertheless drew him to deeper studies.

Following through on his burning wish, making his way doggedly toward his avowed goal of reconstructing the lost teaching, Gurdjieff was to spend many years carrying out a kind of improvised, footsore survey of spiritual schools and traces of schools remaining in the Middle East, Russia, Africa, India, and Tibet. By some accounts he ranged as far as the Solomon Islands. He found traces of the ur-teaching he was looking for, certainly, and by his own account he found treasure-houses, so to speak, of esoteric learning—including the School of Schools . . .

THREE

THE SEARCH BEGUN

You will see that in life you get back exactly what you give. Your life is the mirror of what you are. It is your image. You are passive, blind, demanding. You take all, you accept all, without feeling any obligation. Your attitude towards the world and toward life is the attitude of one who has the right to make demands and take, who has no need to pay or to earn. You believe that all things are your due, simply because it is you! All your blindness is there! None of this strikes your attention.

—Jeanne de Salzmann, "First Initiation,"
in *Gurdjieff, Essays and Reflections
on the Man and His Teaching*

What are anticlerical sentiments, when it comes to one's own son making a living? Gurdjieff's father wanted his son to study at the Georgian Theological Seminary in Tiflis—a priest at least got paid and got his daily bread and shelter. In 1883, at the age of seventeen, Georgei Giorgiades left home for Tiflis, the capital of Russian Georgia. Once in Tiflis, however, he could not bring himself to submit to what seemed to him the lifelessness of the seminary. Instead, he struck off into the world, on his own.

Gurdjieff's first job as an independent adult? He became a stoker for the Transcaucasian Railway. It was a position he held on and off, in those days. Some of the off time he spent studying under a famed Orthodox teacher, Father Yevlampios in the monastery of Sanaine; some he spent on a pilgrimage to the Armenian holy city of Echmiadzin. His real purpose was always there, tugging at his sleeve.

Tiflis was a place of seething black markets and some decadence, which must have tested the young Gurdjieff's character. As a robust young man he might well have done some "experimenting" of his own with Tiflis's more errant women, and its seamy nightlife. But it was also the place where he met two close friends and future fellow Seekers of Truth, whom he names as Abram Yelov, an Aisor,★ and Sarkis Pogossian, an Armenian.

All three shared a desire to know, to understand, to see more deeply into the nature of the world and their own souls. Pogossian had graduated from a seminary and could have become a priest, but he could not resolve the same contradictions that had set up a friction of inner questioning in Gurdjieff, and he felt another kind of calling. Pogossian was drawn to the physical, to machinery—in the external as well as the internal sense—and went from being a stoker to an expert locksmith. Yelov was a scholar but by profession a bookseller, and this was not a profession he'd undertaken lightly: it meant he had broad access to bibliographic wisdom, to "curious volumes of forgotten lore." It can be no accident that one of these young men was centered in his physical nature and that the other's center of gravity was intellectual. It was as if—and Gurdjieff intends that we notice this—they each

---

★A tribe originating in Assyria.

personified an example of two of the three general types of men found in the Gurdjieffian teaching: Man number one, the man centered in his moving center, that is, in his physical/instinctive nature; man number two, the emotionally centered man (was that Gurdjieff himself, in this tale?); man number three, the intellectually centered man. None of the three is superior to the others; they are simply oriented differently toward life—each reacts according to his nature as man one, two, or three. Gurdjieff adduces seven grades of man, and man number four *is* in some ways more complete, higher than man one, two, or three; man five is more unified, higher in several respects than man four, and the gradient continues on up to man seven.

These categories of people dovetail with Gurdjieff's assertion that a human being is three-centered: we have three "minds," governing thinking, feeling, and our body, each with its own set of programming.

A "normal" man will have these three centers working in balance, in harmony. Few of us, after the evident Fall of man, are normal . . .

Before determining his course on ferreting out the prototeaching, Gurdjieff had a more general design in mind: he told his new friends that his aim had crystallized in the determination to understand "the life process on Earth . . . and the aim of human life" in the light of this process.

And he wanted to understand more of this than science alone could give him. Yes, science was valuable, even fascinating. With enough scientific study one could understand something, in general, of the clockwork details of life on Earth and man's place in that biological clockwork. But that only explained some part of the *how*. It didn't explain the *why;* it conveyed no ultimate meaning, no relation of these details to the cosmic whole—and it did not speak to the spiritual self, which Gurdjieff sensed as something quite real.

Gurdjieff's autobiographical inclusion of this aim resonates with meaning. It's impossible to overestimate the importance, in the Gurdjieff Work—and in his life—of having a specific aim, a wish, crystallized as a *question*. In his books and in the Gurdjieffian oral tradition, it's seen as vital to have a living question that drives one's spiritual quest. This question should be as sharply defined, within oneself, as the first equation on the blackboard is to a mathematician working out a formula. The idea relates partly to the Gurdjieffian take on "intention"—which in the Work is ideally something like having a crystal-clear idea before you, like a mental banner; a firm, abiding grip on what you want to achieve, which remains with you as much as you can make it stay. And deeper than that, *intention* would seem to be a kind of benevolent *willing*: felt with one's whole being and illuminated by the energies conducted through that being. As one teacher of the Gurdjieff Work said, "a question has a transformative effect—if it's a *living* question."

Life is breathed into *intention* from this fully felt question. There are layers of significance, from the macrocosmic to the microcosmic, to this demand, this question.

What is your question? What is your aim? What is your . . . wish?

Adventures in Seeking

In 1885 Gurdjieff journeyed to Constantinople—modern Istanbul—to study with Sufi dervishes of several orders. What he found there was of interest to him but seemed incomplete. While in Constantinople he met Ekim Bey, the son of a pasha for whom he'd done a singular favor. The young Gurdjieff had made himself ill by repeatedly diving into the sea to find a precious chaplet, a jeweled rosary, the pasha had accidentally dropped there. He eventually scooped the gem-studded chaplet from the murky sea bottom, and though he might have sold it, he returned it, refused a reward . . . and promptly collapsed on the pasha's doorstoop. Ekim Bey helped to nurse Gurdjieff back to health, and the two became fast friends.

Much later, when Gurdjieff was in the Caucasus town of Suram, he was joined there by Ekim Bey—now a physician—and by Karpenko, Pogossian, and Yelov.

In his accounts of his youth, Gurdjieff is not averse to making fun of himself. With typical Gurdjieffian color, in *Meetings with Remarkable Men* he describes himself and his friends as having been "thoroughly stuffed in all kinds of Don Quixotic aspirations" and says of the hapless Ekim Bey that he was "drawn into our 'psychopathy' and, like us, burned with eagerness to jump over his own knees."

The youthful friends would sometimes go to the ruins of the old city of Ani, finding it a peaceful place to pore over parchments and crumbling books. There they tried to puzzle out the secrets of the ancients. It was in Ani, around 1886, in the precarious wall niche of a long-abandoned monastic cell, that Gurdjieff and Pogossian found antiquated Armenian parchments, one of them alluding to something called the Sarmoung Brotherhood, known to have existed "somewhere between Urmia and Kurdistan" in the seventh century but founded in ancient Babylon.

There were hints in the text that this school was a link to the esoteric schools of a pre-Babylonian antediluvian civilization. They had come across references to the Sarmoung before in "the book called Merkhavat"—by which Gurdjieff may well have meant the Merkhabah texts of esoteric Judaism, essential early texts of Kabbalism. "This school," Gurdjieff remarks in *Meetings*, "was said to have possessed great knowledge, containing the key to many secret mysteries." Gurdjieff made up his mind: he would find this school, and he would find the teaching it embodied. And that aim would become the vehicle for his primary intention: the search for the true significance of life on Earth and in the cosmos.

Gurdjieff and Pogossian deduced from historical references in the parchment that the Sarmoung's school had been founded by Aisors. The Aisors are descended from Assyrians, and are now scattered about the globe. Gurdjieff describes the Aisors as being in line with the Nestorians who do not acknowledge the divinity of Christ.

The two young men decided that the Sarmoung monastery might still exist "somewhere between Urmia and Kurdistan," three days journey from Mosul. Why not go to the area, try to find the school—and enter it?

But how to pay for the trip? I've already mentioned some of the impromptu fund-raising Gurdjieff was capable of. On one occasion Gurdjieff and a friend used mentalist tricks—which he describes in the book—and the decidedly unmiraculous "miracles" of a fakir to raise money; "demonstrations" that were really just entertainments. On another occasion, he tells us gleefully, he made traps and caught sparrows, clipping them a bit and actually *painting* them so that he could resell them as "American canaries." This colorful story has been used against Gurdjieff as an example of his willingness to bamboozle the unwary, but no one was really hurt by this little deception—apart from some inconvenienced sparrows.

No one was really hurt, either, when, on another occasion—as he outrageously boasts in his own account—he went to various towns where he knew a railroad was going to be routed and told the local officials that their town was being *considered* as a possible rail station. For a fee he could see to it that the railroad did indeed come that way. Of course, the railroad was already planned for each of those towns, and these officials, who were by no means impoverished, paid him for nothing. But then again their money paid for something—it paid for his search.

The reader can either sniff self-righteously at these stories or be appreciative of Gurdjieff's nearly unbridled resourcefulness. And it seems to me that we must acknowledge his honesty— paradoxically—in letting us know he was capable of such deceptions. Many would-be spiritual teachers, in their memoirs and biographical releases, paint themselves as purehearted living icons. But when they straightfacedly allege their past to be immaculate they reveal themselves as more like improbable little tin saints.

There's more to Gurdjieff telling these stories on himself. Gurdjieff believed that man was caught up in "the terror of the situation," a world asleep, a world prone to psychotic, mindless fits of rage that men call "war": a world without *objective* conscience. In such a world, anyone with an aim, a wish, that runs counter to the general flow of the world, is always moving upstream, struggling against a cataract of negative influences to keep their quest alive. If along the way Gurdjieff had to stage magic shows, paint some sparrows, or exploit the greed of a few bureaucrats in order to survive long enough to learn what the real meaning of life was, so as to help mankind achieve inner and outer peace—it was well worth it. Along that route he was guided by conscience respecting the things that really mattered.

In relating these tales to us, Gurdjieff would seem to be hinting that real seekers must be determined and resourceful on the precarious path to the truth.

But it was Pogossian who found the means to finance their expedition—he had learned that an Armenian protectionist society wished to send emissaries through the Middle East to communicate with distant Armenian clerics. Gurdjieff and Pogossian talked their way into this courier job and were provided with "a considerable sum of Russian, Turkish and Persian money and a great many letters of introduction." They set out toward Kaghyshman and points East. As they went, they fulfilled their obligations to those who had paid for their trip when they could, but "did not hesitate to leave them unfulfilled" when it was necessary to sacrifice those obligations to their greater purpose. They passed through many adventures in dangerous territory and often found it vital to conceal their real nationality, traveling in disguises. Gurdjieff made this an art over the years, at various times appearing to be an Aisor, a traveling Jew, a Turk, a Russian, a Caucasian Tatar, a Mongol, and a Transcaspian Buddhist.

There are practical reasons he became so good at disguise, especially when entering Sufi and Aisorrian schools where he had to seem "one of them," as certain sects were known to rather spectacularly kill snooping interlopers. A couple of nosy British explorers, he said, had been *skinned alive*.

But his emphasis on disguise suggests this may be another instance where *Meetings with Remarkable Men* is written on more than one level. Gurdjieff was interested in being "in the world but not of it"; he advocated an "outer considering," in which those who follow the secret path in the tumult of life must appear to be what others expect them to be—within reason—while inwardly remaining free of identification. Gurdjieff and Pogossian in disguise represent outer appearance enfolding the hidden, harmonized in the wise man; the dervish who appears to be stained the color of the world but inwardly is pure.

On the way to the region that might contain the Sarmoung monastery, "exactly two months after crossing the River Arax," Pogossian was bitten by a yellow phalanga. The bite of this highly venomous tarantula-like creature is often fatal. In a makeshift operation, trying to save Pogossian's life, Gurdjieff cut a bit too much of his friend's flesh away, effectively crippling him in the short term.

Gurdjieff hired an ox cart in a nearby village and carted his delirious friend to the care of an Armenian priest on their list of contacts. They stayed with the priest for a month, as Pogossian, feverish and limp, was nursed back to health. Here, Gurdjieff learned that the priest possessed a certain ancient map . . . a map that a mysterious Russian prince had tried many times, and with a great deal of money, to purchase.

Persuaded to show the antique map to Gurdjieff, the Armenian priest taxed the young man's capacity for whatever outer considering he'd managed, as suddenly Gurdjieff had to work hard to conceal his excitement. It was a map of "pre-sand Egypt"—that is, the long-ago Egyptian civilization that had existed before the Pharaonic civilization that is known to most scholars, so long ago that Egypt was then not even a desert.

The Armenian priest had charged the Russian prince a small fortune merely to copy this antique treasure, and Gurdjieff had nowhere near such a sum. One day, when the priest was absent, Gurdjieff opened the chest where the map was concealed, took it out, and copied it. Then he replaced it. He could have stolen the map, and after copying it, sold it somewhere for a great deal of profit. But he only copied and replaced it.

So excited was the young Gurdjieff by the find that he decided to set out to discover what he could in Egypt itself, to uncover this ancient civilization. The Sarmoung would have to wait.

With the help of some drunken sailors they backed in a bar fight, Pogossian and Gurdjieff secured a free passage to Egypt. But Pogossian, caught up in shipboard life, decided to go his own way and to become a ship's engineer. His old love of the machinery of the material world called him. Pogossian eventually became a shipping magnate and a millionaire.

Gurdjieff is vague about his doings in Egypt. He merely says that he became interested in the Pyramids and the Sphinx and became a guide to people coming to see Egyptian monuments. And it was in hiring out as a guide that he met two more remarkable men, Professor Skridlov and an older man whom he calls Prince Yuri Lubovedsky and who was to become one of his greatest friends. Gurdjieff soon discovered that this was the same prince who'd tried to buy the map of pre-sand Egypt.

The wealthy prince's taste for the standard rewards of life had expired when his adored bride had died giving birth. After trying to contact her spirit through mediums, he had become caught up in theosophy and occultism and then in a deeper search for spiritual truth.

Between 1888 and 1889 Gurdjieff went on an expedition to Thebes with the prince, looking for confirmation of pre-sand Egypt. With the professor he also went on expeditions into the Sudan and Abyssinia, and what remained of Babylon in Iraq. Gurdjieff would one day speak reverently of the vibrations, the cultivated energies he seemed to sense in the ruins of Babylon; the vibration of abiding *presence*.

Disguising himself as a devout Muslim, Gurdjieff the seeker of knowledge penetrated both Mecca and Medina. This may be where he came by a rather strong aversion for animal sacrifice, which he was to excoriate in *Beelzebub's Tales to His Grandson,* as it was carried out in such places in an excess of animal merchandizing and bloodletting.

Back in Constantinople, Gurdjieff met a remarkable *woman,* through the prince: the beautiful Vitvitskaia. Her family had fallen into poverty, and in order to survive she became first a kept woman for a succession of randy old men, then a sort of lure for a certain unscrupulous physician; her flirtation attracted lonely men to become patients.

Prince Lubovedsky had encountered her as she accompanied an apparently distinguished man on a trip to Alexandria. It was Lubovedsky who, making enquiries, discovered that her escort was known to be a white slaver—unknown to her, this smooth talker planned to sell her into enforced prostitution. Prince Lubovedsky saved her from the slaver and sent her to his estate in Tambov province, commending her to the care of his sister. Both the prince and his sister were spiritual seekers who had learned something of how to "work on oneself," and the grateful Vitvitskaia took up this work with all her heart. She went from being a "fallen woman" to becoming, as Gurdjieff said, an ideal for all women. Like the others who became part of Gurdjieff's circle, she became one of the Seekers of Truth.

Vitvitskaia was not the only Seeker of Truth with a compromised past. Gurdjieff befriended a wretch he calls Soloviev and saved him from the lowest depths of malodorous, alley-sleeping, alms-begging, drunk-tank alcoholism. Like Vitvitskaia, Soloviev was to become a sober, devoted Seeker, and eventually he became an expert on addictive substances of all kinds: the deep study of a problem leads to understanding it, and freedom from it.

Then and now, there are some—alcoholics, addicts, and others—for whom Work on oneself is a lifeline, is the only hope as they thrash in the churning chaos of their lives. Such people may be more deeply motivated than other Seekers. They've been to the bottom—and feel the only way to stay free of it for good is to keep moving steadfastly, if slowly, toward the heights.

Gurdjieff's description of Vitvitskaia, which I have only skirted, has so many telling details it's clear he's talking about a real historical personage and no mere metaphor. But one of her special interests just coincidentally sums up an important Gurdjieffian idea . . . every character in Gurdjieff's memoir, historic or not, serves more than one purpose. Vitvitskaia was a sort of homegrown natural scientist. She was an accomplished musician and was interested in the way that music—and vibration itself—creates special states and conditions, in the air and in its hearers.

She hypothesized that sound vibrations—and by extension, other sorts of vibrations—must have some kind of automatic effect on the inner state of organisms, including people. She began to do harmless experiments on people to see how sound vibrations affected them. Certain compositions and sound progressions, combined with control over atmospheric pressure and other factors in a room, and carried out with subjects of a certain type, made it possible for her to "call forth at will in all of them laughter, tears, malice, kindness and so on." At a certain unnamed monastery in Turkestan, Vitvitskaia, Gurdjieff, and his companions heard a certain "monotonous music," created according to specific principles, that made them all feel like sobbing. Despite their variety of race and type, each had the same response.

But how? How did the brethren of this monastery get such uniformity of response? It wasn't that it was simply sad music. It was as if it affected the listener in some inner place, with its particular combination of vibrations. As if some inner center of feeling was both *designed* and *compelled* to respond according to an unknown law. Vitvitskaia became obsessed with understanding this phenomenon: she couldn't sleep or eat, and she became so frustrated with her inability to fathom the mystery that she bit into her finger, nearly severing it from her hand.

Gurdjieff told her he'd learned from Father Evlissi that by means of an ancient Hebraic music the Essenes were able to "make plants grow in half an hour." This information made Vitvitskaia feverish with a desire for further experimentation. Gurdjieff was much impressed with her character and her obsessive desire *to know,* and he speaks of her death from an apparent pneumonia—much later, after many more adventures—with great sorrow. Gurdjieff is careful to point out that when he first encountered her he felt an initial antipathy, an automatic, inexplicable hatred for her, mixed with pity, perhaps because of the moral compromises she'd made: he was raised in a culture that sometimes judges women more harshly than men, and he was not yet free of his conditioning. Later he seemed to see past his automatic responses and to see her essence, gleaning a sense of Vitvitskaia's inner life, completely changing his estimation of her. So a man's initial, *automatic* responses are often misleading and superficial. They are likely to be the product of a "little I" and not *real I.*

In this tale of Vitvitskaia a theme recurs. Gurdjieff in many places describes a feverish, obsessive drive to penetrate to inner truth. This drive was present in himself, in Vitvitskaia, in Lubovedsky, in the fictional Beelzebub's grandson. Gurdjieff seems to connect this drive with something worth appreciating, even revering. This would appear to be his dramatization of *magnetic center,* something within us that resonates with the Higher and draws us to seek it out.

A more central Gurdjieffian theme is touched on in the story of Vitvitskaia—the primacy of *influences.* Everyone is perpetually subject to influences, both of the grosser sort, as in human historical and interpersonal events, and subtler, vibrational influences. Some of these are *planetary influences*—which, Gurdjieff insists, is one of the fundamental causes of war (though not the sole cause) and of other human automatic responses. Though he says that planetary influences emanate from the various bodies of the solar system and the stars, nowhere does he indicate that the study of these forces is the same as "astrology," at least as astrology is known now.

On a walk with some students, in after years, Gurdjieff deliberately dropped his walking stick. One pupil immediately bent to pick it up; another hesitated, not wanting to get in the way; another wondered at the deliberateness of it and wondered if he *should* pick it up. Gurdjieff pointed out these individual reactions and said that this was a small example of actual "astrology" at work. Their essential characters—formed in the womb from various factors, including "planetary influences"—had decided their courses. In answer to a question by a frustrated student, Gurdjieff, according to a Library of Congress transcription of Gurdjieff's meetings during World War II, said: "Cosmic phenomena for which you are not responsible go against your work. You can only give yourself your word that when life becomes quiet, you will set yourself to work." This suggests that, conventional astrology aside, planetary influences do exert some kind of generalized influence over our lives.

Some vibrational influences are helpful, however. Some originate locally, Gurdjieff said; but some, if man is open to them, and actively turns to them, reach us from a much higher plane of being. Such higher influences have a specific effect on us: influences just as specific as the grosser impulses from lower levels.

According to one of Gurdjieff's French students, Dr. Michel Conge, Gurdjieff's ultimate mission was to awaken people so that they could then become conductors for sublime cosmic influences from the higher worlds—they could then conduct a *current* of a certain kind of energy that would restore balance, and ultimately save humanity. A current of intelligent energy that could save the world.

A PLAYER IN THE GREAT GAME?

The Gurdjieff biographer James Moore, in *Gurdjieff: The Anatomy of a Myth,* tracks him, between 1890 and 1893, in quite another geographical direction than the usual forays into the East. He traces Gurdjieff to Switzerland and then Rome, where he worked as a political envoy for the Armenian Social Revolutionary Party, a group fighting for Armenian rights and territorial recognition. Again Gurdjieff probably did this as a means to an end, since the orthodoxies he might encounter in Switzerland and Italy conceal many esoteric traditions, for example those of the Rosicrucians, sundry Christian mystics and mages, and Kabbalists. But Gurdjieff's work for a "Social Revolutionary Party" nonetheless conjures a Gurdjieffian mystery.

There are various indications that Gurdjieff was involved in revolutionary politics, in Greece and in other places; on the other hand he was, in later years, quite possibly an espionage agent for Tsar Nicholas II. The esoteric writer John Bennett said he saw an extensive dossier on Gurdjieff's activities as an agent. Gurdjieff was at one point denied entry to England because of his alleged past in "the Great Game"—working for the tsar against the interests of England in India and Tibet. Do these political affiliations—revolutionaries on one side, monarchy on the other—seem to contradict one another?

They do. And it's not surprising that the contradiction should arise in Gurdjieff's history. If he had a political leaning, it was probably away from mindless obedience to monarchies and plutocrats, at least. But in his magnum opus, *Beelzebub's Tales to His Grandson,* as well as in his final, incomplete book *Life Is Real Only Then, When "I Am,"* he radiates a disgust with the conventions of human government, as well as with political "movements" and self-righteous social trends. Ouspensky's *In Search of the Miraculous* quotes Gurdjieff's biting irony: "If a sufficient number of people who wanted to stop war really did gather together they would first of all begin by making war upon those who disagreed with them." He speaks with an acid-dripping sneer of "power possessing people"—meaning those whose power grows from the barrel of a gun—and he was equally adamant about the hopelessness of human planning, human society, so long as people remain in their sleeping state of bumbling and even lethal abnormality. He was firm about *nonidentification* with the usual collective endeavors, revolutionary or conservative. Give Caesar what is Caesar's, yes, but give your inner attention to the service of the Higher. Compare Plato: "He whose mind is fixed upon true being has no time to look down upon the little affairs of men, or to be filled with jealousy and enmity in the struggle against them; his eye is ever directed towards fixed and immutable principles, which he sees neither injuring nor injured by one another, but all in order moving according to reason." Gurdjieff gave it out straight from the shoulder, in the Library of Congress's collection of transcribed meetings from World War II: "*The key to everything—remain apart. Our aim is to have constantly a sensation of oneself, of one's individuality. This sensation cannot be expressed intellectually, because it is organic. It is something which makes you independent, when you are with other people.*"★

But Gurdjieff's spiritual convictions do have social implications. In the 1920s, Alfred R. Orage—the noted literary arbiter and pivotal Gurdjieffian—enthused to Gurdjieff about his pet economic reform theory, Social Credit. Gurdjieff told him to concentrate instead on awakening mankind—nothing socially significant could be done until this was accomplished. Men, in their mechanical state, could not communicate well enough to establish a lasting peace. Once enough people were awakened, real communication—and a corresponding hope for world peace—would then be possible.

If Gurdjieff was employed as an agent of the tsar and then as a functionary for a revolutionary group, he probably would have "fulfilled his obligations," as he put it, to these organizations, but his primary purpose with them was likely to use their rubles and drachmas and Swiss banknotes and their connections to gain ac-

★*Voices in the Dark* by William Patrick Patterson.

cess to those places where hidden knowledge might be brought to light.

Not all of Gurdjieff's expeditions bore esoteric fruit. Gurdjieff told Orage that at the age of twenty-one, having read Madame Blavatsky, he believed her enough to journey through India, seeking those places she'd referenced—until he discovered that they did not exist. He gained some experience on the trip, at any rate, and he had learned a valuable lesson: to be skeptical of exotic claims. But the arduous journey through India as an inexperienced youth must have been quite an exhausting, frustrating experience.

It was between 1894 and 1904 that Gurdjieff's most vital seeking was carried out—and this time, guided by maturity and experience, and yes, some guile, it was not fruitless.

SEEK—AND SEEK AGAIN— AND YE SHALL FIND

About 1895, Gurdjieff and his friends formed the Seekers of Truth. "There were all kinds of specialists among us," he said. "Everyone studied on the lines of his particular subject. Afterwards, when we foregathered, we put together everything we found." The Seekers of Truth carried out experiments and expeditions, separately and together, pooling all for the common aim, which is made clear by the name of their little society.

But Gurdjieff was on his own in 1896 when he undertook to search for traces of the legendary Imastun brotherhood in Crete. This time he was apparently riding on the coattails of the Ethniki Hetairia, a Greek "Spartacist" society. Caught in the crossfire of a Greek uprising against the Turks in Sfakia, Gurdjieff received the first of three wounds from three stray bullets (each wound received at well-separated times in his life), "plunked into" him, as he put it, by "some charmer." In each case, as the years passed,

each wound was "nearly mortal." And in each case he was weakened, making it even easier for local microbes that "visited me
and found delight in my body." With typical derisive irony, he lists
some of these "specific 'delicacies' of local character," including
"the honored and famous 'Kurdistan tzinga,' the not less famous
'Armenian dysentery'" and "the honored" Ashkhabadian bedinka,
Bokharian malaria, Tibetan hydropsy, Baluchistan dysentery, and
many others that "left their calling card permanently."

But "animated as always by the *idee fixe* of my inner world,"
Gurdjieff persevered, and in 1897, with the Seekers of Truth, he
set out on a journey through Turkestan to Tabriz and Baghdad.

On this expedition they heard a good deal about a certain Persian dervish. Gurdjieff and some of the others were determined to
find him. Determined they had to be, for it required a thirteen-day
digression from their journey, a side trip on which they spent nights
in the huts of shepherds and in obscure, mud-daubed settlements.

At last they found the dervish, dressed in rags, sitting barefoot
and cross-legged on the ground under a shade tree. The dervish
was at first indifferent to them, until he learned how far they'd
come and how arduous the journey. They ate together, Gurdjieff
eating his food according to yogic traditions, for at that point, relatively inexperienced, he was influenced by certain Indian yogis.
Gurdjieff ate slowly, "trying not to swallow a single morsel without masticating it according to all the rules."

The dervish asked Gurdjieff why he was chewing his food in
this way. Gurdjieff rather condescendingly explained that great
yogis had taught him to eat this way so as to properly prepare the
food for his organism.

The old man shook his head and sadly intoned, "Let God kill
him who himself does not know and yet presumes to show others
the way to the doors of His Kingdom."

The wise old dervish explained that Gurdjieff had been misinformed and was eating in exactly the wrong way. Food should be chewed a little and consumed in large pieces, or the stomach would atrophy. He further said that yogic breathing exercises were even worse than this overchewing and all the "artificial breathing" exercises taught "in contemporary schools" were quite harmful.

He went on to speak at length of the body as a "complicated apparatus," as a machine, and explained that if you tinkered with a machine without knowing its workings down to "every small screw, every little pin," you were likely to harm it.

Gurdjieff's former direction of thinking about the esoteric was here turned around; he had assumed that most "spiritual teachers" knew whereof they spoke. Till now he had cluelessly consumed a great deal of yogic junk food, along with the occasional bite of something nutritious. Now he felt a convincing consistency, a rightness about what the old man was telling him. It meant he'd been not only eating and breathing in the wrong way, he'd been *seeking* in the wrong way. He hadn't used enough discrimination.

In *Beelzebub's Tales to His Grandson,* Gurdjieff's fictional hero tells his grandson that Buddhism on Earth—except for the occasional pocket of purity—is too often sadly distorted. Beelzebub tells of stopping over in a monastery in the Himalayas where, to his horror, an offshoot sect of Buddhism required its adepts to incarcerate themselves voluntarily in small wooden sheds, like coffins standing on end, for the remainder of their days, presumably to conquer desire. Gurdjieff described such distortions of the original teachings as "maleficent"—and the anecdote of the monks immured in their sheds dramatizes the degradation that a spiritual teaching inevitably undergoes. In that story and in the tale of the Persian dervish we see that Gurdjieff had become ever more skeptical, even a bit cynical, about religion and monastic schools.

One had to be selective and work hard at filtering out the noise to get the clear signal of the authentic transmission.

There is more in the anecdote of Gurdjieff's encounter with the old Persian dervish that is redolent of Gurdjieff's overall teaching, particularly the emphasis on the "machinery" of the organism. Gurdjieff's angle on man's mechanicality cuts two ways—cutting one way, we're *wrongly* mechanical: we must transcend our psychological mechanicality, to become free and conscious. Cutting the other way, we are by nature machines—our organism is a complex soft machine—and in order to understand it, both in the physical sense and in terms of its subtler possibilities, we must understand the lower aspects of our nature *as* a machine. In certain respects, we are to rise above the mechanical in ourselves; in other respects, we are to accept it and keep it in good order.

Gurdjieff as a boy had ambitions of a career in "a technical specialization" of some sort. His writing and teaching consistently has the quality of an *engineering* study, even when speaking of the processes of "transforming energies" and "being-foods" for the creation of a soul that could survive death as an individual; in anyone else's hands these energy-transformation processes would seem *supernatural*. In Gurdjieff's presentation they come across as a *higher naturalism*. For Gurdjieff, everything is material, even the invisible world is some form of *materiality,* operating under the authority of clearly defined laws. These laws are unknown to most of us, yet they're as definite as the Newtonian laws of physics.

Even so, his attitude toward the higher realms of the cosmos is reverential. For Gurdjieff, the "machinery" of the cosmos, within us and above us, at some point vibrates with an exquisite fineness that transcends anything that can be described as merely mechanical and becomes the superbly indescribable. Here there are innate laws—but only a few. And starting from Earth, the closer you go toward the ultimate starting place of things—the Absolute—the fewer "laws" restrict us, the greater is the freedom possible, the more sheer divine intelligence is present. Since laws are fewer, on this high, all-inclusive level, presumably even physics is mitigated. So despite his analytical appreciation of system and natural law, Gurdjieff was never any sort of reductionistic slave to scientism, and in *Beelzebub's Tales* he ridicules conventional scientists.

Nevertheless, Gurdjieff seemed drawn to the scientific method, and insisted on applying it—as far as possible—to the esoteric. One of his aphorisms, in later life, stated that only one who had a critical mind could hope to work in his Institute. He exhorted his pupils to experiment—not foolishly but intelligently and carefully— to find out what was true and what untrue, what was imagined and what was real. "I ask you to believe nothing that you cannot verify for yourself."

This insistence on interrogating the esoteric and methodically subjecting it to a form of the scientific method—and certainly to logical analysis—sets him apart from the usual run of spiritual teachers, as does his emphasis on the machine model of the human condition.

The character of the Persian dervish seems to personify the perfect blend of the Western, scientific, engineering point of view and the wisdom of Eastern spirituality.

As with most anecdotes in *Meetings with Remarkable Men,* there is in the story of the Persian dervish the possibility of a parable. Through the process of *self-observation* the seeker ingests *impressions* of himself, sightings of his real behavior and inner responses, observations taken in firm bites, which are not ruminated on but simply taken in whole, to be digested into a new self-knowledge.

Through the Persian dervish advising the eating of food in largish bites, Gurdjieff might have been speaking allegorically of taking in the "food of impressions" without analysis or introspection—a way to see oneself with the cool objectivity that makes spiritual growth possible. And Gurdjieff taught that these objective impressions are literally a kind of food.

Gurdjieff and his companions spoke to the dervish at length. Then they thanked him and returned to their original itinerary, following once more the guiding star of their most heartfelt wish.

THE SARMOUNG

According to both of Gurdjieff's primary biographers,★ it was in the mid- to late 1890s that Gurdjieff became a tsarist agent. Posted to Tibet in the service of the tsar—more important, in the service of his own agenda—the disguised Gurdjieff cultivated a mutually beneficial relationship with a Tibetan official who most likely was Agwhan Dordjieff.

But more epochally, it was in 1898 that Gurdjieff at last found the Sarmoung. His friend "the dervish Bogga-Eddin" came upon Gurdjieff in New Bukhara and told him of having met a member of the Sarmoung brotherhood.

The old Sarmoungian dervish had told Bogga-Eddin that he, the dervish, knew of Gurdjieff—and of course Gurdjieff instantly arranged to meet the old man and obtained an introduction to the monastery for himself and Soloviev.

Four Kara-Khirgiz riders met Gurdjieff and Soloviev at the ruins of the fortress of Yeni-Hissar. The Kara-Khirgiz put blindfolding hoods called *bashliks* over the heads of the seekers so they would not know the way—should it be decided that they were not suitable to remain in the monastery—and took them on a long horseback journey through the mountains of Turkestan.

★Before Moore's book was James Webb's exhaustive but uneven effort *The Harmonious Circle.*

The blinding hoods remained until they camped at night and were taken off en route only twice, once when they needed all their attention to cross a narrow swinging bridge of rope and creaking, rotting planks—just the sort of bridge that, in Hollywood films, usually ends up slashed at one end, falling so that the hapless hero must struggle up the broken, dangling span over the crocodile-infested river. In Gurdjieff's case, there was simply a vertiginously deep abyss, a creaking and uncertain old bridge, and no handrails. He found the crossing all but heart-stopping.

But Gurdjieff and Soloviev at last arrived at the monastery of the Sarmoung, an austere, fortresslike but starkly beautiful structure near a canyon waterfall. They were treated cordially, assigned comfortable, austere rooms, and given good, simple food but otherwise largely ignored, at first. They were allowed to explore, to go wherever they liked in the monastery, and this was itself unusual.

Some commentators have assumed that Gurdjieff's Sarmoung monastery is a fable—or perhaps an amalgam of various monasteries of his experience, a model of the school he'd like to create himself. But certain details of Gurdjieff's description of the journey and the monastery have verisimilitude: the standing stone monuments marking the trail—which he glimpsed when his hood was briefly removed—fluttering with prayer cloths and the severed tails of animals; an old woman who seemed to be warning Soloviev not to leave the monastery but was in fact just gesturing for him to come and have some warm milk; the perfect collusion of sound and quiet around the waterfall. Picking up these and other details, the reader cannot but feel that Gurdjieff genuinely went to *some* such place, whatever it might have been called.

On the morning of the third day among the Sarmoung, a boy brought them an astonishing note. The note was from one of the brethren who turned out to be none other than Prince Lubovedsky, with whom Gurdjieff had lost touch for the last two years. Lubovedsky had recently been sick in bed, with an infected foot (another realistic-seeming detail), and he wrote of his delight in hearing that Gurdjieff had come, especially as Gurdjieff had not merely found the Sarmoung through an introduction from his old friends: "it proves me that during this time you have not been asleep."

Gurdjieff went immediately to his old comrade. Lubovedsky told Gurdjieff that in a lassitude of despair and depression he had encountered a self-effacing old dervish, of indeterminate age, who seemed to plumb him telepathically. The dervish told him that Lubovedsky's forty-five years of seeking had been a waste because the "desire of his mind did not become the desire of his heart." This is a classic Gurdjieffian formulation suggesting the harmonious working of two centers at once.

After two weeks, Gurdjieff and Soloviev were allowed to "enter into the life of the monastery." Their guide at the monastery was an old man alleged to be about 275 years old. The monastery had three courts: an outer, where Gurdjieff and Soloviev had been staying; a secondary court containing intermediary pupils; and a third court in which was a large building "like a temple." It's notable that he doesn't say it's a temple but that it is *like* a temple— that is, it's not religion but has some commonality with religion.

In a side court, called the Women's Court, young priestess-dancers learned sacred dances. Twice a day those who lived in the second and third courts assembled to take in the sacred dances of the priestesses and the Sarmoung's sacred music. The priestesses were taught, from childhood, dances that were thousands of years old, each one a sort of complex somatic semaphore transmitting, to those who could read their choreographed symbology, "one or another truth" encoded into the dance in antediluvian times.

Gurdjieff describes an apparatus used to train the young priestesses, a column higher than a man from which projected seven specially tooled "branches," which in their turn were divided into seven jointed parts. Parts of this device were inscribed with symbols corresponding to symbols of special metal plates kept in a cupboard. The branches were moved into prescribed positions, the young priestesses standing for hours before them, shaped into a particular posture—each posture a coded legominism—which became second nature to them. The emphasis on seven branches divided into seven segments is evocative of the steps of the octave described in Gurdjieff's Law of Seven, which we'll explore in chapter 5.

The dances astonished Gurdjieff with their intricate perfection. These—or other kinds of temple dances seen in diverse esoteric schools—were the models of the challenging and quite distinctive sacred dances Gurdjieff was eventually to teach at his Institute and which are still taught at the Gurdjieff Foundation. There they are called the Movements, or the Gurdjieff Movements. (An authentic sample can be seen in the Sarmoung scenes near the end of the film *Meetings with Remarkable Men*.)

One day, as *Meetings* tells it, Prince Lubovedsky informed Gurdjieff that the sheikh of the monastery had told him that he—the prince—had only three years to live. The sheikh knew this via some form of prescience. With only three years left in his life, Lubovedsky was advised to travel to another monastery on the northern slopes of the Himalayas for intensive inner work.

And so Lubovedsky set out with a caravan, and Gurdjieff, grieving for his dearest friend, never saw him again. But he did not doubt that Lubovedsky was doing the right thing, for "perhaps," said the prince, "I shall be able to make up for the time which I uselessly and senselessly lost when I had at my disposal so many years of possibilities."

We see this warning in Gurdjieff's writing in many places—a sense of urgency, that precious time is being squandered. We have the possibility of being so much more—the possibility of a life beyond life—and too often we don't do the work that crystallizes that possibility into reality.

Gurdjieff's tale of the Sarmoung monastery also offers up probable symbols. He approaches the monastery blindfolded, taken there by men he must trust to guide him along the dangerous route. In a spiritual school, the seeker must submit to guidance, to the point of (figuratively) being led about nearly "blind," at first. In later years, Gurdjieff's intellectual student Orage would be assigned to literally digging unnecessary ditches—and for a while Orage didn't understand why. Eventually he understood, but until then he was, in a sense, led about blindfolded.

In the tale of the journey to the Sarmoung monastery, the blindfold is removed when Gurdjieff must cross the abyss. The abyss is itself a powerful esoteric symbol, relating to the death of vanity, the willingness to let go of the ego though the way seems terrifyingly perilous; to keep faith even across the chasm of death. Yet at this point the seeker guides himself. His blindfold is removed, and *his own awareness* guides him across. Yet the way across the rope bridge is perilous—one false step and he falls. So his awareness must be sharply honed. He must be truly *paying attention* to cross safely.

The Sarmoung monastery has three courts, corresponding to the three circles of spiritual teaching: the exoteric, or outer circle; the mesoteric, or next inmost circle; and the esoteric, the inner circle for the initiated. Gurdjieff at first stayed in the outer court; he then moved inward, just as each seeker must work his or her way inward from the outer. Ordinary spiritual institutions and their teachings—those found in churches, one supposes—are *ex*-oteric. Within some Christian churches exist esoteric traditions, if one knows where to look. The same is true of Islamic and Buddhist traditions. There is an exoteric Buddhism involving shrines and prayers and the trappings of worshippers. Then there are the esoteric methods taught in Buddhist inner circles.

Perhaps Gurdjieff brought some secrets of the esoteric into exoteric view—but much of the esoteric he brought is still only conveyed orally, in special places.

Finally, there is the prince's own tale of encounter with the Sarmoung dervish, who told him to "feel with all your being that you really are empty."

First, to *feel with all one's being*: that phrase alone might summarize a great deal of the Gurdjieff Work. And then to feel with all one's being that one is *empty*—to sense, in the Gurdjieffian phrase, "all one's nothingness"—this is a vital step to take. To fill an urn, you must first know it is empty, and in the Work the "knowing" is the beginning of the filling. Unsentimentally feeling that emptiness is a necessary preface to creating real, lasting being.

This approach is distinctly Gurdjieffian: to desire—that is, to wish, to have intention—with more than one part of oneself, bringing in another of the three centers. And in the prince's case it was particularly important that his intention be felt in his heart as well as his mind.

ABOVE THE STORM ON STILTS: THE GOBI AND BEYOND

Later that year, Gurdjieff and the Seekers of Truth decided to cross the Gobi Desert, off the beaten trails, to search for the remains of an ancient city said to be mostly buried in the desert sands. There they would carry out exploratory excavations under the direction of the Seekers' archaeologist, Professor Skridlov.

Gurdjieff's account of this ill-fated expedition, in *Meetings with Remarkable Men,* is doubtless loosely based on some real journey or journeys—for many of the details, such as the curious death of Soloviev, ring true—but his real purpose seems to be parable.

The difficulties in the route they had to take through the Gobi, crossing great distances and carrying enough food for the long journey, seemed insurmountable. Each member of the expedition brought suggestions according to his or her specialty. Karpenko the mining engineer suggested that the very sands of the Gobi would contain vegetable matter blown there over millennia, mixed in with silica, which, in a pinch, could be extracted and consumed.

Another member, Dr. Sari-Ogli, had worked up a means to survive the terrible sandstorms of the Gobi. He built special stilts, and practiced using them in deep sand under high winds. On stilts, the expedition could look down on the low-altitude sand-storms in safety and with the equanimity of the heights.

The expedition bought poles to be shaped for double duty both as stilts and litters, and after practicing stilt walking, they set out, "amid the bleating of sheep and goats, the barking of dogs, and the whinnies and brays of the horses and asses . . . a long pro-cession of litters, like the grandiose processions of ancient kings. Long rang out our jovial songs."*

They stopped to camp in the heart of the desert, preparing meals and "Tibetan tea, brewed in the stock from the bones of the slaughtered sheep."

Then—disaster. Soloviev spotted a herd of wild camels and set out with his rifle to bag one, for he was a passionate hunter. But he did not return. They finally found him, dead: his neck had been bitten half through by a wild camel.

Meetings with Remarkable Men.

So grief stricken were they, they had not the heart to go on—though they were near their destination—and the expedition was cancelled.

Gurdjieff taught that everything that man ingests, even cognitive impressions and subtle energies in the air we breathe, is literally food, in some way. Compare John 6:27: "Do not work for the food that perishes, but for the food that endures for eternal life."

Keeping in mind the general improbability of an expedition eating sand and poised on stilts, we may assume that Gurdjieff was preparing a dish of truth spiced with tall tales in this parable of the Gobi.

But the tale is indeed the truth, as Gurdjieff sees it—if we decode it.

The goal of the Gobi expedition is a hidden city, the buried truth of a lost civilization: the symbol of secret knowledge. How does one get to buried secret knowledge? Every seeker must undertake a journey, an expedition, to attain knowledge—even if the "expedition" is only carried out at home among his books, and through the idea-landscape of some local spiritual school. That expedition will be long and arduous, so let him not be deterred, *no matter what happens.*

The members of the Gobi expedition each had a specialty—some inborn gift with which they contributed to the general undertaking. As a group they formed a complete *school,* in the sense of an *esoteric school* that adds its individual parts together to create a gestalt of special conditions, making "the journey" after secret knowledge possible.

Stilts? We need not identify with the small and large storms of life—we can rise above the turmoil, the "sandstorms," in our lives, maintaining contact with our objective conscience, through a kind of attentive and *balanced* detachment. A man *balanced* on stilts above a sandstorm is "in the world but not of it" and is liberated from the sandstorm of life.

Obstacles will arise in the path of any expedition. Gurdjieff taught that such obstacles, such deflections from our course, come with a *lawful* inevitability, according to the Law of Seven.

And, lawfully, an obstacle to the Gobi expedition inevitably arose: a herd of wild camels crossed the expedition's path—and a key man allowed his passions to commandeer him. Failing to remember himself, Soloviev was deflected off into the desert alone—where he was bitten by the very object of his pursuit, and died from it. And the expedition, losing heart, died with him—that is, the impulse was deflected from its course; the octave was not fully ascended.

Gurdjieff's delightfully outrageous account of the Gobi expedition reminds me of another story he told, to an audience of distinguished men, and which he barefacedly presented as something he'd seen himself. It seems he knew of a remote place where diamonds are scattered about the unreachable basin of a terribly deep, steep-walled valley. In order to get the diamonds up, the local wise men threw raw meat down into the valley floor, and trained vultures were sent to fetch the raw meat, returning to their trainers with diamonds stuck to the carrion. Gurdjieff's stiff-necked audience was not amused. Gurdjieff, however, was probably amused—by their literal-mindedness.

There are various ways to interpret the story, and here's just one. Vultures are a symbol of death. Gurdjieff more than once urged his followers to keep their own inevitable deaths in mind, so as to motivate them to struggle inwardly for self-observation, and consciousness, before it was too late. *Memento mori.* Through this remembering of death, we're prodded to work. And through work something is crystallized, like a diamond, and the diamonds of spiritual truth may be retrieved.

It may be that not every level of valid esoteric interpretation of a parable was deliberately intended by the storyteller. Yet it's remarkable how they seem fitting in their symbolism down to the last detail, as if a truly meaningful fable resonates with a cosmically connected life of its own.

1899. Disguised as dervishes, Gurdjieff and Professor Skridlov traveled up the river Amu Darya into Kafiristan. On the way Gurdjieff befriended a fellow traveler, a former priest whom he calls Father Giovanni. This ex-priest introduced Gurdjieff and Professor Skridlov to the monastery of the mysterious World Brotherhood. The adepts of this monastery included former Christians, Jews, Muslims, Buddhists, "and even one Shamanist." The Brotherhood was united in service "to God the Truth" and concerned with "transmuting faith in oneself."

Giovanni articulated another important Gurdjieffian idea. "Faith cannot be given to man. Faith arises in a man and increases in its action in him not as the result of automatic learning . . . but from understanding."* Father Giovanni—and Gurdjieff—make a strong case for the distinction between understanding and mere knowledge, and it is not an academic distinction. It is the difference between a man with real possibilities and a sort of man-shaped parrot.

Understanding, as Gurdjieff expresses it, is something consumed, digested, made a part of a person, until *it becomes part of his spiritual being.*

Gurdjieff and Skridlov remained in the monastery until they

Meetings with Remarkable Men.

were simply overwhelmed with what they had learned, and had to go home to digest it.

There was only one more expedition with the Seekers of Truth. In the first year of the new century, they traveled through the Pamir region and India. En route, after going astray and undergoing harrowing privations, the Seekers met a remarkable dervish who taught them all a great deal about healing, and more about the creation of an "astral form" that could survive death.

TIBET, STRAY BULLETS, AND HEALINGS WITHIN HEALINGS

Little is known about Gurdjieff during the first years of the twentieth century. We infer that he spent much of this period formulating and formalizing all that he'd learned, crystallizing the diamond of his grand teaching.

Gurdjieff's outward life, though known only sketchily, could not have been an idle one. He is said to have been presented to Tsar Nicholas II in July 1901. Shortly thereafter, some accounts (James Moore's biography, among others) have him living in Tibet—possibly employed as an agent in the service of the tsar—where he marries a Tibetan, studies with the Red Hat lamas, and even has two children. Gurdjieff alluded to this family in casual remarks to his students Stanley Nott and John Bennett much later.

According to Nott, Gurdjieff eventually had to leave Tibet for good because of illness exacerbated by the high elevation—but he boasted, like any beaming father, that one of his children had ascended at an unusually young age to become abbot of a Tibetan monastery, so he must have somehow kept in touch.

This story of Gurdjieff's sojourn in Tibet has added to the theory that Gurdjieff was working for Lama Aghwan Dordjieff, who was a high functionary for the Dalai Lama. Dordjieff was a spy for

Russia, though quite possibly playing Russia and England against each other for the benefit of Tibet.

Gurdjieff said that he himself was a "tax collector" or "fee collector" for the Dalai Lama, at one point—this may have been through Dordjieff.

And in 1935, Gurdjieff made inexplicable plans to travel to the Soviet Union (which were thwarted by Soviet bureaucrats), exactly when it was most inconvenient and exactly when Dordjieff was said to be exiled in Leningrad and dying there.

In 1902, in "the majestic mountains of Tibet, one year before the Anglo-Tibetan war," Gurdjieff was hit by a second stray bullet picked up in a sort of Tibetan drive-by, one rival mountain clan shooting at another. Gurdjieff states that he was saved from death only by a number of physicians employing a combination of both Western and Tibetan medicine, such a combination being in itself symbolic of his methods in carrying out his life's mission.

Gurdjieff's *Life Is Real Only Then, When "I Am,"* describes an epiphany that came to him when he convalesced on the southwestern edge of the Gobi, near Yangihissar: a place he described as unique in its combination of fecundity on one hand and deadly sterility in a wasteland on the other, so that "if in reality there exist paradise and hell, and if from these arises any radiation, then the air in the space between these two sources would surely have to be similar to this." Air, Gurdjieff says, is a "second food," and here it was "transformed between the forces of paradise and hell," having the effect of helping to create in him—along with the direction of his brooding mentation at that time—a "self-reasoning" of a special character.

Gurdjieff was camped near a spring. Here, on the edge of the wasteland, Gurdjieff found himself between an "awesome silence" and the clamorous sounds of animals and people, "lives of all possible forms," and there arose in him a "critical faculty of unprecedented strength." He seemed to see himself, his blunders and the missteps in his search, with a new, objective clarity.

He went to the spring of very cold water on the edge of the desert, undressed, and poured this icy water over himself, perhaps remembering the childhood regimen imposed by his father—reliving having to strip and pour cold water on himself in the gray chill of the Caucasus morning. Now he was wounded, and beset with uncertainties: a period in life when a man might long for his father's presence.

He dressed and lay down to rest, and he found his mind as clear as that cold stream but his body feeling suddenly weak. With the body too weak to put in its two cents at every juncture, the anxieties normally felt in the moving-instinctive center were reduced to a low ebb.

Then a strange progression of "self-reasoning" ensued in him.

He had survived being wounded again, only to face the excruciating uncertainties of a quest that never quite seemed successful. He tried to live according to the dictates of his awakened conscience. But he never quite got from where he was—to where he wanted to be.

Some things he had achieved. The development of the power of his thoughts—as he puts it in *Life Is Real Only Then, When "I Am"*—had been "brought to such a level that by only a few hours of self-preparation" he could "from a distance of tens of miles kill a yak" or in twenty-four hours "accumulate life forces of such compactness" that he could put an elephant to sleep merely with the power of his mind. And yet . . .

And yet in spite of mastering such phenomena, he could not master *himself*. "I could not succeed in 'remembering myself' in the process of my general common life with others so as to be able to manifest myself . . . according to the previous instructions of my 'collected consciousness.'"

Gurdjieff had achieved supernormal states, had learned to hone and fully utilize his "inherency"—an apparent inborn capability to utilize a form of mesmerism (I use this term to make this distinct from mere hypnotism by suggestion) enabling him to project his will onto others. "Namely, the power based upon strength in the field of 'hanbledzoin' or, as it would be called by others, the powers of telepathy and hypnotism." And he had an *understanding* of what was needed, of the importance of a "collected consciousness," a unified consciousness making decisions; the importance of "remembering himself." But this capability had its temptations—it must have been one of the greatest temptations a man ever struggled with!—and in his dealings with people he had been, as he says, "spoiled and depraved to the core" by succumbing to the temptations of this exquisitely developed inherency.

He could bear it no more. He was stuck below a discontinuity in the octave; he could ascend no farther. He needed to do something that would create the "shock" (to use a term he was later to give Ouspensky) that would lift him past this abyss, this temptation, this gap in the octave. How to transcend this impasse?

But then it came to him. "Why could I not . . . look to a 'universal analogy'?"

He had thought deeply, and he had investigated every discoverable supply of knowledge regarding "world creation and world maintenance." How the world came to be as it is, and what kept it that way; what the "shape" of the cosmos was, what energies continually re-created its material form.

Why not, then, look to the cosmos for help—since, after all, "as above, so below"? Man is a microcosm, indeed a "micro-cosmos." Man is created in God's image, though not in a literal anthropomorphic way. God is not a bipedal primate . . . not particularly.

God is the paramount of being, the apex of the universe. Created in God's image, each of us is also God of our own *inner* universe: "The difference between Him and myself lie only in scale. . . . I also have to be God of some kind of presence on my scale."

What was needed was the insertion of a factor for self-remembering—for being present enough to make conscious, conscience-guided choices—no matter what arose. God had created a reminding factor for mankind in the form of "the Devil," in some figurative sense. As the myth tells it, God had implanted in the world one of his own Angels, Lucifer (*Iblis* in the Muslim tradition), to be the Tempter, to provide a negative, downward-pushing force, so that man would be challenged to provide the upward-pushing force opposing this "devil." In countering the devil, man produced, through the struggle between these opposites, a third force, a particular energy that God used to maintain harmony in the cosmos.

Gurdjieff decided that as God of his own *inner* cosmos, he must also appoint a "devil," a tempter to be consciously struggled with. Thus he would have a constant reminding factor, a constant necessity of conscious opposition to his lowest impulses, the fine energy of this interactive polarization propelling him ever upward on the steep inner path.

And so he took an oath "before my own essence, in a state of mind known to me." He vowed, in *Life Is Real,* to "never make use of this inherency of mine and thereby to deprive myself from satisfying most of my vices. In the process of living together with others, this beloved inherency will always be a reminder for me."

Just envision what he was giving up. He might have been whimsically exaggerating a bit in citing the killing of a yak with his mind at tens of miles—but there's no doubt he was attesting to his having developed powers of this general kind. Imagine having the ability to make people do as you wished with the power of your mind—

without being found out—and yet taking a vow to never again in-
dulge it, to use the potential, the temptation, for exploiting that
power as a reminding factor for a great spiritual path. There really is
something saintly about Gurdjieff's vow, and his fulfillment of it.

He describes the air near this desert spring as "purgatorial." It is
doubly so: it purges him of impurities—and, being "between
heaven and hell," he's also in a sort of purgatorial condition. This
was doubtless the case literally, but it also seems pointed up symbolically, for in Gurdjieff, and in Christian esotericism—as in
"spiritual alchemy"—real progress is made in an in-between place;
through consciously suffering a temptation, an impulse, a negative
reaction, feeling it without giving into it. A friction then comes
about, so to speak, between *yes* and *no,* and from this an energy, or
a "substance," is generated that creates real being. In other terms, it
is the conscious enabling of the interpenetration of opposing
inner forces, one of these forces issuing from the relatively higher
(paradise), the other from the lower (hell): an example of what
Gurdjieff called, as we'll see, the "higher blending with the lower
to actualize the middle." Such a "confrontation" (actually a kind of
cooperation or commingling arising from the right kind of polarization) may provide a "shock" that is used to "cross the intervals"
in ascending an octave of spiritual growth.

Gurdjieff said he made this vow "before my own essence."
That is, his vow addressed the deepest and realest aspect of his
being.

After making this vow he felt reenergized and "reincarnated"—
which is not far from saying that he felt "born again."

An important Gurdjieffian concept, in this tale of epiphany at
the desert spring, is the contrast between having a conscious
aim—arrived at when one is at one's best, in a relatively high state
of presence and our actual behavior in the usual rutted race
track of life.

Even for people trying to work spiritually, remembering one-self enough to be consistent is the exception, if it happens at all. The rule is unrule—an anarchy of inner conditions.

Real I is possible. We are called to make "being efforts," to sacrifice our petty impulses, in order to gain *real I:* authentic self-presence in self-remembering, so that one can truly say *I am.* To achieve this in his own life, Gurdjieff sacrificed something all too dear to him. This is an example of the true meaning of sacrifices and offerings carried out in ritual: esoterically, they represent inner sacrifices. People must sacrifice the "animals" of their lower nature.

Gurdjieff's honesty, in setting all this out—complete with remarks about his having become corrupt—is admirable and resonant of his character. It's true that he was occasionally willing to blow smoke to obtain a goal that would move him farther along the path of his quest; and it's true that he would speak "parabolically" in the service of the Work. Despite the occasional boast—which usually had a meaning of some kind underlying it—he also showed authentic humility, putting himself in perspective, as in the story of the vow in the desert, and in New York when he told his prominent American follower Edwin Wolfe, in the 1940s, that there were "many men on Earth more than me, I have long way to go." In *Life Is Real Only Then, When "I Am,"* he admits to having misused his power in his youth. But it is clear that he regretted his misuse and exulted in rising above it.

Gurdjieff was to return to the same area to convalesce again, after being shot a third time by a stray bullet.

But first he returned to Tibet, perhaps to be with his purported Tibetan wife and children. In the same year Colonel F. E. Younghusband led a small but well-equipped British army into Tibet to put down an uprising. Younghusband slaughtered all who resisted and many who didn't, including a highly initiated lama. According to James Moore, Younghusband's military murder of a great lama filled Gurdjieff with disgust and contempt. It was then that he made for himself another aim, a sort of extension of his original aim: to understand the nature of humanity's propensity for war and thus to find a way out of the "mass hypnosis" that leads to collective violence.

Yes: Gurdjieff vowed to try to wake up all mankind enough to bring about an end to wars.

In his last known stay in Tibet, Gurdjieff became ill with hydropsy and was forced to go to a lower elevation to recover. He tried to return to Tibet in 1904 but seemed warned away by vicious mischance: near the Chiatura tunnel in the Transcaucasian region, he caught another stray bullet fired by "some 'charmer' from among two groups of people." He had been caught in a conflict between Gourian revolutionaries on one hand and Russian cossacks putting down yet another rebellion. It is typical, and not without importance, that he doesn't know who fired the bullet. It could have come from the Russians—those under the influence of "national psychosis"—or it could have been fired by those "under the influence of revolutionary psychosis." It didn't matter which. From Gurdjieff's point of view, there are no good guys in a war; there are only madmen striving to kill one another and innocents caught in the crossfire.

To protect him from the cossacks, a friend put the wounded Gurdjieff in a cave and went to get help. When he returned, Gurdjieff was gone, and could not be found in the moonless night. The next day they followed the trail of his blood and found him some distance from the cave, unconscious in a cleft of rock. They returned him to the cave and nursed him. When he was well he found that the cave contained a great number of mummified Khevsurian tribesmen. Ironically, he had knit himself back to health in the company of these silent remnants of lives.

Is it strange that Gurdjieff was wounded three times by stray bullets? He thought it strange. In a certain respect it's not surprising—he was drawn to those places where human energy was quickened and released, where he might study human beings in their terrifying state of mass suggestibility: that is, the fringes of wars, the areas of social ferment where bullets are likely to fly. And he might have regarded himself as personifying all victims of humanity's waking-sleep.

More practically, each wound was a challenge to Gurdjieff's constitution, his determination. It was almost as if War itself was afraid of him, trying to kill him. He would not be killed, he would not be deterred, and it must be supposed that with fighting his way back from each wound, his will and his sheer psychic being increased.

After resting and recovering in Yangihissar, he is said to have had two more years in an unknown Sufi community, perhaps finalizing his synthesis.

A Pause to Consider: Synthesis or Revelation?

Was Gurdjieff's teaching a synthesis? Later in answer to questions from British students at the Institute he was to create in France, he said that it was his own system, formulated through research and the aid of other researchers—the Seekers of Truth, we take it. But there is another school of thought, which he supports in *Meetings with Remarkable Men,* that says in effect that he had discovered a font of the primeval teaching, the ultimate spiritual, cosmogonic, and psychological system, and was merely brilliantly articulating it both in his own terms and in the language of the modern world. According to this interpretation, Gurdjieff was only saying that it was his own synthesis because he was trying to protect its source, in accordance with a vow: he hinted as much to Ouspensky. In the 1930s, Gurdjieff's muttered comment to one of the "Ladies of the Rope," a group of women students he taught in Paris, seems to reinforce this view: "I am small man compared to those who sent me."* Those ten words have enormous implications. If Gurdjieff was *sent*—then he was sent on a specific mission, by specific people, even greater than himself.

Which people? The research of Gurdjieff's student John Bennett seemed to indicate (to Bennett, at least) that Gurdjieff's famous esoteric symbol, the nine-pointed geometric form he called the enneagram, came to Gurdjieff from the Naqshbandi Sufis, one of the most profoundly mystical schools of Sufism. And "Bogga-Eddin" might be a play on Bahauddin, who was one of the Naqshbandi's greatest teachers.

The Christian esotericist Boris Mouravieff claimed that Gurdjieff's teachings were all Christian mysticism derived from the Eastern Orthodoxy. He quotes some fairly Gurdjieff-like remarks from the Orthodox mystical classic the *Philokalia*.**

On the other hand—and when speculating about Gurdjieff's sources we're as multihanded as a Hindu deity—Professor Thomas Mether argues that the enneagram, some Gurdjieffian practices, and much of Gurdjieff's cosmology derive from Syriac esoteric Christianity, which in turn is informed by proto-Hindu "alchemy" and the Gnostic-influenced astrologer Bar Daisan.

Ladies of the Rope by William Patrick Patterson.
**Ironically, it appears from accounts of Mouravieff's note-taking during Gurdjieff's lectures that Mouravieff's own teaching may be more derived from Gurdjieff than Gurdjieff's is from Orthodox mysticism.

Gurdjieff's account of having sampled many monasteries and teachings gives us an image of the seeking George Giorgiades often studying quite deeply but never committing to one place forever. This suggests to some that his teaching was a synthesis. But there is a "reconciling" possibility: that he found much of the ultimate teaching, perhaps through Syriac-Christian Sarmoung, but found it not quite complete and completed it himself through his research, incorporating Naqshbandi and Tibetan methods. Certainly the system he taught seems both self-contained and self-confirming. All this is reckless speculation—we just don't know for certain, and he offered no inarguable proofs of his sources.

What finally remains to us is the Gurdjieff teaching itself, which has within it the life to become its own, vital tradition.

1907. Gurdjieff turns up in Tashkent, which apparently served as a sort of staging area for the esoteric school he had in mind. He spent several years there as a freelance "professor-instructor," studying his students to try to determine what made them tick, what kept different types of people asleep. Here, too, he accumulated wealth—trading in various goods, everything from oil to cattle to carpets.

By 1912 he was ready to teach his system. He took himself to Moscow, where, sometimes calling himself "Prince Ozay," he found his first serious pupils, including Sergei Mercourov and Vladimir Pohl.

The same year Gurdjieff met a mysterious woman of Polish descent, Julia Ostrovsky (may also be spelled Ostrowska) and made her his wife. Not a great deal is known about her, or the circumstances of their acquaintance, though she remained with him until her death in France many years later. Some say he "saved" her from ruin of some kind. Others maintain that she was merely a beautiful young woman who came from a fine family that had

had a run of hard luck. She is said to have moved with unusual grace and economy of motion—"like a queen, exactly," according to the British writer Katherine Mansfield, who died at Gurdjieff's school Le Prieure. Gurdjieff said that his wife was "an old soul" who had been incarnated many times. A later student, Fritz Peters, in *My Journey with a Mystic,* said that Madame Ostrovsky was one of the few at Gurdjieff's Institute at Fontainebleau-Avon who carried herself—innately, not imitatively—as Gurdjieff did: with conscious grace, bringing attentive exactitude and presence to every small thing she did. She is said to have kept the surname Ostrovsky as a sign that she did not elevate herself above the station of being "merely one of his students."

Also that year Gurdjieff read an intriguing and fashionable book called *Tertium Organum,* by a certain freelance philosopher, journalist, and explorer-mystic, P. D. Ouspensky. Apparently Gurdjieff saw potential in Ouspensky, for he made it his business to recruit him, through intermediaries.

In St. Petersburg, in 1913, Gurdjieff took the colorful Englishman Paul Dukes as a student, and in 1914 he attracted a physician, Dr. Leonid Stjoernval, who was to become one of his most devoted followers. Gurdjieff wrote the book for a "ballet," *The Struggle of the Magicians,* which he began advertising in 1914. It was in that year—the year Germany declared war on Russia—that he also supervised the composition of the earliest Gurdjieffian work written for the public, *Glimpses of Truth.*

In the grudging Moscow spring of 1915, with World War I as an instructive backdrop, Gurdjieff accepted P. D. Ouspensky as his student, and two powerful minds came together, both mingling and clashing, with epic results.

FOUR

IN SEARCH OF
THE MIRACULOUS

Is a candle brought to be put under a bushel, or under a bed, and not to be set out on a candlestick?

For there is nothing hid which shall not be manifested; neither was anything kept secret, but that it should come abroad.

—Mark 4:21–22

Born in Moscow in 1878, Piotr Demianovich Ouspensky was the son of middle-class parents steeped in the enthusiasms of the intelligentsia. He grew up against a backdrop of political instability—the republicanism of France and the United States was looking better and better to the masses under the heel of a Russian privileged class that clung with white knuckles to its tsarist monarchy. Anarchism and early forms of communism were taking shape too.

Ouspensky was expelled from school at the age of sixteen for leaving mocking graffiti on the wall for a visiting inspector, and he studied more or less informally thereafter, always vacillating between deep intellectual penetration and a dreamy rebellious-ness. But his intellect and perception were both strikingly power-ful, and when he encountered Gurdjieff, Ouspensky was already the author of *Tertium Organum* and other successful books.

Tertium Organum was an attempt to show that there already ex-isted an "instrument" of thought other than the first two classic instruments posited by Aristotle and Bacon. It argues against pos-itivism, saying that "science must come to mysticism," and takes off from Kant and the theories of the English writer C. H. Hin-ton (whose work also inspired H. G. Wells) to arrive at the idea of the Fourth Dimension as not only the office of time but the doorway to the numinous: the objective world beyond our sub-jectively deceiving, limiting senses. Ouspensky had also absorbed the ideas of Nietzsche, with his belief in "eternal recurrence," and, perhaps with the Nietzschean superman in mind, seemed to believe in a spiritual elite: "a new race CONSCIOUS OF ITSELF . . . will judge the old race." This alarming vision of something akin to spiritual fascism also appears in the idiosyncratic Christian eso-tericism of Boris Mouravieff: a kind of "Gurdjieff spinoff" mys-tic who envisioned a world governed by a spiritual aristocracy.

As described in *A New Model of the Universe* and *In Search of the Miraculous,* Ouspensky carried out his long search on long trips to India and the Far East. Though a former member of the Theo-sophical Society, he was unimpressed with the top Theosophists he encountered in Madras and with the gurus he met. But he did encounter wonders on the contemplative level—gazing at the Taj Mahal he had a vision of the magnificent edifice as symbolizing the soul's place in the grand dimension of pure spirit that activates the universe; pondering a sapphire-eyed statue of Buddha, he seemed to see himself as the Buddha would see him, a particle of cosmic consciousness trapped in the dilemma of the embodied.

Returning to Moscow, Ouspensky gave lectures on his travels—one lecture was entitled "In Search of the Miraculous," later also to be the title of his exegesis of the ideas of Gurdjieff. Some of these lectures were attended by more than a thousand people.

But Ouspensky was far from content. He'd had mere peeks at the miraculous. He'd squinted through a sealed window at that other world. But he had found no one who could show him where the *door* was. He wanted more than glimpses, and he wanted something more than the theoretical. At last he heard of a man who might know the way to the real thing: a certain Gurdjieff.

In the spring of 1915, having heard many intriguing rumors about Gurdjieff, Ouspensky met him at last. He describes his meeting with Gurdjieff in his book *In Search of the Miraculous,* published decades later. This book constitutes the best existing single description of many of Gurdjieff's ideas, insofar as they can be conveyed intellect to intellect. Another superb resource for information from Gurdjieff's Russian period is *Our Life with Mr Gurdjieff* by Thomas and Olga de Hartmann. Consulting both books, I'll hazard a sketch of some of the ideas Ouspensky brought us from G. I. Gurdjieff.

Gurdjieff evidently did not wish to take just anyone as a student: he seemed to have specific methods for discouraging people who didn't show the persistence and spiritual acumen to look past superficial appearances. Ouspensky was almost discouraged.

Gurdjieff had arranged a meeting in a rather shabby, noisy St. Petersburg café, and the man Ouspensky met, in his bowler hat and black overcoat with velvet collar, seemed strangely in disguise. He seemed to be acting a part. Many people felt this peculiar sort of "acting" with Gurdjieff, and Ouspensky remarked on it in more than one place—but he made it clear that it was not the acting of a charlatan but a kind of acting that, on the contrary, paradoxically gave you confidence: the role-playing of a man consciously masking a higher, more powerful self. Revealing only a little bit at a time . . .

Gurdjieff often played "the charlatan" when people first met him. His meeting with the composer Thomas de Hartmann paralleled Ouspensky's experience: it was in an establishment so tarred with the reputation of the demimonde that the embarrassed Hartmann might have been ostracized by certain members of his social set if he'd been seen there. The man Hartmann had been told was a spiritual master gleefully pointed out the whores to Hartmann and generally went out of his way to give a mixed impression.

Not only did Gurdjieff wish to discourage the easily discouraged, he did not wish to make it easy to acquire his ideas, even for those who persisted a bit more, since people do not value what is easily acquired. What was acquired easily was just as easily shed; it was not fixed in the *being* of the seeker unless he had brought his Will in play in searching for it. Gurdjieff made it a point that the seeker had to "pay" in some way—not only with money but with inner payments. The character of the first meeting with Gurdjieff hinted that there were intervals to be crossed before the teaching could proceed.

Gurdjieff suggested that he and Ouspensky depart the café for an apartment he kept for meetings, where certain students were waiting. He implied that the apartment would be splendid and his students would be important people, professors and scientists and artists—but again, Gurdjieff had dramatized the dichotomy between expectation and reality: Ouspensky found a barely furnished, mildewed flat and a group of ordinary, not particularly accomplished people who did not match the buildup. Here Ouspensky listened to a reading of a work "written by a student"—actually a tract created under Gurdjieff's supervision—called *Glimpses of Truth,* which Ouspensky found rather fanciful, "pretentious and tedious," at first hearing.* All this disheartened Ouspensky, as perhaps it was supposed to. But during the meeting in the apartment he was impressed with a sort of leonine presence, a consciousness in Gurdjieff's smallest movements. "In G himself," Ouspensky said he "felt something uncommon." When he was going to take his leave, the thought flashed into Ouspensky's mind that he "must at once, without delay, arrange to meet him again."

In a later meeting, Ouspensky asked Gurdjieff if he should travel again to the East in search of knowledge. Gurdjieff told him to go there for a vacation if he liked—but the knowledge he sought was right here in Russia. Gurdjieff had already done the seeking for Ouspensky, and he had compounded the hidden teaching into one system. There was no need to go anywhere. After establishing the ground rules of his Institute, Gurdjieff accepted Ouspensky as his student.

MANKIND REDEFINED

Gurdjieff instantly set about disabusing Ouspensky of his most cherished notions, many of which are everyone's most cherished notions. Ouspensky was summarily informed that the author of *Tertium Organum*—Ouspensky himself—did not understand his own book. "You do not understand either what you read or what you write."

As we've seen, Gurdjieff went on to inform Ouspensky that nearly all humanity is perpetually asleep, and Ouspensky was no

Glimpses of Truth is actually fascinating and can be found in *Views from the Real World* by Gurdjieff.

exception. He informed him that he was a machine, as nearly all of us are. And he informed Ouspensky that he didn't mean this figuratively, and that Ouspensky might think himself awake and free . . . but he simply wasn't. "Man's possibilities are very great," Gurdjieff said, speaking to Ouspensky and other students in St. Petersburg. "You cannot conceive even a shadow of what man is capable of attaining. But nothing can be attained in sleep. In the consciousness of a sleeping man, his illusions, his 'dreams' are mixed with reality. He lives in a subjective world and can never escape from it . . . he lives in only a small part of himself."

Gurdjieff went on to say something that Ouspensky felt was even more "hard to swallow"—the result of this sleep and this mechanicality is that a person cannot *do*. He can do nothing of his own accord. Everything simply happens to us. If a person decides to launch a project, that decision is a reaction to something, and the carrying out of the project is itself more reacting, which only *seems* like conscious doing. Something gets done—but it's not done by the man, or his associates, regardless of his very genuine toil and sweat; it is done *through* him. It merely happens to him. But no one wants to believe such a thing: it is offensive and unpleasant to people "because it is the truth," Gurdjieff said, "and nobody wants to know the truth." Which is, perhaps, another reason Gurdjieff ruefully named the hero of his great allegorical novel *Beelzebub*—the reviled presenter of ideas that, true or not, seem to many to be offensive.

The declaration that people cannot *do* seems related to the idea of predetermination, of predestiny. We are trapped in the chain of mechanistic cause and effect spawned by our own behavioral fixity. That is in effect predestination—or karma, if you like—until we're conscious enough to transcend it, to *do,* breaking the chain of endless reacting; at least, of reacting to influences that exist at the lower levels where human beings usually dwell. When we are conscious enough and unified enough so that we can *do,* we will in certain respects find ourselves in another medium entirely—a place of more freedom, but still a medium with its own laws, rather like an amphibian emerging from muddling about in the mud, first to the clear upper water and then farther upward to the possibilities of dry land. Each new place is a medium of activity with its own limitations, but there is, nevertheless, more freedom in these upper realms than in the muck under heavy pressure at the lightless floor of the sea.

It seems to me, at least, that through some unknown intervention involving the grace of God, men and women sometimes find themselves *doing*—perhaps Joan of Arc was one such; perhaps Martin Luther King. But apart from such exceptions it almost never happens unless one works on oneself in a long-term, committed way.

This is not to say that people shouldn't try to improve their lives and the world before they can "do." Of course it's worthwhile to start a food bank, to work in politics for peace, and so forth. There may be fitful moments of "doing" in taking up such causes—Gurdjieff had a forceful way of speaking of these things that did not admit of exceptions, or mitigation, necessary because people are so prone to illusion—and one can give oneself to a series of "reactions" that are flowing in the direction of a good goal. Being involved in activities also generates possibilities for self-knowledge, if we are watchful.

But how to really *do* in the fullest sense? Gurdjieff said that the only real magic that exists is this *doing.* But in order to *do,* one must first *be.* And what does it mean to truly *be?* In Gurdjieff's teaching the idea of *being* is a critical one. A person with *being,* in the Gurdjieffian sense, has various characteristics—but to list them does not actually explain what that *being* is. Our attempted inventory may include the recognition that someone with *being* has crystallized an actual substance (or highly organized field of energy) that actually makes him or her *more* than before. A person with *being* is capable of retaining individuality despite the usual surrounding influences. A person of real *being* has something that makes it possible to be the recipient of higher, finer influences: that is, he or she is more in touch with God.

But none of my wiseacreing can accurately describe what I have not experienced. Real understanding of what *being* is requires enough *being* to contain that understanding. We can only hope for indications, lampposts along the way to understanding that state.

And when we say that a person with being has Will, it is not will as it is usually understood. What most people suppose to be the "will" of a "strong-willed man" (or woman) is merely the persisting strength of one or another of his or her desires. Real Will would make it possible for a person to conquer that desire, when appropriate. (I prefer to write Will with a capital *W* to emphasize the distinction between what we usually think of as will and Will of this order.)

Gurdjieff did his best to set out some lampposts for Ouspensky. He even provided charts and astonishingly complex breakdowns★ to give a *theoretical* sense of the gradations and characteristics of these states, and their inner functions—and perhaps he provided this aspect of the work to exercise the intellectual center, so that

---

★I won't be setting out or interpreting those complex tables and breakdowns, such as the charts of exchanges of "hydrogens," or the calculations of octaves, or enneagramic permutations. I'm not qualified. I refer the reader to Ouspensky's *In Search of the Miraculous* and to the multivolume *Psychological Commentaries on the Teachings of G. I. Gurdjieff and P. D. Ouspensky* by Maurice Nicoll.

as other centers were worked on, the Intellect too was properly engaged.

Gurdjieff also provided motivation: for he made it clear that real immortality, authentic and individual life after death, is only possible to people with a permanent and unchangeable I, consciousness, and Will.

Again, we think we have these characteristics—and we don't. Until we sense with all our inner attention that we don't have them, we cannot hope to have them. It is tragic, since we have magnificent possibilities that usually go unrealized.

A person who has attained the full potential possible, and with it immortality, has developed four bodies, one incorporated into the next. Each of the four bodies is composed of a finer substance than the previous body in our list. Gurdjieff often speaks of the esoteric *substances* composing the higher bodies, without quite defining them, but we understand that they are definite and palpable, on some level; subtle bodies they may be, but they do not exist as merely spiritual, "supernatural" states. The four bodies have various names in various traditions. Christian mysticism calls the first body the Carnal Body: this is the physical body, the *carriage*, in Eastern parlance; the second body is the Natural Body, the *horse* in Eastern terminology, which contains higher feelings and desires; the third body is the Spiritual Body, or the *driver* of the horse and carriage, corresponding to the mind; the fourth body is the Divine Body, or the *Master:* called the Causal Body in Theosophy, it has crystallized Unchangeable I, consciousness, and Will.

Many in the traditions that speak of the higher bodies may be unaware (because this knowledge was forgotten or distorted) that man is not born with the second, third, and fourth finer bodies. We don't have them unless we make them; they must be cultivated in the right sort of internal and external conditions.

Compare this with the work "From Hermes Trismegistus to

Asclepius: Definitions," a text that is said to be more ancient than the seminal mystical text the Corpus Hermeticum: "Likewise the soul, once it has gained perfection, goes out of the body. For just as a body as it goes out of the womb while it is still imperfect can neither be fed nor grow up, likewise if the soul goes out of the body without having gained perfection it is imperfect and lacks a body; but the perfection of the soul is the knowledge of the beings."* Note the phrase "once it has gained perfection," suggesting it cannot survive long outside the body unless it has been properly developed in the womb that is the harmonized body, mind, and feelings of man.

For Gurdjieff, to be sure, the human body is the crucible of transmutation. An active work with turning attention to the sensations of the body—combined with taking conscious "impressions" of one's inner and outer state—is the beginning of the transmutation that creates a lasting soul. Compare the Gnostic Gospel of Thomas: "Jesus said, 'If the flesh came into being because of the spirit, it is a wonder. But if the spirit came into being because of the body, it is a wonder of wonders.'"

We don't need these higher being-bodies to live as sleepers. But we do need them for continuation as a conscious individual in the afterlife. They are a consequence of lives lived fully and freely—in the esoteric sense of "fully and freely." Then again, it's the only real fullness, the only real freedom.

Gurdjieff said that the functions of a person who has only a physical body are governed by that body, but one who has higher bodies, or "Permanent I," is governed by this higher "I."

In addition, the realized individual will have a fully matured essence. Such a person identifies with their perfected essence—not the superimposed claptrap of personality.

---

*The Way of Hermes.

Distinguishing *essence* from *personality* is a vital step in the Gurdjieff Work. Essence is what we are born with, it is our natural state, our real feelings, our real affinities. Personality is what is imposed on us by conformity to parents, peers, schools—in trying to please and to avoid discomfort, we develop the outer, masking machinery of personality. It's as if we have by degrees created a marionette, and we make this puppet dance according to what we suppose are our real desires, and what people want of us—and we make the mistake of identifying with it. We become the puppet.

It is necessary to have an external, role-playing appearance, often simply for the sake of kindness but also to perform the necessary social dance so as to not be out of step with the world (unless it's really important to be—as when Gandhi was "out of step" with the British).

Consciously playing those roles, and responding appropriately to others, is "external considering." It is necessary to the Work, requiring much development. The student of the Work seeks to observe how we "consider" outwardly with others, and then modifies it with right *outward* considering. Gurdjieff also spoke of *inner* considering.

When we let ourselves get caught up in inner reactions—that is, the mistake of "inner considering"—allowing ourselves to identify with the capering marionette of mere personality, then our lives become a puppet show, played out according to a script that does not represent our real feelings.

Because of this identification with personality we'll ironically find ourselves doing what we most dislike—deep inside—and not doing that which is natural to our essence. In C. S. Lewis's masterpiece *The Screwtape Letters,* a man just arriving in Hell remarks: "I now see that I spent most of my life in doing *neither* what I ought *nor* what I liked."

And that more ancient text, the Corpus Hermeticum, seems to

agree: Those with reason, who, as we have said, are led by Nous [i.e., detached spiritual intelligence], do not suffer as others do . . . they suffer as men who have been released from evil."

Because a man identifies with his personality, his essence becomes numb, paralyzed, and it will not develop as he grows older but will remain immature—though his personality may appear to be sophisticated, full of glib witticisms and charm, his essence is infantile. Essence, sufficiently suppressed, may die entirely. Which brings us to another one of Gurdjieff's characteristic startlers:

It happens fairly often that essence dies in a man while his personality and body are still alive. A considerable percentage of the people we meet in the streets of a great town are people who are empty inside, that is, they are actually *already dead*. It is fortunate for us that we do not see and do not know it. If we knew what number of people are actually dead and what number of these dead people govern our lives, we should go mad with horror.*

Ouspensky relates a story of an experiment in observing essence and personality, carried out by Gurdjieff. He chooses not to reveal Gurdjieff's experimental methodology, but it may well have been hypnotism. Two men were chosen: one was an older man, fairly sophisticated, fond of talking of Christianity, of the politics of the war, of scandalous immoralities; the other was a younger man, flighty, prone to argument and playing the fool. Both men were somehow reduced by Gurdjieff to their essences, their personalities put aside for once. The older man became rather vacant-eyed and distant. He was unable to remember his

In Search of the Miraculous.

assertions of opinion, very seriously given just a little earlier, about the war, though he'd only just spoken them. When pressed on what he really wanted in that moment, he said, very seriously and thoughtfully: *"I think I should like some raspberry jam."*

The other, however, was no longer flighty—he asked seriously about what was going on and was seen to be sharply observing everything. Later he remembered these events, but the older man remembered nothing. For *personality* remembers nothing. The younger man had some intact essence—which can remember. The older man had almost no essence remaining, and what endured was arrested in an infantile state.

One can think of many television pundits—sophisticated, articulate men with arched brows and glibly ironic wit—who in the right conditions might well be revealed as empty but for a desire for . . . some raspberry jam.

INQUIRING ABOUT GURDJIEFF'S METHODS

A well-known American-born guru once said that Gurdjieff's teaching was "only theory; without practice." He was mistaken; perhaps he had read only *Meetings with Remarkable Men,* which offers background and theory, and hadn't troubled to find out what Gurdjieff's actual methods were. A loose sketch of a few of these methods is provided in Ouspensky's great exegesis of Gurdjieff's ideas: he speaks of conscious suffering, self-observation, self-remembering, Sacred Movements, and *the overall use of attention* as a tool in self-development, and he gives a general theoretical overview of some of these procedures. But for practical application of these and other methods brought by Gurdjieff, one must find the students Gurdjieff personally taught—and those taught by his close students—who then pass his methods on only in person and only in the proper conditions.

When Gurdjieff speaks of conscious suffering, he isn't talking about wallowing in life's miseries—indeed, he says that we are all reluctant to give up our suffering. That is, we're reluctant to give up pointless, *subjective* suffering, which we use to keep from facing our real dilemma. One of his aphorisms was "Only conscious suffering has any sense." But being present to one's condition—intentionally conscious of the friction between the negative and positive—is not misery at all, and it's certainly not masochistic. It's a kind of sublime bearing of what is.

Gurdjieff had other methods that only he was capable of employing with any success. His life was half over when he started teaching, leaving him with insufficient time in which to begin—or renew—the current that he hoped would someday awaken enough of humanity to end war and restore humanity to its birthright. Hence he was in a hurry to create students who could follow in his footsteps. In the service of that urgent mission he employed methods of his own innovation—along with some associated with so-called crazy wisdom masters—involving direct psychological challenge to the student. Some of these techniques entailed a kind of verbal guerilla warfare against students' sleep and vanity, forcing them to see themselves and to struggle with what they saw. Teaching methods of this kind are inherently risky and can be pulled off successfully only by a master. Students of the Gurdjieff Work are still challenged in various ways, but this personal-confrontational methodology of Gurdjieff is not attempted by those who came after him, at least not in anything like the lengths to which he took it.

Nevertheless, the hundreds of other, nonconfrontational exercises and methods offered by lesser but authentic teachers of the Gurdjieff Work appear to do the job, judging by certain very accomplished students who never met Gurdjieff. These students—who have in turn become teachers—studied under such figures as Jeanne de Salzmann, her son Michel de Salzmann, P. D. Ouspensky, Maurice Nicoll, A. L. Staveley, Henriette Lannes, Paul Reynard, Thomas de Hartmann, Olga de Hartmann, William Welch, Louise Welch, Henri Tracol, William Segal, Lord Pentland, and Lady Pentland—all of whom worked with Gurdjieff himself. Most of the figures on this off-the-cuff list of some of Gurdjieff's prominent students lived to a great old age (in defiance of statistical probability, many lived into their mid- or late nineties and longer, with Madame de Salzmann active past 100), and most were alive and teaching until very recently. At this writing, of the teachers listed here, only Paul Reynard and Lady Pentland are still living. Both are still teaching.

THREE WAYS AND A FOURTH

Gurdjieff asserts that each spiritual way has the same ultimate goal: the creation of an immortal soul. The defeat of death. But each tries to attain that goal with its own idiosyncratic method.

The way of the fakir is the way that *attempts* to create an immortal will through conquering the desires of the body. The fakir puts himself through excruciating physical difficulties, outrageous postures held for outrageous periods of time, the suffering of self-inflicted pain, near-fatal fasts, asceticism and privation of all kinds, so as to build up his Will and spiritual power. The way of the fakir corresponds to the instinctive-moving center in man—to his carnal nature.

The way of the monk is the way of devotion to God, through work on the emotional center. It is a "way of the heart" and of faith, as faith is usually thought of. The monk spends decades struggling with himself, with all his attention focused on his *feelings*. He does create a kind of unity in himself, but it is lopsided, and his physical and intellectual aspects may remain undeveloped.

The way of the yogi is the path of developing the mind and knowledge. As Gurdjieff put it, "he knows everything but can do nothing." He has developed his intellectual center to some unity and acuity, but in order to learn to *do* he must, according to Gurdjieff, develop his physical and emotional centers as well. The yogi often knows he must do this but fails to do so, having spent all his "money," so to speak, in one place.

The three ways have one thing in common: renunciation. The yogi, the monk, and the fakir must each give up home and family, surrender all attachments—must remove themselves from the world.

But there is a fourth way, which does not require renunciation—which in fact profits from "work in the midst of life." The fourth way was known to certain esoteric schools and was systematized for the modern world by G. I. Gurdjieff. He sometimes called it "Khaida Yoga." *Khaida* is Russian; one translation is "hurry up" (it's also been written "Haida"). The fourth way is an accelerated path, though by no means actually easy or rapid in the way usually understood by "modern people": for we are all spoiled by the instant gratification of modern life, and our idea of "rapid" is currently more or less that of a small child's unrealistic expectations. "Are we there yet? I'm tired of being in the car."

There is also a "hurrying way" known to Sufis, which may or may not be related to Gurdjieff's fourth way. At any "rate," if Gurdjieff is correct, the fourth way may be the only fully effective path for the creation of all three creatable bodies, resulting in immortality. For Gurdjieff, in his seeking, encountered many who had worked exclusively with one way or another, but they were spiritually misshapen, like bodybuilders who'd developed enormous arms but retained wobbly, spindly legs. If creation of the second, third, and fourth being-bodies required man to learn to be present to and to master all three aspects of his nature, then a way that developed only one of those aspects was inadequate. It was like drawing a single line, slanting to one side, and calling that single stroke a triangle.

Always, the fourth way involves *self-remembering*: The foundation of the edifice of Self-Remembering is *sensing* the self physically—really *inhabiting* the body in a way we don't normally do; that is, we inhabit it with a consciously directed portion of our attention. The next level is an effort at *being present* enough so that one isn't *taken* by dreaming and free association. There are of course more floors to the "building"—there always seems to be more to observe. But the foundation and first floor are all-important; the rest would fall down without them. We rarely feel ourselves in the present moment; normally we're dreaming of something we wish to do or thinking of the past. Our attention is rarely in the Now. The present moment, C. S. Lewis remarked, is where Time contacts Eternity. In the light of attention actively turned to the present moment, we find it difficult to lie to ourselves; things are revealed as they are in the Real World. Our whole relationship to our life in Time is changed; struggling to be present, we can include another dimension, the *I Am* dimension, which perceives phenomena from a vantage point outside time.

Returning again and again to the present moment is a tool for self-remembering, for sheer consciousness, an asset that is always available, no matter what. When the spiritual teacher Ram Dass had a stroke, much of his capacity was impaired; but afterward he indicated that his ability to contemplate his essential presence in the present moment remained intact. The true present moment is ever-renewing because Eternity is a bottomless reservoir, a limitless resource.

Attentive self-remembering is an inner work that can be discreetly done in almost any surroundings and can be sharpened by the challenges of ordinary life. You can be doing a profound *inner* work while outwardly engaged in a discussion at the PTA or passing the time of day with a grocery cashier.

A student of the fourth way is a student of *his or her self*, really, since it all begins with self-study. The student first begins this self-study by utilizing *divided attention*. Normally—as in the diagram we saw earlier—the "arrow" of our attention is outward, to the world, turned to all that happens around us, so that we tend to simply react to it. When we learn to make the effort to turn some *part* of our attention always inward, to our physical sensations and to taking impressions in self-observation, we reach by slow degrees the possibility of occasional experiences of fuller and fuller self-remembering. We have created a capacity in ourselves for sensing, seeing, consciously suffering ourselves as we are, at least some of the time.

We've seen that we tend to lose ourselves, to forget our goals, to slip into rote activity. Gurdjieff speaks of two overall currents in life; normally it is as if we're being carried along by the "downward current," or passive current, of life's free association and automatic behavior. Both currents have their place; the downward current is part of life's creative energy. But if we are engaged in the Work, we are flying with our falcon into "another current," a relatively upward movement, by moving actively against the "stream" of automatic behavior. Working on him- or herself in life, the student of the fourth way does what is required and expected by society and people encountered, within the limits of conscience, but all the time internally trying to remain present to the moment, self-observing and struggling to stay nonidentified.

When the ordinary frustrations of life in the world arise, carrying with them the temptation to get caught up in irritation and anger and depression, a longtime practitioner of the fourth way actively chooses not to *identify* with negative reactions within, though consciously aware of them; externally, the practitioner chooses not to negatively act out. From this comes a powerful spiritual benefit: the creation of Being. So the student of the fourth way is *taking advantage of the difficulties that arise in ordinary life.* He or she is reaping the benefits of working with *life as it happens.* The more challenging life is to us, the more we can work with it and profit by it spiritually.

CALLING ATTENTION TO . . .

All serious esoteric work would seem to have one common theme: the use of attention as a "thing in itself." Attention is awakened, summoned, strengthened, refined, and directed. This is not the vague attention of "something caught my attention" or "the movie had my attention." That is a subjective, passive use of attention, valuable primarily for relaxation. The attention of esoteric work is an *active,* objectively directed attention, an attention that is refined as we struggle against the usual impulse to daydream, to free-associate, to get caught up in negativity. Attention becomes a form of light, somehow, in this effort. It has always been clear to me that *conscious attention is itself a form of light.* Working by observing what takes place in our inner world, what characterizes the activity of centers, separating our essential selves from our superimposed "personalities"—all is done with the turning of attention, like a softly shining living spotlight, on all those manifestations.

Attention used in this way seems to slowly "sort things out" on its own. Gurdjieff was very clear that the Work is *not there to solve your problems.* It exists for a higher aim. Still, over a long time, this persistent mindful attention demonstrates a mysterious power to correct wrong work of centers, in fact to ease neurotic behavior, even to alleviate needless emotional pain.

The main point here is that deliberate, mindful attention is always a part of the Work, as a grow-light is always necessary in hothouse farming, even though the hothouse farmer will engage in other more complex activities like seeding, watering—and harvesting.

THE ALCHEMIST'S LABORATORY

Ouspensky does give us clues as to the esoteric workings of Gurdjieff's deeper methods—many of them quite ancient esoteric techniques—for developing real *being* and permanent "I." One fundamental method is something glimpsed earlier, at that wellspring in the desert with Mr. Gurdjieff.

The following is something one should only attempt under the guidance of a reputable teacher, after an adequate period of preparation. I give it as an instance of certain kinds of work.

Gurdjieff told Ouspensky of "an Eastern teaching" that described a person's possibilities for developing the four bodies as analogous to an alchemist's glass vessel filled with metallic powders. The powders are disconnected from one another and are subject to constant change within the glass vessel, depending on conditions—if the vessel is tapped or shaken or turned, for example, the various sorts of powders shuffle about randomly with each of these influences. There is no definite internal structure within the vessel. But if a "special kind of fire" is lit under the vessel, the "metallic powders" are melted and fused together. They have now become one solid substance: individual and indivisible. This analogy roughly describes the way one creates the "second body"—through creating a transformative "heat" from the "friction" of "a struggle between yes and no."

"One needs fire," says Gurdjieff in the Library of Congress transcription of his talks during World War II. "Without fire, there will never be anything. This fire is suffering, voluntary suffering, without which it is impossible to create anything. One must prepare, must know what will make one suffer and when it is there, make use of it . . . the fire cooks, cements, crystallizes, *does*."

Let's take a theoretical example. A woman, say, tends to berate her husband and belittle her children. This is a powerful tendency in her. But she is unaware of this destructive habit in herself, as her defenses don't allow her to be aware of the tendency, no matter how much she is told of it. She is somehow drawn to take up work on herself, and—*guided by a teacher who truly knows what he or she is doing*—begins a process of self-observation, trying to see herself as she really is.

Our well-meaning but venomous lady has spent a fair amount of time practicing a method taught by Gurdjieff and others: *divided attention*. In this process this hypothetical *yenta* takes inner *impressions* of herself, and these *impressions* are used as "food," feeding a growing capacity to see herself as she really is: part by part, little "I" by little "I." She also observes her external behavior, trying to see her interactions with others as it is. This enables her to begin to see past her defensive *buffers*.

Thus, one day she sees it, can no longer deny that it's true. *she really does unfairly and habitually berate her husband and belittle her children.* Objectively seeing this tendency in herself gives, for the first time, the possibility of working with it. She feels the beginnings of real remorse—but she only waits, and watches. She observes that this tendency arises along with certain interior sensations and from certain external provocations. Always certain sets of stimuli bring the tendency out in her. So one day, as she remembers herself, she's ready for those stimuli, and her own reactions. That day, as usual, her husband annoys her; her children annoy her. Her usual reaction to this annoyance would be to overreact, to berate him and belittle them.

But now, she actively chooses not to identify with the impulse to do as she usually does. She is, to be sure, aware of the impulse. She sees it and feels it. She does not suppress it, exactly . . .

She simply does not *act* on it. Though provoked, she does *not* berate, she does *not* belittle. She *suffers* the annoyance and the impulse to react, and she suffers it *consciously*. She has set out to suffer it for a purpose—as part of her intention. She is intentionally suffering.

Her habitual self is saying, "Yes! Go for it! Snarl at them as usual! Express yourself as you usually do! Give 'em Hell, you'll feel better!" But her conscious response is: "No!" That is, she inwardly says, "No!—I will not snarl at them as usual! I see and experience the urge to do that, and I suffer it, but no, I won't *do* it." (She doesn't literally say this even in her mind, of course; "No" is merely her inward response.) And in the struggle between that yes and that no—that lower, passively arising automatic impulse and the higher active impulse coming from her consciousness—there is a kind of "friction," in a manner of speaking, that produces an energy of a particular quality. This struggle is the awakening of *authentic conscience,* which is the "heat" that is produced by this friction. Since this energy has a particular defining quality, it is also a *substance.* This new substance is produced in her by her struggle and takes its rightful place in her. Or, turning again to the analogy, some of the "powders" in the "vessel" are heated by the friction, melted, and fused into unity, in the crucible that is the body; she has a tiny bit more individual substance than she had before. A related analogy is found in alchemical formulations; something low, dark, *leaden* within her has been transmuted into something finer. Lead has been turned into gold.

Each time she says *no* to this lower impulse and consciously suffers it with the proper attention, she builds up a little more of the desired substance—she turns a little more lead into gold. And by slow degrees this *lower* impulse, which comes from some mis-placement, some misuse of energies of her inward self, will cease to trouble her. Its energies will find their way back to where they were supposed to have been in the first place, and she will no longer tend to treat her husband and children this way.

In facing herself, seeing herself through self-observation as she is, she has the possibility of beginning the removal of *buffers*. Buffers, according to Gurdjieff, are defense mechanisms that we develop from childhood in order to bear the contradictions be-tween what we feel is right—that is, what our conscience tells us—and how we actually are. Buffers cushion the shock of con-tradictions, keeping us comfortable enough with ourselves to re-main asleep, enabling us to believe we're always in the right. They are to some extent practical, protecting us from feeling contradic-tions that would otherwise drive us mad. If we have the courage, we can end these contradictions in our nature, learning to *consider externally*, to treat people as they need to be treated, to do unto others as we would have them do to us, to play the expected roles in a conscious fashion—while remaining inwardly free of identi-fication. But to do this, we must *see* those contradictions, and consciously suffer them, building up something capable of behav-ing differently: real being. And so this hypothetical woman, on seeing her behavior with her husband and children as it really is—seeing the contradiction between the way she thinks she has been and the way she really has been—has begun to remove one of her many buffers. But the destruction of buffers must be balanced with the creation of Being.

In the creation of this being—and the diminishing of a buffer—she has also ceased to waste at least some energy on mindless reactiveness. This energy is then freed up to be used for higher purposes, to be redirected toward more work on herself, and for the benefit of the organism. She has not set out to change her bad habits but only to carry out inner work—but a change for the better may well occur in due course. And because she's treating her family better, her life improves in other respects. What goes around comes around! There may be other, indefinable spiritual benefits as well.

And there's a deeper consideration. Gurdjieff spoke of "work with emotional center," and he subjected students to powerful emotional experiences that they had to consciously suffer. This not only increased their Being but also gave them a chance to cultivate something more than kneejerk emotional responses (which the philosopher Jacob Needleman calls "ego emotions"); it made it possible to cultivate *real* emotions: genuine love and compassion, a function of the higher emotional center.

Having worked through this particular mechanical behavior, this imaginary student of the Work will have to find some other way to challenge herself. Observing herself, she sees past another buffer, noticing that she tends to resent her boss and to gossip about him because of her resentment—so without telling anyone, she commences to work with that tendency . . . and so on.

She may say *yes* to counter an undesirable *no* also. *"No,"* her body says, "I don't want to get up early and sit in meditation. I want to sleep. No I won't get up."

"Yes," consciousness counters, "I *will* get up and meditate." She consciously suffers the body's frustration, its desire to go on sleeping, but successfully directs the body to get up and do what it must. In this case consciousness says *yes,* the body says *no.* The friction again arises from the struggle between yes and no, and an energy— that certain substance—is lawfully produced. A little more real Being is created, bringing with it the possibility of real Will.

We can also think of this transaction in monetary symbolism.

We pay with the "money" of conscious suffering, moving in full awareness against the tendency of our usual lower impulses. That effort and the follow-through is our "investment," and we reap the profit, the "gold," that is *being*.

For this hypothetical seeker, the experience of awakening conscience, and experiencing herself as she really is in the fire of that conscience, at first ranges between uncomfortable and painful. But if she persistently sustains her contact with conscience, Gurdjieff tells us, "an element of very subtle joy, a foretaste of the future 'clear consciousness,'" gradually appears.* The unity and freedom—a typical paradoxical combination—the contact with the Higher, the joy that will eventually come, all this is worth waiting for, worth bearing much for.

The actual Work with attention that achieves all this has not been given here: I am equipped to offer only a description of the general theory of the method.

The method of "fusion" creates singularity—being—in the vessel.

One last remark about this seeking lady. With the help of her school, and her own observations, she may be able to determine if this bad habit she's working with is part of her *chief feature*. Gurdjieff maintains that we each have a defining characteristic that is "like the axle round which all false personality revolves." Much of work on oneself consists of locating and struggling with this chief feature. People are typically unaware of their chief feature—even if constantly told of it by others. They look around in puzzlement for a forest they're told is there, but they can't see it—because all those trees are in the way.

Gurdjieff told one of his students that the fellow's chief feature

In Search of the Miraculous.

was a proclivity to argue. The student immediately and vehemently responded: "But I never argue!" Of course everyone laughed at this automatic, kneejerk display of his argumentiveness.

This reminds me of a piece I read about a psychologist who specializes in helping celebrities with their neuroses. He believes that most of them suffer from neurotic narcissism—surely a good candidate for *chief feature* in a celebrity. He "gently broke it" to one of his patients—a movie star—that he was neurotically narcissistic. The patient's face lit up, and he said, "Wow—that's really a *special* kind of problem, isn't it?" He had been told of what may well have been his chief feature—yet he avoided coming to grips with his narcissism by incorporating the diagnosis *into* his narcissism! And this dogged slipperiness is typical of chief feature.

Chief feature is the key to the lock chaining our essence away from us. If only one could find that key; if only one could know . . .

KNOWLEDGE EYE-TO-EYE WITH BEING

Related to the "harmonious development of man" offered by the fourth way is Gurdjieff's assertion that knowledge depends on being and must not outweigh being. A person who has developed the intellectual center but neglected the emotional and physical centers is out of balance; that is, knowledge has outweighed being.

A person may have theoretical scientific knowledge, but if it outstrips being—spiritual substance and Will—it becomes harmfully abstracted from life. One thinks of brilliant men who expend vast mental energies developing ever bigger nuclear bombs, neutron bombs, and biological warfare, most of them without a flicker of doubt about the morality of creating these murderous devices. One major scientist involved in the development of the neutron bomb even expressed a great deal of frustration that it was never used! Could such a man be high on scientific knowledge—but low on *being*?

Another case might be the government-sponsored Tuskegee syphilis experiments: black men were the subjects of a syphilis study in which symptoms and their rates of decline were observed and meticulously clocked. But no one treated these men, even though penicillin was available; they were allowed to become syphilitically demented—and die. They were human beings who had somehow become laboratory animals in the minds of the researchers. Gurdjieff emphasized again and again that a key to becoming a fully realized person is being able to put yourself in someone else's place—to put aside your own point of view and experience real empathy. This is the opposite of dehumanization. It is humanization—and it becomes natural to a man or woman if they have *being*, and with it contact with objective conscience. Had the Tuskegee researchers been *present* enough, on several levels, they might have put themselves in their research subjects' place, realized the monstrousness of the study, and cured their "lab animals."

Gurdjieff was also clear that we need knowledge to temper and direct *being*; and we need *being* to contain the kind of knowledge that cannot be really understood without it.

People wildly out of balance push the world itself out of kilter: a terrorist may have courage enough to carry out what he supposes to be an act of sacred martyrdom; had he enough knowledge, he would know that the *actual* laws and teaching of his own religion (which might be based on Christianity, Islam, or any other source) are opposed to the mass destruction of innocents; he would have enough knowledge to be skeptical of those who would prey on his suggestibility, who fan extremism through theological distortion.

But both men—the scientist and the terrorist—will need more than knowledge to break free of their mechanicality. They will need to develop *understanding*. "Understanding," as Gurdjieff explains it, "is the resultant of knowledge and being. . . . Understanding grows only with the growth of being."

Being completes knowledge; completed knowledge is understanding. It is as if another dimension has been added to knowledge: when it becomes understanding, it has become holographic.

But more specifically, mere knowledge may include the involvement of *one* center; but "understanding is the function of *three* centers." Understanding appears only when, in addition to mental grasping, we also *feel* and *sense* the idea—that is, all three primary centers are brought into the act.

This emphasis on rediscovering our inner wholeness is the unifying motif of Gurdjieff's psychological teaching.

FIVE

THREE MIRAGES: PROGRESS, EVOLUTION, AND UNITY

World War I was raging in Europe, and its conflagration had spread to Russia. To Ouspensky it was a stunning example of an utterly senseless war. Men who regarded themselves as enlightened moderns were destroying one another even more barbarously than men had in the "primitive" past. Ouspensky pointed out to Gurdjieff that most people would find it hard to believe that "an ignorant fakir, a naïve monk, a yogi retired from life"* may have some possibility for evolution while, judging from the war, modern men who were the product of scientific progress evidently had no such chance.

Gurdjieff answered that people only imagined the supposed progress of modern life, without understanding that "there is no

*In Search of the Miraculous.

progress whatever." Mankind, he said, is the same as thousands of years ago—only the outward form changes. "Modern civilization is based on violence and slavery and fine words."

Ouspensky was struck by these remarks because the only "progress" he could see was the slaughter of men with the wholesale efficiency of a harvesting machine. Technological and medical progress there may have been, but humanity's social progress seemed only superficial. He told Gurdjieff of seeing a convoy of enormous trucks piled high with new unpainted wooden crutches headed for the front—for soldiers who hadn't yet lost their limbs. The planners had calculated for maiming on a massive scale. This casual cynicism horrified Ouspensky. *In Search of the Miraculous* has Gurdjieff replying with a verbal shrug:

> "What do you expect?" asked Gurdjieff. "Men are machines. Machines have to be blind and unconscious, they cannot be otherwise, and all their actions have to correspond to their nature. Everything happens. No one does anything. 'Progress' and 'civilization' in the real meaning of the words, can appear only as the result of *conscious* efforts. . . . And what conscious effort can there be in machines? . . . And the unconscious activity *of a million machines* must necessarily result in destruction and extermination. It is precisely in unconscious involuntary manifestations that all evil lies."

There, against the backdrop of World War I, and now, in the midst of our own violent times, we can feel the truth of Gurdjieff's words—even the statements we don't want to believe—about mankind's sleep and mechanicality and inability to *do*. But if he's right, they are truths that must be faced before there can be any real progress; before any one man or woman can evolve. What we normally think of as mankind's progress is just a modification; what is progress in one respect is a decline in another.

Evolution—in the spiritual, not the Darwinian, sense—is not possible, Gurdjieff avers, until a human being has developed something within himself or herself that is capable of evolving.

Evolution is usually understood as a kind of refining and empowering of the organism, or spirit, that comes about naturally over time. But again Gurdjieff challenges the popular notion. We cannot evolve mechanically; we can only evolve through conscious effort. And nature is not inclined to help us—our spiritual evolution is not necessary to nature.

Gurdjieff taught that all matter is alive, and that the planets of all solar systems are themselves evolving entities. But "the evolution of the planets proceeds, for us, in infinitely prolonged cycles of time." He told Ouspensky that all life on Earth—including humanity—is a sort of living coating or membrane of organisms over the planetary surface; the membrane is a device for refining energy. Via this membrane, life serves to create energies needed by the planet and the cosmos, in accordance with the needs of "Great Nature." Within the mechanism of Great Nature, a single person is no more important than any other organic matter. In our degraded state, we serve no higher purpose than to be part of this transformer for cosmic energies. Only the evolved man or woman becomes something more than a mindless part of this film of organic matter.

In envisioning something like the "biosphere" and emphasizing the interdependence of man with nature, Gurdjieff anticipated both the Gaia Hypothesis and the concept of ecology by several generations. And he said bluntly that one of the great mistakes of Western civilization was to suppose that we're engaged in a *conquest of nature*. "Even in struggling against nature man acts in conformity with her purposes."*

In Search of the Miraculous.

Our lack of respect for nature is symptomatic of a *wrong orientation toward the universe itself*. We have a good and rightful place in the cosmos, a just place to begin, but we can't *feel* that place as we are now. We have no sense of our place in the *scale* of existence. We're looking down—thinking we're at the top—when we should be looking up. Our disorientation leads us to identify with sheer appetite, which takes its toll on the natural world.

As Jacob Needleman puts it in *Time and the Soul*, "The need is for the connection to nature within ourselves; only then can we understand how to act toward nature outside ourselves. Along with the obvious crimes our culture is committing against the natural world, we would be wise to remember that the main crimes are the crimes against our inner nature. From these inner crimes all the outer evil arises."

Gurdjieff indicated that it's possible for only a relatively small number of people to evolve spiritually. Partly this is because of human limitations, partly because of limits imposed by nature. A certain balance holds sway. He tells us shockingly that "special forces (of a planetary character) oppose the evolution of large masses of humanity and keep it at the level it ought to be." The cosmos uses the energies of human life, as men die, to nourish the development of life on the cosmic scale (e.g., as "food for the moon,"★ for Gurdjieffian literalists) so as to keep certain forces in balance. Men who are sufficiently evolved are vibrating at a level too fine to be absorbed in this way. They go on to serve the cosmos in other ways. But in the meantime the cosmos has its own agenda with life as it stands, and that agenda too must be served.

★For one interpretation of the "food for the moon" idea, see appendix B.

The *possibility* for evolution does exist for everyone. But the seeker of spiritual evolution must be willing to sacrifice day-dreaming and illusions, and must recognize that she is moving "upstream," against the usual current. The Way is difficult. The serious seeker must, in a sense, struggle up a steep mountainside against the forces of gravity; must rise above avalanches and plod onward through icy conditions. A man climbing a steep mountain expects to have to struggle, to make sacrifices to get to the top.

Gurdjieff's teaching with respect to evolution may seem cold to some people. Many contemporary spiritual seekers come to a teaching looking for "sweetness and light." Gurdjieff offers truth and hope, real hope—but there isn't much sweetness, as such, and the light he offers isn't a very warm one. Gurdjieff is honest about the difficulties—and it's the painfully honest man who can be trusted. And while the warmth of sentimental comfort is not there, the crackling, white-hot *energy of real life* is abundant in his teaching.

"The evolution of man is the evolution of his consciousness," Gurdjieff said. "And consciousness cannot evolve unconsciously. The evolution of man is the evolution of his 'will' and Will cannot evolve involuntarily."* In both instances we're called to an effort—a conscious effort, a voluntary effort; to trudge up that steep grade, barking our shins on rocks but never giving up. That's why it's called "work."

If Gurdjieff's insistence on the narrowness of the Way sounds distasteful, it's probably because the first obstacle to our evolution is *us*. We are all lazy, prone to "not following through" unless food and shelter are at stake. And we're in denial about our actual state.

Knowing our actual state takes a lot of seeing; a great deal of the nourishment of self-observation. We have to *see* our three

In Search of the Miraculous.

centers—intellectual, emotional and moving—working according to the influences coming from outside. We see them interacting, perhaps in disharmony, one usurping the place of another. We help bring them into harmony with this seeing—which has a harmonizing effect in itself. We see that our essence self, our real, personal, *honest* nature, is buried beneath all the claptrap and bad habits and fears programmed into us. And we see how little we are present—how much our spirit, our soul, needs to grow, to be truly free. All this is helped by seeing our place in the cosmos. Somehow, understanding how influences from the higher, finer part of the cosmos can transform us, if we're open to them—seeing ourselves in right context in the scale of being we're about to discuss—makes evolution more likely. In fact, the process of seeing initiates evolution. It begins with knowledge of our component parts, and our place in the universe.

There's an inner world to see—and an outer world to be in right relation with. Let's start with the inner world.

THE SUM OF THE PARTS

Here's a quick overview of some aspects of our inner world that we may observe as levels of ourselves, inside, which react to outer stimuli in particular ways—absorbing energy, redistributing it, guiding or confusing us depending on our degree of inner unity and overall consciousness.

The three centers within man or woman—the thinking center, the emotional center, and the moving-instinctive center—are there for three overall functions. According to Gurdjieff, the thinking center governs ideas, thinking, and the usual sort of memory. It is analytical, coordinative, and involved in planning—its lower part is the "formatory apparatus," which is like a secretary who takes dictation and types it up but doesn't understand what it means; the formatory apparatus is free-associative, automatic. It's also typified by black-and-white, either/or thinking—and we can see the result of its dominance in human intolerance and narrow-mindedness.

The emotional center governs feelings, emotions, values. The usual "emotions" are associated with it—many of these, such as fear, are actually not part of the emotions but are instinctive reactions taken as "emotions"—and our likes and dislikes are ranged within it. We react positively or negatively to input within this center. Our temporary selves, the many fickle faces of our personality, take part in this center's emotionality, using its energy to animate their small transient agendas. But a man with *real I,* who is present within his emotional center, has developed a fine state of energetic being that can include a higher emotional center and conscience, and that *feels* in an active way, without negativity, and far beyond the shabby reactive emotions of our temporary selves.

The moving center supports the physical organism and its movement; it is essentially passive, having to be taught to imitate a model of movement. It does possess the potential for a complex range of "physical intelligence." The instinctive function includes automatic maintenance of our physicality and our instincts.

The sex function and instinctive functions are in effect centers too, though in some way subsidiary to the moving center. So there are three overall centers—thinking, emotional, and moving—broken down into other subsidiary centers and functions.

The sex center works with a very fine energy, which is all too often stolen and used wrongly by other centers. Various mechanical, useless behaviors are associated with the theft of sex energy by the emotional and moving and intellectual centers: political persecution, religious fanaticism, obsessions with sport, and so forth. The sex center is more than just an organic sexual function. Fine sexual energy can be used for spiritual transmutation. This may be the true origin of the tradition of celibacy in many monasteries: it might originally have been more a matter of preserving a precious resource than worrying about sex as sinful. Possibly the real purpose of this celibacy—which is not necessary in most cases for the right utilization of sex energy—was forgotten over the centuries.

Each center has its own memories, in which everything that happens is recorded, sometimes deeply, sometimes temporarily. These recordings are linked by associations, so that new, related impulses bring about associated responses in the organism, in all three centers; in the absence of guidance and parsing from a higher self, these recordings add to the general tendency toward habituality and automatic behavior.

Because of the confusion that comes from the reign in one's inner kingdom of an incompetent sovereign, King Personality, one tends to fall into "wrong work of centers." For example, the emotional center may mistakenly try to do the work of the intellectual center, resulting in an emotional fuzziness, giddiness, or overreacting fearfulness, confounding what should be coolly controlled work of the intellect; the intellectual center may mistakenly try to do the work of the emotional center, trying to work out something very slowly that the properly functioning emotional center would know what to do with instantly.

Which brings us to the higher centers: the centers-within-centers. We are too often unaware of them, and we're incapable of accessing higher centers without long preparation by inner work—this is partly due to higher and lower centers' different speeds in processing information. We have occasional experiences of them, but the centers are, unfortunately, likely to be "out of the loop" of our usual activity. Especially of note are the higher emotional center and higher intellectual center. Gurdjieff maintains that without access to the higher emotional center, all of our emotions are "negative," that is, subject to polar swings and without real meaning. We don't feel authentically since we're always reacting on the fly. By contrast, the higher emotional center is the seat of real feelings, of authentic contact with the divine. The higher intellectual center is a lofty aerie within every human being, where the falcon of objective reason roosts, the *nous* of objective spiritual intelligence spoken of in the Hermetica. A person asleep is not capable of taking flight with that falcon.

Spiritual evolution begins with self-study, with understanding the machinery and energy exchanges that make up our inner world. To understand what we are, we must first see, honestly, what we're *not*. We return again to a theme now becoming familiar: the absence of unity, of *real I*, in mankind. We return to this theme for a reason—it's so hard to see the reality of our absence, *our nothingness*, in Gurdjieff's terms. That is, when we see our "nothingness" we see our lack of true volition, our tendency to react mechanically, to fall trancelike under the control of subsidiary selves and impulses. Seeing these truths is part of "taking impressions," seeing ourselves inwardly and outwardly—but nonjudgmentally, without "beating ourselves up" about it. Gurdjieff's great disciple Lord Pentland counseled against getting caught up in "secondary emotions" about what we observe in ourselves.

"Every thought, every mood, every desire, every sensation," Gurdjieff said, "says 'I.'"* We assume that each of these momentary manifestations are expressions of a whole man or woman. The Whole, however, "never expresses itself." Every person is a plurality; man's name is Legion, as the New Testament put it.

In Search of the Miraculous.

A human being evolved enough to have a permanent and un-changeable *I* deals with both mother-in-law and IRS agent with the same equanimity as they greet the arrival of the weekly pay-check. This is not to say that a nonidentified practitioner of the fourth way is bland, boring, monotonous; a fully realized human being may even seem mercurial, if that's what his or her essence—real nature, unaltered by programming—is like. Such a person will know the value of a sense of humor—and may perhaps show a lot of apparent "personality." But inside he or she is untouched, in the usual sense of being *taken* by a feeling, though they feel authentic love and remorse very deeply indeed; externally such a person deals with things consciously, with reference to authentic con-science, playing the expected roles but always in a way that's for the best, given the particulars of the situation, and deriving spiritual good from every intentionally suffered moment.

If we're honest with ourselves we can see how terribly far we are from this kind of evolved individuality, no matter how "spiri-tual" we suppose ourselves to be.

We can't find our way across a land unknown to us until we're ready to ask directions—and that requires that we admit we are lost.

THE LAW OF THREE . . . AND THE RAY OF CREATION

As if he hadn't already done enough to transform Ouspensky's spe-cific point of view, Gurdjieff went on to forever blow apart Ous-pensky's entire view of the world by informing him of cosmic laws of which he—the famous "expert" on the esoteric—had been quite unaware.

Let's begin with the Law of Three—which Gurdjieff called "Triamazikamno" in his masterwork *All and Everything: Beelze-bub's Tales to His Grandson.* According to Gurdjieff, this law is the basis of all phenomena—everything arises from it. It is the law of three forces, which is symbolized by the Holy Trinity: Father, Son, and Holy Ghost. Gurdjieff's own Holy Trinity is: *Holy Affirming, Holy Denying, Holy Reconciling.* A force advancing, a force resisting the advance, a force reconciling and fulfilling the interaction of the first two. "The three forces together," as Ouspensky sums it up, "form a trinity which produces new phenomena."

Science speaks of positive and negative charges, a force and the resistance to it, male and female—but we rarely hear of a third force that interacts equally with the first two, at the same point of juncture.

In the Law of Three, an active force is lawfully and inevitably met by a "denying" force—but these two forces are not enough to create phenomena. A third, reconciling force must be called into play. One example is the atomic nucleus interacting with electrons: they are reconciled into an atom by an electromagnetic field. The field is the Third Force.

Another example is the interaction of a teacher and a student: the teacher is Holy Affirming, the student is Denying, the teaching itself is Reconciling. The student has learned—but the invisible part of Reconciling is within him, in the dimension of what he will do with the teaching. This level is perhaps one where we can see another aspect of the Law of Three: "the higher blends with the lower to actualize the middle." That is, there is a kind of "involutionary" force from on high that reaches down and vibratorily enlivens the next step down. Involution is as much a part of the process as evolution. The teacher explains things simply—involutionarily—in order to bring the student up to the next level.

I find myself picturing the three basic dimensions. A point is asserted, a plane is the response, and third-dimensional space is the third component that activates the first two into some three-dimensional object. But can we see space? We infer space—because things move through it. But space itself? We cannot grasp space *it-self,* except abstractly; it cannot be done. Likewise the third force is usually invisible to us, unless we know how to look for it.

The basic pattern of the Law of Three can be observed all through nature. Take a walk and observe how the leaf of each plant is symmetrically divided into two opposing parts; the two parts are united and harmonized by the stem and fine branchings running up the middle, and by the parts being equally balanced out in the overall shape.

Cut a photo of a human face in half, down the center. With-out the other side it looks like a more-or-less random arrange-ment of shapes. Push the two halves back together, and now one is opposed by the other, which, in its opposite symmetry, brings about a harmony. The "oppositeness" becomes harmony—the two contrasting sides working together make a pleasing pattern that makes sense to us.

Spiral patterns are fundamental to nature, too—from DNA to ice crystals to geometric arrangements found in trees—and spirals are made up of a *force* pushing one way, a *modification* that turns that impulse into a curve, the impulse seamlessly continuing on-ward, still shaped and curved by the opposing force. The spiral shape as a whole is the Holy Reconciling.

Picture a vast chain of such interactions, of the playing out of the Law of Three, throughout the cosmos. This cosmic chain of interac-tions—the Ray of Creation*—begins at the Absolute, which is the sum total of all created things, *and* of "the uncreated"; it is the cos-mos in totality and in unity. In the Absolute there is only one law: its unconditional Will. The Absolute, in an act of divine Will, separates its one law into a trinity, three interacting laws in the next level down; these three laws, or states of being, interact to produce the

---

*An amalgam from various sources appears in figure 2.

FIGURE 2

THE RAY OF CREATION AND CONSCIOUSNESS
A creative current flows down the Ray of Creation.

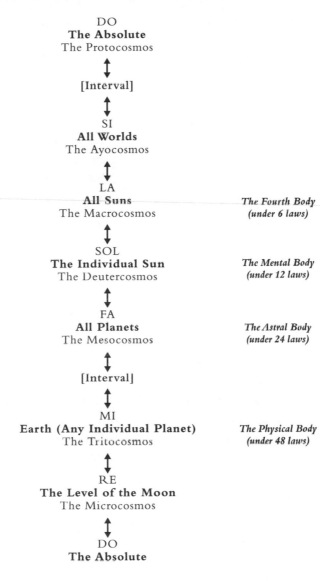

DO		
The Absolute		
The Protocosmos		
↕		
[Interval]		
↕		
SI		
All Worlds		
The Ayocosmos		
↕		
LA		
All Suns	*The Fourth Body*	
The Macrocosmos	*(under 6 laws)*	
↕		
SOL		
The Individual Sun	*The Mental Body*	
The Deutercosmos	*(under 12 laws)*	
↕		
FA		
All Planets	*The Astral Body*	
The Mesocosmos	*(under 24 laws)*	
↕		
[Interval]		
↕		
MI		
Earth (Any Individual Planet)	*The Physical Body*	
The Tritocosmos	*(under 48 laws)*	
↕		
RE		
The Level of the Moon		
The Microcosmos		
↕		
DO		
The Absolute		

The Ray of Creation, with intervals indicated, and the four
bodies possible for man, with their correspondence to levels of the
Cosmos. We begin with the physical body and work our way up,
with greater freedom as each higher body is achieved.

next level below, which Gurdjieff calls All Worlds. This world's laws interact in accord with the Law of Three, producing another created world, All Suns, where six laws interact also in accordance with the Law of Three, ramifying to produce the next step down the Ray to the level of the individual Sun, where there are proportionately more laws . . . and so on down to us, and past us, infinitely subdividing into the familiar complexity of life's dilemma.

A friend of my young son wondered aloud "why the world sucks so bad." Here's one answer. Gurdjieff said that at each ascending level of creation, we are subject to different sets of laws—more laws down "lower," at the level of the Earth and moon, fewer laws up higher, closer to the Absolute. At the higher levels, there are fewer restrictions on the movements of conscious beings. At our level, down at the roots of the cosmos, the planets, we labor under the burden of forty-eight of these laws, each law increasing the difficulties of life.

There is less freedom at our end of the universe—and less access to the grace, the benevolence of the Absolute. One teacher explained this aspect of the Ray of Creation by pointing to a tree and noting that the top of the tree was bathed in sunlight, the leaves just below the top had a little less sunlight, and the leaves and branches and Earth below had even less, the light being "stepped down" through the intervening foliage.

The will of the Absolute cannot reach us directly, at our lowly level; we must ascend, through work on ourselves, to obtain more and more of its influence and, with it, freedom. We ourselves have to bridge the intervals, the gaps in the ladder, that lead us back to the will of the Absolute. But we do get help getting there—if we're open to that help.

In his book *A Study of the Ideas of G. I. Gurdjieff,* Dr. Michel Conge suggested that "the real struggle is to be actively still and permeable, allowing the free circulation of energies in their dual complementary movements of ascent and descent." This stillness, this permeability, this receptivity to the current, the higher energies, and the full reality of our place in the Ray of Creation, is accomplished through a cultivation of consciousness itself, with methods involving an increase and directing of attention to the self in a certain alert, objective way.

There are obstacles—things are difficult down here—and it's that way for a reason: without that resistance, without intervals to cross, Conge tells us, "no created being would have the opportunity to learn how to become conscious or volitional." There is a famous story about a rare butterfly, observed by entomologists emerging from its chrysalis. They saw that it had to struggle furiously to get out. Someone carefully cut it free, prematurely, so it wouldn't have to struggle. As a result, it was unable to fly, since the full struggle to break out of the chrysalis was what pumped vital fluids into its wings. Without that struggle, first, it soon died.

Seeds are used in another classic analogy. Many seeds need to be buried in the ground in order to grow. They must have the soil to resist the probe of their root, or they have no orientation; and what buries the seed also nourishes it.

What the butterfly and the seed need human beings also need. Self-help counselors like to point out that our difficulties are opportunities for psychological growth—but they're more than that. On an esoteric level, they are an indispensable part of the recipe for *spiritual* growth.

Yet even at our low level, the current of life reaches us, though filtered, by way of the long-term playing out of the Law of Three. And that current animates our world.

"In this way everything is created," says the Corpus Hermeticum. "The Sun bestows on the immortals their everlasting life and he nourishes three eternal regions of the cosmos with the ascending light sent forth from the side that faces heaven; with the descending light that illumines the entire hollow realm of water, earth and air, he enlivens and sets in motion birth and death. The creatures in this region of the cosmos he remakes and reshapes in a cyclical movement."★

We can see the Law of Three manifesting in our own attempts to grow spiritually. Let's take the hypothetical case of one man, in this case a seeker. The law manifests in the outcome of the seeker's desire to attain a higher level. His initiative, his effort—this is Holy Affirming. His lassitude, his laziness, his inertial tendency to watch the morning news instead of taking up his morning meditation, is for him Holy Denying, the negative response to the positive of his initial effort.

But attention, informed by knowledge, enters the picture. He knows that in forcing himself to work when he doesn't feel like it, he will make some headway toward attaining that higher level. So his knowledge, remembered, provides just enough motivation to get him to do the work after all, and he implements that work with *attention* directed toward himself: with self-observation. Knowledgeable attention in this story is Holy Reconciling: the third force.

The intertwining or polarization of two forces, a productive dualism, is everywhere in philosophy and religion. We think immediately of yin and yang. But is there a third force to apprehend, along with yin and yang? What activates yin and yang, what is produced by yin and yang—but also produces their unity?

We intuit . . . the great Tao.

★ *The Way of Hermes.*

The Law of Three, Planets in the Octave, and Tearing Down an Old Fence

In the Gurdjieff Work there are "Work days" and "Work weekends" and even "Work weeks" in which, now and then, students gather to be directed in crafts, the arts, Gurdjieffian sacred dances, and even some fairly major construction projects—along the lines of what was done at Gurdjieff's Institute in France, though generally less rigorously. The object is to work while self-remembering, at least as much as one can, to keep some attention for the sensations of the body, while working with a measure of conscious intelligence and sensitivity for others and the world, thus attempting to engage all three centers—and there are other purposes in all this, too.

A student of the Work provided this account of the Gurdjieff teaching arising during a minor demolition project carried out on a "Work day."

We were tearing down a fence, and tearing up a very large redwood deck, at this place in the country, and working hard under the hot sun. Most of those working on the project were young, and the tendency was to chatter about this and that, to make the toil pass more quickly—intellectual speculation along with a great deal of silly joking—rather than doing the work with some degree of consciousness like we were supposed to. A longtime, very experienced work-teacher came to help a while.

Observing this mindless chatter in us, our teacher said that we were wasting an opportunity, throwing away energy chattering that could be used on conscious work. He tried to call our attention to the spiritual significance of working physically with other people who had the same goals, the same wish in mind: "It's just my interpretation of things," he said, "but it's my experience that

the work is real—call it a sacred physics—and what I see is that
something happens when we work together. We are asked to try
to think about Gurdjieff's ideas, even working out here, and
what I wonder is if the Law of Three applies here, to what we're
doing right now, this second, working and sweating on this
project. The Law of Three—and the Ray of Creation.

"Just consider this—the law is that the Lower meets the
Higher to Actualize a new Middle. And this is important to us,
here and now, in this moment. The Ray of Creation starts at the
bottom with the moon. What is the moon? A planet with no life,
or light of its own, just reflected light. Isn't that where we live
most of the time? We live on the level of the moon: a world of
thoughts, reactions, dreams. All reflections of life. No life of
their own.

"But then on a hot afternoon like this, say, we work with
some others and something comes together and lifts us to the energy of all planets: he is a planet, she, him. Something comes
when we work together consciously. It calls me up from the
moon to here—the Higher calls the Lower to a middle energy—
to occupy my body, to really occupy it *now*, a real contact within
all my parts. Mind incarnated in body, is a way to put it. And
when I am trying to be really *here,* with other people who are
also trying to be *here,* I become "the Earth"—I'm then at the
level of the Earth, alive now, under the Sun. And if I—and you,
and him—become "the Earth" in this scale, we have a new
"low" to work from. A new low that calls to a new high—the
sun—and what is the new middle? The energy of all planets—
yes? We know it as relationship in the Work, real exchange. Call
it brotherhood, fellowship. Something new.

"So doing this, it happens that sometimes we really arrive
here—*together.* A real moment of work together arises. And that

in turn is a new "low" that could call a vibration higher than the Sun to help us.

"That's maybe why we're here, man on Earth. Any less than this and we don't serve our real purpose. Now let's shut up and get back to work."

THE LAW OF SEVEN . . . AND AGAIN THE RAY OF CREATION

A defining aspect of the Ray of Creation, the Law of Seven—or law of Octaves—says that all matter and energy in the universe is ultimately vibratory, and those vibrations oscillate in measurable patterns, crucially including a repeating pattern of discontinuity between certain levels.

The late Gurdjieffian sage William Segal put it incisively in his book *Opening*: "According to the law of seven, every transformative process in the universe, from the life of a cell to the life of a solar system, unfolds as an octave in seven successive steps. The progression of each octave is determined at two intervals by the presence or absence of appropriate shocks."

The octave, in the Gurdjieffian and in the musical sense, is divided into seven steps and then the *entre* to the next octave: *do, re, mi, fa, sol, la, si,* and then *do,* onward. The Ray of Creation begins with the Absolute as well as ending with it ("I am the Alpha and the Omega, the beginning and the end.") The Absolute is *do,* the level of the moon is *re,* the Earth is *mi*—then comes an interval of discontinuity (the term *interval* is used in Gurdjieff's teaching a little differently from its use in music, always meaning specific places of retardation of vibration), till we arrive at the level of All Planets, which is *fa;* then comes the Sun, which is *sol;* and above that is All Suns, which corresponds with *la;* then All Worlds, which is *si;* and then comes . . . *do* again, the Absolute. Passage up the scale requires a "shock," or additional conscious push, to carry us over the interval and upward, as we move against the restraints of the accumulated laws of the lower levels.

Gurdjieff said that to the astute in ancient times, the octave scale represented more than a musical formulation, and he has restored its original symbology. In fact, Gurdjieff-like formulations on the octave and other ideas are found in the teachings of Pythagoras.

Gurdjieff described the vibratory aspect of his teaching as "more materialistic than materialism." Everything, he said, is a form of "matter" in some way, but the various forms of matter are relatively more or less vibratorily dense, depending on their place in the Ray of Creation and where they are relative to us. Even the apparently miraculous is only a function of definite material laws—but laws of a level we're unfamiliar with. A miracle is the insertion into our world of the vibratory possibilities of a world higher on the Ray of Creation; it is that world interpenetrating our own in a way that, however unusual, is nevertheless lawful according to laws beyond our ken at our low level of development.

Authentic evolution creates within us a self that can move ever more freely in the cosmos, with a Being that is receptive to higher influence in the form of finer energies. It is a complete self, and its completion liberates it from the great weight of the General Laws that oppressed it before; it is liberated from what Gurdjieff calls the "Law of Accident." Our evolved spiritual bodies—the third and fourth bodies discussed in the previous chapter—are capable of surviving death as individuals. The Divine Body has the possibility of relative immortality within the solar system, and potentially beyond.

The Laws Within and Around Us

How else does the Law of Seven apply to us as individuals? The same mechanisms hold true in a "lateral" direction, in life, and vertically within us. Any force—human or not—on its way somewhere must in some manner conform to the Law of Seven: it must pass through an octave to get where it's going. But it does not necessarily get where it's aimed and neither do we. It is just as likely, or more likely, to be deflected by other influences, unless there's what Gurdjieff called a "shock"—a nudge of directed energy, really—at the right moment, to help us up the scale, past the intervals. For it's at those naturally occuring intervals in the scale that we're easily turned aside from our goals by wayward influences.

We can apply the Law of Seven to our movements through the world, and to social movements. The Law of Seven explains why we usually do not act consciously, why we tend to stay mechanical, why we tend to stay asleep thinking we're awake, why what actually happens is not what we expected. Indeed, in the absence of a "shock"—a conscious impulse carrying us through to the next level—we tend to go around in circles.

All human efforts—all efforts of any kind—are directed through a scale of seven steps and two intervals, according to this Law of Seven. Even in something as literal as shooting an arrow at a target, the intervals that must be crossed presumably include a nearly imponderable combination of such factors as crosswinds, whether or not the archer had coffee and enough protein for breakfast, whether some part of the archer's mind is on a disagreement with a lover, the presence of distracting ambient sounds, inadequate training, and so forth. All these factors and the weakening of the archer's attention might accumulate in the intervals, in the octave of the attempt to hit the target. But if the archer provided *additional shocks,* to carry intention *across* the intervening intervals, accurately to the target—shocks such as working at making attention sharper than usual, special preparatory training, using more strength than usual in drawing the bow, say—then the arrow may fly "past the intervals" and strike the target dead on.

The organizer of a big rock concert for charity ran into trouble partway through the event when the planned venue fell through. But he kept his focus, calling persistently on the goodwill of others till he got the help he needed, thus crossing the interval, and the concert took place after all in an even better venue.

"Nothing can develop by staying on one level," Gurdjieff tells us. "Ascent or descent is the inevitable cosmic condition of any action."★ If a movement doesn't go up it goes down. Horizontal motion is highly conditional, and temporary. But again we're in denial about this—so we expect spiritual evolution to happen without real efforts and we expect good efforts to stay good without maintenance. The very existence of the created worlds, Gurdjieff said, is a matter of perpetual "reciprocal maintenance." In order to maintain itself, despite the enervating, decaying effect of "merciless Heropass," a.k.a. Time, the Absolute must create worlds that restore its equilibrium.

Remember the seeker, who was our example of the Law of Three? He is also engaged with the Law of Seven. His effort at moving upward is a movement from *do* to *re,* to *mi,* on the octave— and then he feels tired, he's caught in laziness and inertia, and forgets himself . . . unless through self-remembering he brings an act of conscious effort into play, making himself do inner work when he doesn't feel like it. If he does this instead of riding the downward current, his effort provides the additional shock neces-

★*In Search of the Miraculous.*

sary for driving the original effort across the interval. Thus he crosses the interval—the rope bridge over the abyss—and moves up the octave, to *fa, sol, la, si,* and on to the challenge of the next interval. The shock in this case is an inner effort—it may at other times be an impression of oneself as one really is: invariably a shocking impression.

We recall Gurdjieff's emphasis on following through on an aim, on the power of real *wish,* of the weight of *being* behind intention . . . all this relates to the necessity imposed by the Law of Seven.

When a movement up the octave is stymied by the intervals, the original impulse can eventually become its own opposite.

A well-known example of a movement becoming, in effect, its own opposite is the current that Jesus created to pass on a teaching that was both pragmatically compassionate and esoteric. The force of Jesus' teaching degenerated, over the centuries, in the absence of the necessary additional "shocks"—the necessary conscious guidance across intervals of resistance—to become its own opposite: his call for *non*violence became the violence of the Inquisition, the persecution of Jews, the Crusades, and Christian fundamentalism. Without the guidance of objective consciousness, good intentions become their own opposite—lawfully, in accordance with the Law of Seven and the fallen state of humanity.

But again, the "downward" movement, into the material world, into identification, is in other frameworks also a creative movement, a necessary part of the fabric of life. If we are not to some extent involved, identified, with our attractions, we cannot fall in love and procreate; if we are not identified—up to a point—with hunger, we can't become motivated to feed ourselves and survive. We accomplish nothing spiritually if we die from hunger! We must interact with the world, and be part of it, yet be capable of stepping back from it. We learn to be "in the world but not of it."

The Enneagram and the Symbols Within Mankind

With Gurdjieff, philosophical symbols—like the triangle, the Seal of Solomon (or Star of David), and the enneagram—represent the stages and movements of a person's inner development. It is almost as if in developing we incorporate these symbols into the very fabric of our being: "the union of knowledge and being."

The enneagram has become the best-known symbol of Gurdjieff's ideas. As it stands with the public, it may be another practical example of the negative side of the Law of Seven: Gurdjieff brought us the enneagram as a symbol designed to provide clarity, to avoid blurry, subjective interpretations and confusing terms. But people can distort anything, and in many quarters the enneagram has come to represent the opposite of what Gurdjieff intended.

In Search of the Miraculous quotes Gurdjieff's sharply worded warning on metaphysical symbols: "in the hands of the incompetent and the ignorant, however full of good intentions, the same symbol becomes an 'instrument of delusion.' . . . Symbols which are transposed into the words of ordinary language become rigid in them, they grow dim and very easily become 'their own opposites.'"

Gurdjieff also warned Ouspensky and his companions that "one thing incompatible with Work . . . is 'professional occultism,' in other words, professional charlatanism." Self-professed spiritualists, so-called "channelers," fake clairvoyants, and the like will take some small, half understood element of a teaching and "use it to make fools of other people."

So it has proved. Always in search of a new gimmick, certain individuals have latched onto Gurdjieff's enneagram symbol and

FIGURE 3
THE ENNEAGRAM

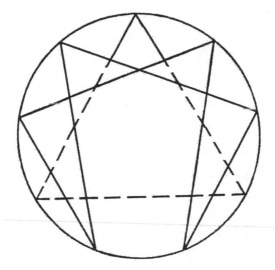

THE ENNEAGRAM NUMBERED AND WITH
OCTAVE AND INTERVALS

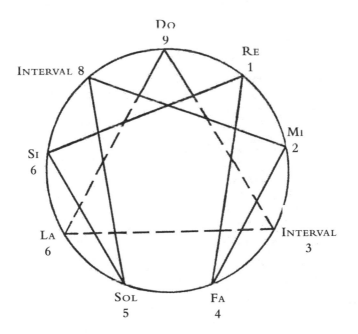

turned it into an industry of vague reassurance. Gurdjieff said nothing about using the enneagram as a personality assessment device, or for "readings."

"Everything in the universe has a place in a scale," Gurdjieff said. The nine-pointed figure of the enneagram is the "fundamental hieroglyph of a universal language," a schematic for the transformation of energy within man and in the cosmos, and a means for further understanding the Law of Seven and the Law of Three. The enneagram has many levels. One level can be glimpsed in considering that the octave is counted around its points, from *do* at the top, going clockwise to *re,* and onward through the octave, with the intervals counted at the fourth and eighth points around the circle. Seven notes plus two intervals equals nine points. The triangle within the figure relates to the digestion or transformation of certain fine energies, and to the Law of Three.

One type of "food," whether air, food for the stomach, or impressions, will be counted on the enneagram as entering the organism in its given place on the scale set out around the enneagrammic circle; the food then interacts with other aspects of the inner world of the organism, transforming according to the laws of Three and Seven and the inner workings of man, and inventoried within the enneagram according to an esoteric system taught only in certain places.

The same system uses the enneagram to monitor the laws of Three and Seven in the outer world. The enneagram, Gurdjieff said, "is perpetual motion and . . . is also the philosopher's stone of the alchemists." Why the philosopher's stone? This legendary creation could be used to transform one substance into another— for example, lead into gold. The enneagram graphs the transformation of substances—vibrations and other foods—within a human being.

In some quarters Gurdjieff's work will inevitably be watered down and then distorted. All this happens lawfully, according to the Law of Seven.

But his essential teaching is intact, and can be found, because, as we will see, Gurdjieff made the requisite sacrifices and exerted enormous efforts to keep the transmission going—the current flowing.

SIX

FINLAND AND THE MIRACULOUS

The Caucasus and Revolutionary Psychosis

We never reach the limits of our strength.

—G. I. Gurdjieff

When he was on the point of committing himself to study with Gurdjieff, Ouspensky asked Gurdjieff for direct evidence of the miraculous. Gurdjieff promised him that he would have it, but "many things must happen first."

Gurdjieff, Ouspensky testified, was "as good as his word." It happened in the summer of 1916.

Ouspensky said that he found most of what happened to him in the realm of the miraculous, that summer, to be indescribable. He also said he used to be indignant when people wrote that they could not describe the miraculous clearly or in detail—but having experienced it himself, he now understood the difficulty. It is hard, as Gurdjieff warned, for a higher level to communicate its experience to the lower level, if not impossible. Still, some of it Ouspensky did describe.

It happened in Finland, where Gurdjieff's group was to meet for a sort of retreat in the country.

Just prior to this retreat, Ouspensky had begun a series of exercises, an experiment that apparently incorporated some of Gurdjieff's methods with some of his own. Ouspensky carried out a series of short but intensive fasts, combining them with breathing exercises and "'repetition' on the method of the 'prayer of the mind,' which had helped me very much before to concentrate my attention and to observe myself." He used, as well, complicated mental exercises for the concentration of attention. The prayer of the mind presumably had effects in the emotional center; the mental exercises were very intense; the body was incorporated with breathing and fasting. Being Ouspensky, he of course added his own methodology to Gurdjieff's.

In August 1916, in a state of nervous excitement and physical weakness, Ouspensky arrived at the Finnish country house of another student. Gurdjieff and eight other students were already there.

One of Gurdjieff's methods—utilizable only by a master—was the provocation of powerful reactions in students, which they must then consciously suffer and which also provide work in nonidentification and outer considering. Forced to experience these reactions without acting on them—without expressing negativity—students are then able to glimpse themselves as they are; they see their reactions as the manifestations of little *I*'s, the spurious expressions of false, temporary selves; their usual "emotions" as the kneejerk responses of a man asleep. They see their dual nature. Ouspensky and the others endured a rather harsh session of this kind, that day, Gurdjieff ridiculing their accounts of their lives, pointing up their "cowardice and laziness of . . . thought."

Ruthlessly, Gurdjieff repeated before Dr. Stjoernval and Ouspensky something that Ouspensky had told him "in absolute confidence": what Ouspensky privately thought of Stjoernval. Something quite negative. Ouspensky had always condemned people who talked about others behind their backs—and yet he had himself gone behind Stjoernval's back to ridicule him to Gurdjieff. In exposing this, Gurdjieff had shown Ouspensky his own hypocrisy so starkly he could not look away.

Seeing ourselves as we really are is an important stage in awakening. And as we were warned, "awakening is bitter" at first.

During a special session with two other students, in which Gurdjieff taught special movements and positions, Gurdjieff began to discuss sleeping man's dishonesty with himself. A man cannot even tell his own story without lying . . .

Suddenly, *Ouspensky began to hear Gurdjieff's thoughts.* One of these thoughts was intended for Ouspensky, who replied to it, speaking aloud in the ordinary way. Gurdjieff nodded to Ouspensky—and then came a communication conveyed in silence. "I heard his voice inside me as it were in the chest near the heart." Gurdjieff was asking "a definite question."

Ouspensky responded aloud in the affirmative. Gurdjieff turned to the others. "Why did he say that? Did I ask him anything?"

Then Gurdjieff asked Ouspensky other questions, which Ouspensky again answered aloud—to the astonishment of the other two men. The questions and responses concerned "certain conditions which I had either to accept or *leave the work.*" Gurdjieff gave Ouspensky a month to make up his mind.

Unnerved, Ouspensky went for a walk in the forest. Here, some distance from the house, he found himself in a welter of contradictory feelings—and then, somehow synthesized from the contradictions, came an epiphany: he saw that Gurdjieff had been right about him, about his hypocrisy, his dishonesty, his lack of self-knowledge. Knowing such things theoretically was not much help: now he concretely understood that "what I had considered to be firm and reliable in myself in reality did not exist." He saw his own nothingness.

Returning to the house, the exhausted Ouspensky went to bed but was unable to sleep. Then "a strange excitement again began in me, my pulse began to beat forcibly, and I again heard Gurdjieff's voice in my chest." (It's interesting that he heard it *in his chest,* the seat of the emotional center.) Ouspensky replied mentally, and a strange conversation ensued, an exchange of questions and cryptic answers.

Gurdjieff then asked Ouspensky a question so powerful he felt paralyzed in trying to answer it. Ouspensky does not tell us what the content of this telepathic conversation was—he declines to attempt to articulate it. That it took place at all is remarkable enough.

Finally Gurdjieff telepathically told Ouspensky that he must rest, and to go to sleep.

But sleep was not so easy, after all that had happened. For days he was to be both troubled and illuminated by an unusual intensity of feeling.

The next morning Ouspensky found Gurdjieff and three students in the garden. "Ask him what happened last night," said Gurdjieff to the others.

This made Ouspensky angry, though he wasn't sure why, and he stalked off toward the terrace. "As I reached it I again heard Gurdjieff's voice in my chest."

"Stop!"

Ouspensky turned toward Gurdjieff, who was smiling. "Where are you going? Sit down here," Gurdjieff said in his ordinary voice.

Ouspensky couldn't concentrate on conversation. He was in a state of "extraordinary clarity of thought" and tried to use it to further his understanding of the Law of Three and the Ray of Creation. Mentally, saying nothing aloud, Ouspensky struggled with these questions—until suddenly Gurdjieff said aloud to him, "Leave it. This is a very long way away yet. You cannot find the answer now. Better think of yourself, your work." Once more Gurdjieff had telepathically entered Ouspensky's mind—and apparently was quite comfortable and facile in the process.

Ouspensky's exquisite intensity of feeling continued as the days in Finland passed, and Ouspensky began to find his state "burdensome." He asked Gurdjieff, "How can this be gotten rid of?"

"This is what you wanted," Gurdjieff said, "make use of it. You are not asleep at this moment!"

But there was a quality of mockery in Gurdjieff's response. Ouspensky had induced a state of heightened consciousness without having the Being to bear it.

At last they returned to St. Petersburg. But the strange psychic link between Gurdjieff and Ouspensky continued for a time—even after Gurdjieff had departed for Moscow on the train. "Late in the evening of that day I 'conversed' with him while seeing him in the compartment of the train going to Moscow."

Telepathy is of interest: it demonstrates phenomena of a certain order, and we may infer much from it, as a small flash of heat lightning suggests the burgeoning electrical charge in storm clouds—but insight is more important. Truth. Revelation. These came to Ouspensky when, soon after the trip to Finland, he was walking in St. Petersburg and suddenly saw that a man walking toward him was asleep. The man seemed to be sleepwalking with his eyes open—though there was nothing about him that would ordinarily have made one think so. He was "walking along obviously im-mersed in dreams which ran like clouds across his face." Then everyone Ouspensky saw walking and driving about seemed asleep. Later when his attention was diverted: "I ceased to see 'sleeping people' because I had obviously gone to sleep myself." But, for a time, Ouspensky had *witnessed* the sleep of humanity.

Other insights washed over Ouspensky in the wake of the miraculous. He realized that his own character had changed in some fundamental way. The emotional intensity of the experi-ence had awakened a new compassion and a sense of the unity behind all things—that classic insight of the hardworking spiritual seeker. This perception of underlying unity seemed to revitalize his feeling of community with people. And now he understood in a new, objective way, what he called "the esoteric principle" behind the philosophy of nonviolence: if we're all interconnected you cannot harm another without harming yourself, on some level.

It was as if his higher emotional center had begun to awaken . . . and the perceptions natural to that center had begun to awaken as well. This resonates with William Segal's remark: "We seek to awaken to the point where fine energies penetrate, transform, grow, and steer our everyday lives to our hidden reality."*

Ouspensky remarked on another change that took place in all of Gurdjieff's regular pupils: that *they were not afraid to keep silent,* even around other people. This is more significant than it sounds at first. They came to his apartment and sat down and often did not speak a single word for hours, as they waited for Gurdjieff to-gether, and were quite comfortable that way. Pointless talk, small talk, is a function of sleep and seems jarring in a place appointed for the striving to awaken. Some visitors to the apartment thought

Opening by William Segal.

that this silence was put on, or hostile, or they simply found it unbearable and consequently began to chatter. One man, unable to
bear the silence for more than five minutes, began to tell Ouspensky a spurious story of an interesting fellow he'd met on the street,
and all that fellow's opinions about the war. Ouspensky suddenly
knew that this visitor was lying: he had met no one, had heard no
opinions, he was making it all up just as an excuse to talk. The
other students knew the man was lying too, and this underscored
something nearly miraculous that Ouspensky had noticed about
Gurdjieff's apartment: *it was impossible to tell lies there.* "A lie at once
became apparent, obvious."

A high quality of attention, maintained in silence, somehow
makes authenticity shine out clearly. A person who's nervously
chattering cannot distinguish lies from truth in himself or others.
But someone engaged in self-remembering, in silence, has awakened a little, and in his new state lies are immediately apparent,
particularly in a place—like the home of a master—where certain
vibratory subtleties are present, conditions that help one struggle
for authentic presence.

Gurdjieff himself invariably knew when someone was lying.
He emphasized the great difficulty people had in recognizing
their own lies: they lie to themselves and others often without
knowing they're doing it. So basic a thing as sincerity is far more
difficult to achieve than we realize.

Gurdjieff's students came to see him and his wife Julia Ostrovsky off
at the station after his final visit to St. Petersburg. He was on his way
via Moscow to Alexandropol, to see his family. On the platform,
said Ouspensky, Gurdjieff was "the usual Gurdjieff we had always
known." Then Gurdjieff boarded the train and sat by the window in his compartment, to gaze out at them—and was somehow

transfigured. It was "as though he had suddenly become a ruling prince or statesman of some unknown kingdom." This impression lasted a few seconds, as the train left the station. Afterward someone remarked on the "transfiguration," and everyone agreed that they had seen it, had felt something extraordinary. There was a sense that Gurdjieff had momentarily revealed himself.

This impression was to be repeated, over the years. Now and then Gurdjieff would lift a kind of veil, step out from behind the often dismaying role-playing of his outer considering, and show something of his actual Being. There was a quality of radiant compassion in it, and something else that certain esotericists speak of: an intrinsic "kingliness." One who has this quality, which Gurdjieff called Hvareno, is paradoxically required to hide it, at all costs, even to the point of making himself seem quite the opposite. But he may have cause to show Hvareno to select people, when the time is right . . . perhaps on a railway platform.

EXPERIMENTS IN ESSENTUKI; THE CROSSING OF THE MOUNTAINS

1917 was to be traumatic for Russian aristocrats—the Revolution would kill many, drive survivors from their homes, deprive them of their fortunes and titles. Yet Thomas and Olga de Hartmann quite willingly gave up their aristocratic status for quite another kind of revolution: the inner insurrection, wherein the true Self overthrows the false self.

Thomas de Hartmann was born to privilege on his family's estate, near Kiev in the Ukraine. A composer who was later to collaborate with Gurdjieff in the composition of sacred music, he graduated from the St. Petersburg conservatory, under the direction of Rimsky-Korsakov, in 1903, as well as graduating from military school. In 1906 Hartmann married Olga Arkadievna de

Schumacher, the daughter of a high government official. In 1907 Thomas's ballet *The Scarlet Flower* was performed by the Imperial Opera with Nijinsky in the cast; in the audience was the tsar himself. Impressed, the tsar authorized Thomas de Hartmann's release from active service in the Guards so that he could concentrate on composition.

Both Thomas and Olga de Hartmann had deep family connections in Germany, and from 1908 to 1912 they lived primarily in Munich, where Thomas studied with Wagner's student Felix Mottl, director of the Munich Opera. There Thomas came into contact with the youthful energies of modern art, taking in the first great exhibition of van Gogh, Gauguin, and Cezanne and becoming close friends with the painter Kandinsky.

In Munich the Hartmanns brought into focus an interest that had always been hovering in the background for both of them: the esoteric and spirituality. They began with Blavatsky's doctrine and later had an intriguing experience with spiritualism, but they felt no indubitable quality of realness in the usual theosophical suspects.

Then Thomas's friend Andrei Zakharoff, a mathematician, told them about a startling new teaching, and in due course he introduced first Thomas and then Olga to G. I. Gurdjieff. "Mr. Gurdjieff," Olga wrote, in *Our Life with Mr. Gurdjieff*, "was an unknown person, a mystery. Nobody knew about his teaching, nobody knew his origin or why he appeared in Moscow and St. Petersburg."

They followed this mystery for the next twelve years, through the social minefield of the Russian Revolution; into and out of poverty several times; and through many adventures in Armenia, Turkey, Europe, and America.

In March 1917 Tsar Nicholas II was forced to abdicate. The Russian Revolution—at this time more a civil war—was fomenting chaos everywhere. One never knew where one might be safe. Gurdjieff had planned to return from Alexandropol to continue teaching in St. Petersburg, but it became evident that the Revolution was not going to go away. He settled on Essentuki, on the isthmus between the Caspian and the Black Sea, and summoned his core students there by telegraph.

Thomas De Hartmann pulled some strings and got himself transferred to Rostov. The Hartmanns entrained for Rostov for appearance's sake but instead went on to nearby Essentuki, where Gurdjieff awaited them. The army of the White Russians and other factions held various territories in Russia; nothing was yet definite, although the tsar had stepped down. Though he was careful to get the necessary papers in Rostov later, Thomas recognized that his obligation to the Guards was no more, as the monarchy was no more. The day after the Hartmanns left St. Petersburg, soldiers came to Olga's parents' house, looking for Thomas to arrest him for being a reserve officer of the guard and a favorite of the tsar. They had narrowly slipped the Bolsheviks' murderous net.

Gurdjieff had divulged much of the theory of his teaching, complete with his cosmology, symbology, and the arithmetical details of his system, in St. Petersburg, over the course of 1916. He taught method there too; but the real transition from theory to practice took place in 1917, in Essentuki.

The first evening, at a house Gurdjieff had taken in Essentuki, he had a room cleared and then lined his pupils up and—to the astonishment of the Hartmanns—told them to march. They marched around the room; then he directed them to run and to perform a series of exercises. He seemed to be preparing the ground for another level of physical instruction. It went on and on, as Gurdjieff's physical work and exercises typically did—until at last he told them to rest.

Observing that Thomas liked a lot of sugar in his tea, Gurdjieff rather arbitrarily told Thomas to give up sweets of any sort. On the surface this was for Thomas's health—but in fact it was, Thomas knew, "to produce an inner struggle with a strong habit. Mr Gurdjieff often gave this exercise—to struggle with habits—to those who were beginning to work on themselves." Where better to see one's mechanicality, one's machine-conditioning, than in struggling with a habit? Just giving up a habit in the normal course of life has value, but the exercise has more hope of succeeding and has more significance in a work environment—in the supportive, reflective atmosphere of a fourth way *school*.

Zakharoff was forced to kneel in a corner, from time to time, and when someone asked him why he was kneeling, the normally mild-mannered mathematician was *required* to snarl a response— "None of your bloody business!" Both behaviors were the opposite of what he would normally be inclined to do, and therefore Gurdjieff *for a time* required him to do just that. In the tension between his normal inclination and this new activity, a possibility for self-knowledge and conscious (intentional) suffering was generated.

Some of Gurdjieff's prescriptions for new behaviors were minor, like giving up sweets; others were life-changing challenges: he told the Montenegrin aristocrat Olgivanna Hinzenburg to give up her servants, even her cook, and do all the cooking and cleaning herself! To most Americans this may not seem so intimidating, but imagine having been raised with servants and a cook and suddenly to have to voluntarily give them over and learn their skills. Perhaps the most humbling part would be in realizing how difficult and skill-intensive the work had been all along. Olgivanna was not only taking on physical drudgery—she was taking on a whole alteration of her psyche. Scrubbing out chamber pots will induce a new humility in pretty much anyone, at least for a time. But of course this sacrifice was only the beginning. She must not only do these tasks herself—she must do them as consciously as she is able. She must do them in the present moment, with full attention.

The fundament of Gurdjieff's work, Olga de Hartmann confirmed, was work with *attention*. It is as if efforts at conscious attention and real Will are the building blocks of Spiritual Being itself.

The day after arriving in Essentuki the Hartmanns were introduced to the famous "stop exercise." When Gurdjieff shouted "Stop!" everyone had to freeze in whatever position, whatever expression, they held at the moment. Gurdjieff used variations of this exercise in many contexts, including in the Movements demonstrations, when people engaged in dynamic physical activity were commanded to "Stop!" and all tumbled one over the other . . . but tumbled down or not, keeping the postures they'd held when the stop was called; the end result is startling to observers. The "Stop!" exercise, reported to be of Sufi origin, brings about a cessation of inner momentum, along with the stopping of the outer self: the mind is momentarily stopped in its tracks, its usual free-associations derailed and piled up before the mind's eye. For a brief moment, shocked by "Stop!" out of the sleep of daydreaming and rumination, one might glimpse oneself as one really is . . .

Mr. Gurdjieff soon announced an expedition "to Persia"— though as it happened a literal trip to Persia itself was not the point and was not in the offing. A core group of pupils met Gurdjieff in Tuapse and set out on a trip along the Black Sea and over the mountains toward Sochi. The luggage was piled up in a horse-drawn wagon, on which Mr. Gurdjieff and Zakharoff rode; the others had to walk, taking a different route. In entirely inappropriate shoes and clothing they tramped with excruciating difficulty over a mountain pass. At last they met Gurdjieff at an inn. Here they hoped to rest for the night, but Gurdjieff said, "The night is so wonderful, the moon is shining. Is it not better to continue?"

They continued, trudging on and on, with their feet blistering and swelling out of their shoes. Each step for Olga in her high heels must have been a lesson in itself. The hours passed—one in the morning, two—and sometimes Gurdjieff actually made them run to catch up with the wagon. At last, in the scrubbiest, stoniest, least comfortable place Gurdjieff could find, they were given bread and tea and told to sleep. Except for Thomas, who had to stay awake on watch. It was not long till dawn; they had barely slept when Gurdjieff woke them all and moved the expedition out again. Olga's feet were so swollen she was unable to put on her shoes. This elegant lady, at whose wedding the tsar's sister had been in attendance, was forced to tie pieces of cardboard on her feet to serve as sandals. These soon fell apart, and she began to trudge barefoot, like a peasant—but without a peasant's toughened feet.

That morning, Thomas, who hadn't slept, was told he could ride on the wagon. This only sounds easy; if he fell asleep he would fall off the wagon and down the rocky mountainside. So he had to stay awake, sitting up, though the day was hot and the rocking of the wagon threatened to lull him to sleep. It would have been easier to stay awake walking; now he must stay awake with sheer force of Will. And Gurdjieff knew this.

All of this would naturally evoke the expected inner responses: anger, rebellion, self-pity. Yet the whole point was to bear such feelings, to endure them, to consciously suffer them, and to go on, pursuing an aim, a wish—to complete the expedition exactly as they were directed to carry it out, and to do it without shirking, without giving up. Following through despite everything. Of such efforts Being is made.

Soon after midday Gurdjieff sent someone to a village for a pot of lamb and green beans. The expedition stopped in a shady green meadow; they ate their fill, and Gurdjieff told them to sleep.

Though Gurdjieff often pushed his students past what they had supposed was their limit of endurance—to the altitude of what he called "superefforts"—he always knew when they had reached their actual limits, and he then rewarded their organism with food and sleep. He followed the same course in his assaults on his students' psychological mechanicality: he would role-play seamlessly, appearing to be enraged; he would shout at people, "press their corns," going right for their psychological weakness, pushing them to their apparent limits and just beyond, but he always, later, gave them ease and support, and they understood that what they'd endured had been an exercise, not some dictatorial cruelty. All of it played out meaningfully in the context of the Gurdjieff Work.

Resorting to one of his favorite metaphors, Gurdjieff remarked that he was like a coachman: so long as the horse was on the road—that is, so long as the pupil was on the Way—he gave the horse free rein. But if the horse turned toward the ditch on the right, Gurdjieff directed him left; if he turned left toward the hill, he urged the horse right.

We may assume what Gurdjieff did not bother to say: that in due course of the lawful magic of the Work, this "horse" eventually transforms into a coachman himself, and guides *himself* along the Way . . .

For as Gurdjieff later told Thomas de Hartmann, "Today you are a fool for me, but tomorrow I will be a fool for you."

After a long, deeply refreshing nap in the meadow, they continued onward—and found they were no longer weary. Olga barefoot, the others with their shoes crumbling, they trudged on into the night. At last they camped in a glen. They were in a dark and wild place in the Caucasus; there were wolves and jackals and bears in the woods. During the night they saw the animals' eyes shining . . . and a wolf killed a cow not far away. But the stars were brighter than they had ever seen, and they were "happy in a way we had not known before."

After resting a couple of days in a posthouse abandoned to the Revolution, they started again. As the road became more mountainous, Gurdjieff assigned Zakharoff and Thomas to push the cart from behind, aiding the horses. As it became harder and harder, he added an additional task: a simple counting exercise to be carried out in their minds as they struggled to help the heavy cart up the mountain. Two centers were then actively engaged— the moving-instinctive and the mental.

In St. Petersburg and Essentuki Gurdjieff had engaged them in work in self-observation, which led to "discovering America," Gurdjieff's whimsical term for the discoveries they made of their inner New Worlds. The expedition "to Persia"—which in fact only went to Uch Dere, near Sochi—was another stage of learning. De Hartmann later wrote that on this expedition, "by creating all kinds of emotional and physical difficulties, he was creating . . . a ladder of obstacles over which we had to pass to reach a certain little *do* in ourselves."

In a house rented in Uch Dere, Gurdjieff told Thomas to help Zakharoff clear a great deal of hay from some sheds. The hay was full of thorns, and they had to move it with their arms. It took a day to finish the work and by sunset their arms and hands were covered with scratches. Here was the aristocratic composer of *The Scarlet Flower,* the prodigy of the Munich opera, spending the day moving hay with his bare and bleeding hands . . . and not minding at all. It seemed quite right to him.

But soon Thomas came down with typhoid, which was spreading in the area. Gurdjieff—who before had made him stay up all night on watch, push carts up mountain roads, and drudge in hay barns—now lovingly nursed the sick composer, then found him a hospital bed when none was readily available. He took Thomas to the hospital in Sochi himself. Still, Thomas nearly died, more than once. His recovery was a long one. But by January 1918 he was hale again, and the Hartmanns were back in Essentuki with Mr. Gurdjieff.

There Gurdjieff told his students to work up a suitable name for his Institute, but it must as precise a name as possible, a difficulty since—and there is a complex Gurdjieffian teaching on this problem—the ambiguity of language itself is a constant barrier to understanding. They pondered the title of the Institute through their time in Essentuki and Tbilisi. Much later they evolved a name that Gurdjieff approved—and that Thomas de Hartmann felt Gurdjieff had had in mind all along: The Institute for the Harmonious Development of Man.

While in Essentuki, one day, walking with Dr. Stjoernval and Gurdjieff, Thomas saw a poster for a night club and muttered something nostalgic about how he'd enjoy such an evening. "Doctor, you hear?" Gurdjieff said. "He's inviting us to the club this evening. What, Thomas? Will you invite us to supper?"

Thomas was dismayed: his financial resources had withered away in the flames of the Revolution, and now with post-Revolution inflation, what had once cost 2 rubles now cost 500. But Thomas did not have the courage to demur, and so they went to the club. "And now my Hell began," Hartmann wrote: Gurdjieff insisted on ordering the most expensive items, and the bill ran far higher than the already painful 500 rubles Thomas had brought. Thomas tipped the waiter and sent him, a stranger, in the middle of the night to his wife for more money; she sent another 500 rubles.

The bill of 1,000 rubles consumed most of their resources. Gurdjieff was unapologetic.

But the next morning Gurdjieff gave him the money back, explaining that the evening had been a lesson. Thomas had behaved like a lamb when it was appropriate to be a wolf. He should have stood up to Gurdjieff and said no, but he had failed to bring the whole of himself to bear. He had reacted to the situation mechanically and without maturity. It would not happen again: overnight Gurdjieff had matured Thomas de Hartmann enormously.

Similarly, Gurdjieff told Olga that she must give up her jewels to him, as the school's finances were at an ebb. The jewels were heirlooms and gifts from Thomas's mother, precious to her for sentimental reasons. She agonized; she wept through the night. But she knew she must surrender her identification with the jewels, for Mr. Gurdjieff said he had need of them. He was more precious to her than the jewels—so the next morning, still struggling with herself inwardly but outwardly composed, she gave the jewels to Gurdjieff. He casually told her to put them in a box, and turned away. But after she'd gone downstairs—having well and thoroughly given the jewels up—he called to her . . . and simply gave them back to her. He hadn't wanted the jewels—he'd wanted to provoke her struggle within herself over them.

On another occasion Gurdjieff needed paper for a craft project, to earn money for the Institute. Thomas wincingly admitted that he had some rare music paper, which he intended to use for an orchestration. He had given some of the same sort of paper to Prokofiev himself, who had come all the way from Kislovodsk to get it, so rare was it in the present circumstances of civil chaos. But with characteristic ruthlessness—that is, a conscious, meaningful ruthlessness—Gurdjieff instantly demanded the composition paper for the crafts project. It must have been inner torture for Hartmann the composer to give it up for a crafts project. Thomas's vanity, his self-importance, had to be sacrificed, along with the opportunity to work on the orchestration, and Gurdjieff knew this.

The same vanity was again shattered soon afterward, when Gurdjieff commanded Thomas to go to the square in Kislovodsk to sell rolls of silk on the street. Thomas was horrified—he didn't mind working in hay and pushing carts when only other students and strangers were about, but in Kislovodsk he would see his aristocratic friends and acquaintances from St. Petersburg, who would perceive him as having fallen to the state of a curbside flea-marketeer. Gurdjieff knew this full well, which is exactly why Thomas was chosen and why Gurdjieff insisted he must go, over his protests. Thomas went, sold the silk—and felt a change in himself. Until this moment Thomas had not seen his own "insurmountable sense of class pride" before. Once more he had a strong impression of himself, a truth about himself he'd never before seen.

Gurdjieff was constantly teaching his students about themselves and always looking for unexpected ways to do it. A person who anticipates a teaching may have a mechanical, animalistic response to it; a man surprised by being shown himself as he is may wake up enough to respond like a real, fully developed Human Being.

SACRED GYMNASTICS, A.K.A. THE MOVEMENTS

Soon Gurdjieff began in earnest to teach an early form of what we now call the Gurdjieff Movements; at the time the students called them Sacred Gymnastics. They "absorbed the attention of the whole person." The whole body was engaged in a sequence of complex movements, which by their nature also called for the full attention of the mind.

Visually, the Gurdjieff Movements are startling. One has a sense of each dancer's sharply defined individuality paradoxically contained in a conscious uniformity of purpose. The Movements rarely involve solo dancers—picture them always as rows of dancers wearing identical white costumes with sashes, moving either identically and simultaneously as a whole, or identically in their own section; sometimes the dancers are divided into rows that move differently with respect to one another but always in an overall symmetry. Other formations besides rows are adopted, at times, with equal precision. The effect of this collective replication of symbolic movement is eerie and enigmatic. Observed today, the Movements look like dance, march, and intricately choreographed calisthenics all at once, each pose symbolic—and there is something in their display that is teasingly like hieroglyphs or pictographs. Many are adapted from temple dances Gurdjieff saw in the East—for example, Tibetan, Sufi, and Aisorian dances—and are somatic codifications of ancient teachings. Some of them refer to the movement and transformation of energy within us, a choreography of the workings of the enneagram.

Gurdjieff said that every dance has a certain meaning, a certain content. There's something else at work besides the study of the symbolic: "If one moves without being stimulated from without, it is the movement of heaven," says the Taoist *Secret of the Golden Flower*. The Gurdjieff Movements are said to provide access to a different kind of movement: a movement that flows from *a current* reaching us from somewhere higher than our usual dull, reactive world of mechanical associations.

René Daumal, the great essayist and author of the allegorical novel *Mount Analog*, beautifully described the experience of the Gurdjieff Movements:

A whole other landscape, which opens in the self, appears to him who takes part (if only once) in these "lessons." First, there is an internal chaos, a profound confusion; everything is put back into question. They ask you to make very simple gestures; your body no longer obeys as soon as you step slightly away from your old habits. They ask you to express a very simple feeling and you remain expressionless, or with appropriate expressions, as soon as you are stripped of your learned attitudes and conventional masks. They ask you to make a very simple effort of memory, reflection, calculation, and your intelligence works only with great pain as soon as your associative mechanisms, your set expressions and your clichés have fallen in cold ashes on your brains and tongues. . . . You will know what this joy can mean from real contact with yourself, when it rises up in you, when not only a simple pace but an entire rhythm comes to life in your body.*

The usual physical movements of life—even of dance, for the most part—are merely a mechanical response, Jeanne de Salzmann tells us.

And this whole event takes enough to perceive it at the very moment it happens . . . it has been conditioned by the automatism of our associations, by all the habits and clichés engraved on our memory. We have nothing in us to respond with except these accumulated memories. So our life is endless repetition. . . . We must first of all see the difference between unconscious movements, which operate entirely under the control of the moving center, and those that are set in motion by the intervention of thought. . . . There is however a movement of still a third kind. When we see that the mind can no longer control the movement and the moving center is about to take over, at this very moment, when our ordinary consciousness does not know what is going

*From *Powers of the Word* by René Daumal.

to happen, a feeling of urgency may appear. This feeling of urgency mobilizes a new energy in us—an attention hitherto unknown to us because we were ignorant of our need for it. If we can *move* consciously—we can learn to *live* consciously.

Yet it all begins with the simple process of bringing the normally inharmonious three parts of a man or woman into inner harmony. Gurdjieff summed it up in *Views from the Real World:* "Dances and movements, are a means of combining the mind and the feeling with movements of the body and manifesting them together."

Sacred dances are described in the unpublished scenario for Gurdjieff's ballet—if it can be called a ballet—*The Struggle of the Magicians:*

Immediately the pupils leave their work and place themselves in rows, and at a sign from the magician they go through various movements resembling dances. . . . These "sacred dances" are considered to be one of the principal subjects of study in all esoteric schools of the East. . . . The movements . . . have a double purpose; they express and contain a certain knowledge and, at the same time, they serve as a method of attaining a harmonious state of being. Combinations of these movements express different sensations, produce varying degrees of concentration of thought, create necessary efforts in different functions and show the possible limits of individual force.

In attempting to perform the Movements there is a sense of inner struggle for ever more attention, more intelligence, in one's connection with the body; and at times it's as if the kaleidoscoping Movements—radically restoring engagement of two centers, moving-instinctive and intellectual—are the shifting tumblers of a lock, by degrees unlocking an inner door and opening the possibility of passing through that door to the higher emotional center.

The Sacred Gymnastics were demanding and often exhausting. They were also another chance to push out the limits of endurance, to summon superefforts, thus to strengthen genuine Will and one's Wish and to give another possibility for the growth of Being—for the cultivation of the tiny mustard seed, as Jesus had it, from which "the Kingdom of Heaven within us" grows.

For six weeks Gurdjieff carried out intensive cultivation. Lectures on the System alternated with Sacred Gymnastics; there was craft work, cooking, and housework, and one strove to do these things while remembering oneself and without wasting energy on muscular tension that could be utilized for something higher; there were carefully controlled fasts; and there were "inner exercises," sometimes for the whole group but often given individually. Always the unifying motif involved striving for a new "collectedness" of the self—a collectedness composed of efforts at restoring attention to its rightful place.

And there were "shocks" to help jump the intervals of personal struggle up the octave, episodes of "Khaida yoga" in the form of Gurdjieff's artificial creation of nearly intolerable emotional situations. He would play a role, sometimes screaming at people like a drill sergeant, sometimes acting the sighing, disappointed parent; he would play the Unjust Man, for example, and play it so effectively that, despite all previous experience, his students were usually taken in and would react in kneejerk fashion—occasioning *actual* disappointment on Gurdjieff's part. But sometimes they would suffer his "abuse" intentionally, seeing their automatic reaction to his roleplaying without identifying with that reaction, without being taken by it, and something needed was then lawfully produced within them. Gurdjieff would occasionally later confirm that he had been role-playing—and had given them a chance to learn something about themselves by seeing their automatic reactions. He had set out to create a sort of hothouse for the accelerated growth of certain substances in people—and he truly had to turn up the heat on them to do it.

The heat on Gurdjieff himself was great, in the spring of 1918. The Russian civil war—from the Bolshevik perspective, a revolution—was spreading. He and his followers often had to evade it. Then came word that the Turks were moving against the Armenians, threatening his family in Alexandropol. Gurdjieff found himself having to try to save both his family and his followers from two different vectors of mass psychosis. He arranged for his family to join him in Essentuki. All came but his father; the elder Giorgiades stoically refused to be driven off his land.

In July, Gurdjieff's eldest sister arrived with painful news. Gurdjieff's father had been murdered by Turkish soldiers when he tried to drive them off his property. His father must have known what would happen . . .

Gurdjieff's inner torment can only be imagined. Ouspensky had observed him with his father and had remarked on the warmth and heartfelt respect Gurdjieff showed him. Gurdjieff's belief in honoring one's parents was so strong that it became a byword with him, a dictum. But he had been able to spend only a little time with them since first leaving home, and now in his absence his father had been shot down.

But Gurdjieff had to think of the living. It was time to take some essential core of his students out of the reach of the Revolution. The route he was to choose was not one he could take his elderly mother and family on—these he would send for later. He may have calculated that they were "proletariat," and were not likely to be targeted by the Reds, whereas the "plutocratic" Hartmanns and other students might well be executed if they ran afoul of the Red Army. And who knows what the Reds might make of Gurdjieff himself, if perchance they found he *was* (no one is quite sure about this) a former foreign agent of the tsar?

Any guesses we have of his thinking at the time are speculative. What we're sure of is that Gurdjieff created a cunning disguise for his own and his followers' exodus from the madness of the Russian Revolution. In July 1918 he arranged for a newspaper story to say that he was leading an archaeological expedition to Mount Induc. With this camouflage, he took fourteen followers in the direction of Sochi, with plans for points beyond.

Though he would eventually rejoin Gurdjieff, in a detached sort of way, Ouspensky didn't go with the "expedition." He had begun to worry that he could not entrust himself to Gurdjieff any longer, that there were too many evidences of Gurdjieff's human fallibility, such as his alienation of the faithful Zakharoff. Indeed, it seemed to Ouspensky that Gurdjieff had needlessly placed Zakharoff's life in danger—for he had rather arbitrarily sent Zakharoff away into a dangerous territory seething with revolutionary and counterrevolutionary violence.

It may well be that Gurdjieff was simply showing the strain he was under. His burden was great. He must somehow find a temporary pocket of safety in Russia for his family and his followers; he must take fourteen people past the hostile "power possessing people" of both the Red and White armies.

They were to make the exodus in stages—first over the mountains to Sochi, where they would stay for a time and wait to see which way the political wind blew.

As it happened—as Russian Georgia became untenable—they were destined to leave Russia altogether, and for good.

As much as Gurdjieff was phenomenally capable of living in the moment—more literally and fully than the casual use of that expression can transmit—he also had a gift for planning ahead. Six weeks before the trip, he shocked his followers when he told his student Shandarovsky, a lawyer, to apply for a government position with the Soviet authorities—the very people who would have had Gurdjieff's followers shot on the spot if they knew their backgrounds and sympathies. Soon the efficient Shandarovsky managed to get himself appointed to the office that issued passports and travel papers, and Gurdjieff instructed him to issue Soviet passports to all of them—and himself—designating them "citizens" with such occupations as gardener and laborer.

Gurdjieff had instructed them in the manufacture of linen rucksacks, for they would be able to take only what they would carry. He trained them to carry 100-pound loads in the rucksacks, and "how to walk consciously": On a night-dark mountain trail one could tumble into a ravine unless one learned to walk by feeling the way ahead with one probing foot, one's weight carefully balanced on the other. He knew they would have to travel, at times, by night—and in due course this conscious walking saved them from disaster.

Gurdjieff's students were following him from somewhere that had been safe—and away from the possibility of taking up offers of an even better haven with, for example, the former prime minister. To follow Gurdjieff into the mountain wilderness, across lines of battle, with no certainty of being able to return, seemed sheer folly, and Madame de Hartmann, among others, felt a piquant uncertainty. In his memoirs, her husband reminds us that at the time the

Hartmanns and the other students believed the Soviets temporary and assumed that some semblance of the old order would return. They had learned that, regardless of immediate appearances, Gurdjieff had reasons for everything he did—but even so, to follow him now required real faith, and more. In *Beelzebub's Tales,* Gurdjieff explains that most of what man usually thinks of as faith is mere blind inertia; what he thinks of as hope is something anxious, fearful, and weak; what he thinks is love is a feeble automatic reaction. Instead, mankind can aspire to *faith of consciousness, hope of consciousness, love of consciousness:* the true essence-feelings of faith, hope, and love experienced with a profound, connective resonance. So it was that Thomas and Olga de Hartmann, and the others, followed G. I. Gurdjieff, against all the apparently saner arguments, behind horse and donkey carts, even bringing two children along. . . . Despite all their reservations, even terror, they followed him in faith of consciousness, in hope of consciousness, in love of consciousness.

A CAUCASIAN GREAT DIVIDE

Just before the expedition embarked for the foothills in two railway baggage cars, Thomas encountered his friend General Radko-Dmitriev. The general spoke wistfully of his regret that he could not go along on what he supposed to be their scientific expedition. Thomas later learned that after the departure of the expedition, the Soviets arrested the general and other officers familiar to the Hartmanns, made them dig a mass grave, and then shot them in it; they were then haphazardly covered with earth and buried, though many of them were not yet dead. Had Thomas stayed he would have died with them, or in some other purge boiling out of the revolutionary psychosis.

When Gurdjieff and his followers reached Maikop, the area was surrounded by cossacks fighting the Red Army. The noose was closing. Gurdjieff handily turned some Soviet soldiers into allies by involving them in a playful card game. Won over by his apparent joviality, the soldiers told the expeditioners about a deserted farm-house they might use. There Gurdjieff and his people stayed, as the battle lines raged around the "expedition" for several weeks. Though bullets screamed over the house, the fighting never quite engulfed them.

At last the White Army retook Maikop; now Gurdjieff and his followers needed a new set of papers to get through. Through Dr. Stjoernval's connections with an admiral friend, they got the nec-essary papers and became, for a time, a different sort of expedi-tion. They found ways to be whatever sort of expedition was expected of them by whatever "power possessing person" they encountered.

They passed through various vicissitudes only to come to the greatest challenge: a climb through the mountains, carrying heavy packs. Though they had toughened up, over the last two months, the slender Olga de Hartmann found climbing a steep mountain trail—hour after hour, bent double under a 50-pound pack—something beyond her experience. Her tears were "flow-ing in torrents." More than once she was about to give up—but she forced herself to go on. Just as it became utterly unbearable, Gurdjieff at last called a halt for the night.

They stayed in a hut, keeping a fire lit all night to scare the wolves away, and Gurdjieff remarked: "Now I am at peace. We do not have to deal with men anymore, just wild animals." This re-mark speaks volumes about his general attitude toward humanity—something that would emerge even more clearly in *Beelzebub's Tales*.

They traveled on through forests and across muddy, slippery areas where the horses were given their head—this was Mr. Gurdjieff's suggestion, the voice of experience; the pack animals instinctively picked the best routes with pure horse sense. The weather turned harsh, the food began to run out—and here were the doctors, professors, and composers, the aristocratic intelligentsia of Gurdjieff's following, in tattered clothes, eagerly foraging for berries in a wilderness . . .

At one point, hungry and bone-weary, they were given bread by some traveling peasants they happened on. In these conditions, the taste of this simple bread was "indescribably delicious." Gurdjieff remarked that "the trip had been worthwhile if only to experience the real taste of bread." They had experienced something of real consciousness—in simply tasting bread.

Later Gurdjieff told the Hartmanns to wait with the luggage while he went with the others to find supplies and check their route. Eventually, Petrov—one of Gurdjieff's ablest Russian students—and a boy were sent back with some food and to fetch them. But just after they'd eaten, bullets smacked into the ground around them. Shots were being fired at them!

Mountain brigands were firing warning shots; outgunned, the Hartmanns and Petrov reluctantly surrendered to them. The robbers were heavily armed men with blackened faces and brutal speech. But Olga de Hartmann, this lady at one time trained only to sing light opera, to "defend" herself with repartee in drawing rooms, refused to be cowed by murderous mountain bandits; she seemed determined not to give up anything more than necessary. First she hid her jewels in her bodice. The brigands went over their luggage, looking for anything of value. Astonishingly, she "argued with them over every piece." She even talked these grimy, gun-toting men, who'd fired shots at them minutes before, into letting her keep a silver toiletry set. She tricked them with a honeyed tone into letting her go through a pair of the boy's pants to get the lad's "passport"—in fact extracting and hiding the boy's watch from them. Then she *made the brigands write a note* for their compatriots that they had already been robbed of "everything useful"! Somehow, Olga de Hartmann had taken command of the situation, never losing her nerve, minimizing the damage.

Would she have been so self-collected, so calm as to be able to do this—to take control of the situation when being robbed by mountain bandits—had the robbery happened to her before working with G. I. Gurdjieff? Probably not. It puts me in mind of Ouspensky's remark about seeing a change in himself after his work with Gurdjieff: he felt a "new confidence" that he was capable of facing and dealing with whatever circumstance life set before him.

Just before reaching Sochi, they took a side trip to examine some dolmens—which were always of interest to Gurdjieff. Guided by local hunters through the surrounding mountains, they found a dolmen almost covered with underbrush. The dolmen was a stone box about 8 feet high, roofed with a flat stone, its insides hollowed out. Some researchers believe them to be merely tombs; others feel that their use was ceremonial—or they might have had both uses. This dolmen's builders (or grave robbers) had bored a hole into the dolmen's side, and Gurdjieff sent Madame Olga de Hartmann squirming with great difficulty through this narrow aperture. Inside she found only an empty chamber—which might symbolize, in the symbolism that life itself composes for us, the struggle to seek inward, only to discover one's own inner nothingness.

Through some system only Gurdjieff understood, he "took some measurements" and pointed the way through the undergrowth, and after a difficult penetration of virgin forest, came to another dolmen that no one had known about, and then a third one.

Their guides were astonished. *How did Gurdjieff calculate where the additional dolmens were to be found?* Is not this successful calculation some kind of confirmation of a portion of Gurdjieff's claims? A practical demonstration of secret knowledge originating in a primeval epoch?

In Sochi, Thomas de Hartmann looked forward to sleeping late after so exhausting a journey. But Gurdjieff made him get up at dawn and tend the horses, though he had to do so with one foot in a slipper because of an injured, festering toe. Fairy tales had always been deeply meaningful to Thomas de Hartmann, and among other things they seemed to promise that "you will reach your goal only by overcoming all obstacles." He kept this in mind at all times, with Gurdjieff, remembering that "in spite of all apparent tiredness, when one takes the right course one finds that inner energy increases, new force appears and it begins to be easier to make new efforts." Later that week when he had to look after the horses, Thomas found that "many fashionable people" at the hotel, including old aristocratic acquaintances, watched him in ragged clothes limping with buckets to the stables, but now it didn't bother him at all. He had gained a measure of inner freedom—for which he was ever after grateful to Gurdjieff.

FREEDOM, WANTED AND UNWANTED; CONSTANTINOPLE; A NEW INSTITUTE

Soon Gurdjieff announced that that the expedition was finished and, essentially, so was the "institute" as it now stood.

Gurdjieff never hesitated to use financial resources offered by followers—but he was just as likely to support them when it was necessary, as it often was. Now he announced that they should make their own plans, as he had no money left to support them. He seemed to be rethinking his methods, as if discouraged by his progress. And he was probably overburdened by responsibility for others, to the detriment of his mission.

The Muscovites returned to Essentuki and points beyond— including Zakharoff, who wanted to rejoin Gurdjieff; but he died of smallpox before it became possible. Petrov became the director of a state school and was absorbed, at least outwardly, into the Soviet body politic.

Ouspensky had moved on to Constantinople. The students who remained in Sochi scrabbled along as they might, selling things in the market; the great composer Thomas de Hartmann was reduced, not for the last time, to giving piano lessons.

When the fighting came closest to Sochi, Gurdjieff and his nucleus moved on to the Georgian capital Tiflis. And a small nucleus it was, then: the Hartmanns, the Stjoernvals, and Madame Ostrovsky. A cold, uncomfortable sea trip took them there, where they found further cold and discomfort, aggravated by their meager financial resources. Things improved when Thomas encountered an academic friend from the old regime who hired him as a professor of composition.

Soon Olga de Hartmann found herself singing opera in a production of *Carmen*—which led to the most important development for the Gurdjieff Work, in Tiflis: the advent of Alexandre de Salzmann and Jeanne de Salzmann, two important figures in the Gurdjieff Work. Alexandre de Salzmann was the set designer for the opera. A well-known painter, he was the son of the state architect; he had designed a new theatrical lighting system and continued to innovate in theatre. Jeanne de Salzmann had been an assistant to the famous Emile Jacques-Dalcroze, and she was teaching the Dalcroze system of dancing.

The Salzmanns were fascinated by what they heard of the Work from the Hartmanns and asked for an introduction. Gurdjieff was immediately impressed by these two, calling Alexandre de Salzmann, after their first meeting, "a very fine man," and about Madame de Salzmann he said, "She . . . is intelligent." He must have perceived something extraordinary, that evening, as these sorts of compliments were unusual in him.

Madame de Salzmann invited Gurdjieff to a Dalcroze demonstration. Gurdjieff watched briefly, and silently departed. It was Jeanne de Salzmann who was impressed—by Gurdjieff. Two weeks later Gurdjieff had arranged to appropriate a number of her dancers, teaching them his Sacred Gymnastics, which they were to demonstrate in "An Evening Programme of the School of Jeanne Matignon-Salzmann: Part I—Method of Jacques-Dalcroze; Part II—System of GI Gurdjieff." Gurdjieff's Sacred Gymnastics were very different from the dancing the pupils in Madame de Salzmann's class had done before—they even included, among many other directions, formations adapted from military drill.

The first demonstration was a success—and then Gurdjieff asked for Jeanne de Salzmann's pupils to be utilized purely in demonstrating his own work. The pupils, who'd signed on for Dalcroze, rebelled—and refused. But Madame de Salzmann had seen her destiny in Gurdjieff, and "with the whole force her authority and the feeling of the rightness of Mr Gurdjieff's Work," as Thomas de Hartmann tells us, she persuaded her pupils to undertake the excruciating difficulties of training and demonstration of Gurdjieff's Sacred Movements.

1919, 1920, and 1921 were eventful, tumultuous years, alternating feast with famine for Gurdjieff and his pupils, soon growing in number again. The Salzmanns became an integral part of what was now officially his new Institute for the Harmonious Development of Man. It was in Tbilisi that the Institute's name was finalized—and along with teaching his system, work was begun on rehearsing his "ballet," *The Struggle of the Magicians*—which he had been planning for many years. First announced in 1914, it was rehearsed only in parts, and was never publicly performed. There are indications that Gurdjieff was not particularly concerned with putting this "Manichean revue," as James Moore calls it, into public production—his main purpose apparently was to use it to stage something else entirely: instruction and spiritual work for the students who were tasked to learn and rehearse it. The same performers, he told Ouspensky, who will be "attractive and beautiful" in the first scene will be "ugly and discordant" in the second. "You understand that in this way they will see and study all sides of themselves."

The Struggle of the Magicians tells of one Gafar, a wealthy man, who wishes to marry the beautiful and mysterious Zeinab. She repeatedly spurns him; frustrated, he goes to a black magician to get help in bewitching her. But she is under the protection of a white magician—hence the struggle between the white and black magicians commences.

The ballet's elements are an esoteric allegory, with its suggestions of hieratic initiation and its light and dark magicians corresponding to the Holy Affirming and Holy Denying of the Law of Three; Zeinab may represent the Reconciling force. Within each man, too, is a dark and a light magician, forces that must be reconciled.

Along the narrative way, *The Struggle of the Magicians* showcased dervish dances and temple dances, and a lecture by the magician encapsulated some of Gurdjieff's cosmological ideas, neatly tied in with self-study:

What is above is similar to what is below. . . . Every unity is a cosmos. The laws which govern the Megalocosmos also govern the Macrocosmos, the Deuterocosmos, the Mesocosmos, the Tritocosmos, and others, inclusively down to the Microcosmos. . . .

The nearest cosmos of all for our study is the Tritocosmos and for each one of us the nearest subject of study is oneself. Knowing oneself completely one will know all, even God.

At the end of the tale, Gafar meets the good magician and is shown two possible paths for himself—he sees the vile Gafar he might become and the good one, beloved by all. Gafar experiences remorse and reverence as the magician intones: "It is the duty of every man in every moment of the present to prepare the future, improving on the past. Such is the law of fate. . . . Lord Creator and all you His assistants, help us to be able to remember ourselves at all times in order that we may avoid involuntary actions, as only through them can evil manifest itself."

In a kind of liturgical response his followers sing: "Forces become transformed to be." In *The Struggle of the Magicians* Gurdjieff's profoundest convictions are acted out, in larger-than-life symbols.

Gurdjieff had recognized that the Soviets were not going to go away. He decided that he must leave the country, before he was "purged" and his work purged with him. On April 27 the Soviets moved to seal off the eastern route he might have taken, leaving him with the western route: Constantinople. Though robbed by a militia of the valuable carpets he had planned to turn into financial substance in Turkey, Gurdjieff and his core followers made their way as best they could on vermin-infested ships, steerage class, to Constantinople, which had become a magnet drawing the educated classes fleeing the Bolsheviks.

Here they renewed contact with the Ouspenskys, who were living just outside town with their infant child. Ouspensky had his own students by now—a forewarning of things to come—but for now he turned them over to Gurdjieff.

In Constantinople, Thomas de Hartmann studied the dance and music of the Mevlevi dervishes, and Gurdjieff convened a temporary home for his Institute, giving lectures and demonstrations of the Sacred Dances.

There wasn't a lot of free cash floating around in Istanbul, though occasionally they gave performances for the pasha. The Hartmanns found themselves so low on funds that when Thomas's music student didn't bring her fee with her, they went without supper.

Now that the "Great War" had run its murderous course, Gurdjieff had his eyes on Europe as a more stable home for his Institute. When the Salzmanns wangled an invitation from Jacques-Dalcroze to settle the Institute in Germany near Dresden, Gurdjieff quickly accepted and began the process of accumulating the necessary visas for himself and his entourage.

Before leaving Constantinople, Gurdjieff made the acquaintance of Captain John Godolphin Bennett, an adventurer and engineer—and some say a secret agent—with a nagging interest in the occult and spirituality. His first brushes with Gurdjieff (described in his memoir *Witness*) did not entangle him in the Work but lit a pilot light that never went out. Eventually he spent ten problematic years studying with Ouspensky, and in 1948 he was to study intensively, though for less than a year, with Gurdjieff. At Gurdjieff's death Bennett went on to found his own idiosyncratic variant of Gurdjieff's teaching, melding it with Sufism and the Southeast Asian teaching known as Subud.

Gurdjieff and his followers left Turkey in August 1921 by train, and then traveled on more trains, through Bulgaria, Serbia, Hungary, and Czechoslovakia, arriving at last in Germany. Gurdjieff lectured in Berlin and then went on to Hellerau, where he was involved in a legal dispute over donated property. It seemed the property had been promised to quite another institute first. Indeed, the man who had originally offered the property claimed that Gurdjieff had somehow hypnotized him.

Because of this fiasco, and for other reasons, Germany didn't seem to offer fertile ground for Gurdjieff's work. Perhaps Britain, then . . .

After all, willingly or not, Ouspensky had prepared the ground in Britain. With his independent nature chafing against Gurdjieff's seemingly arbitrary decision-making, Ouspensky had gone to London to find his own pupils. The translation of *Tertium Organum* had made him a minor culture hero in some quarters, prompting offers of support from elements of the British nobility. He quickly accrued students, not least of whom was Alfred R. Orage, the editor of the literary and political journal *New Age*.

Orage has been described as the British Saint Paul to Gurdjieff's Jesus; perhaps he was more like Plato to Gurdjieff's Socrates.

Fifty years old when he met Gurdjieff, Orage had sidled up from an obscure lower-middle-class family with an even lower working-class income to become a powerful literary influence on Ezra Pound, T. S. Eliot, James Joyce, G. K. Chesterton, and others. Orage was never to achieve anything like wealth, but he was destined to gather "diamonds" from the valley floor for Gurdjieff and for English letters both. Brilliantly articulate, personable, and socially idealistic, Orage had always been drawn to the esoteric— to theosophy, Vedanta, Hermeticism, and the ancient Greek philosophers. He was also an aficionado of Nietzsche, who had at least some ideas in common with Gurdjieff.

When Gurdjieff lectured in London—with Olga de Hartmann standing beside him translating from Russian to some version of English—many of the intelligentsia were confused, and unimpressed. But among the smitten were Maurice Nicoll and A. R. Orage. And Orage was to give the next ten years of his life over to Gurdjieff.

England was not to be home for the Institute. The British authorities scowled over Gurdjieff's visa and ultimately rejected his request for a living visa, despite attempts by Orage to pull strings. Someone had remembered Gurdjieff from the days of the Great Game, and he was still regarded as a foreign agent. In the absence of a tsar he seemed a loose cannon at best.

France was an agreeable compromise. In 1922, with the financial help of English students—students by way of Ouspensky—Gurdjieff "leased with an option to buy" a beautiful former priory at Fontainebleau-Avon, 44 miles from Paris. His Institute was to remain at "le Prieure" until 1932. There he oversaw his grandest experiment in creating conditions for the awakening and harmonious development of human beings.

SEVEN

BEELZEBUB IN FRANCE AND AMERICA; G. I. GURDJIEFF BEYOND

Freedom is the ultimate goal of all schools, consciously or unconsciously.

—A. R. Orage

The Prieure was a primly decaying country estate; a commodious, quiet place to work, with a rural lane on one side, woods and fields on the others. In that quiet setting, Gurdjieff consciously provided the necessary turbulence for work. The personalities who swirled around G. I. Gurdjieff, the eye of that hurricane, at le Prieure d'Avon and in America and Paris, are so many and so dramatic that I cannot hope to survey the period with any verisimilitude in this slim volume. Some of these personalities, like the writers Jane Heap, Katherine Mansfield, Jean Toomer, Orage, and Kathryn Hulme, are so "larger than life" that their time with Gurdjieff deserves (and in some instances has gotten) specialized books.

So let us take the final phases of Gurdjieff's career in anecdotal jumps, and hope that we at least capture some of the atmosphere: of the hurricane and of the calm at its center . . .

Olga de Hartmann had been trained as Gurdjieff's secretary. She had received special instruction from Gurdjieff in attention, memory and remembering herself. He had also prompted Olga to an exercise in *doing,* in persuading the owner of the Prieure to rent with an option to buy, when the woman wanted to sell the property: she had been told "to hold in mind at all times what she wished to get from her and not for a single moment to lose this thought."★ And she got what she needed; the woman agreed. Olga employed the same means when asked to persuade the same skeptical lady to dismiss the ground's gardener—the woman had wanted to keep the gardener on the property to keep an eye on the Prieure's furnishings and grounds. Gurdjieff wanted no interfering outsiders. So Olga went to see the lady, keeping in mind Gurdjieff's instruction: "Even if you speak with her about the most trivial things, but have uppermost in your mind that the gardener has to leave, she will do it." Olga spoke to the woman about trivialities for the space of half an hour, until the lady suddenly said, "Yes all right, I will send the gardener away . . ." And Olga had said nothing to her about it! At least, not aloud.

And so the Institute had a home. Once a seminary, the Prieure had been remodeled into a three-story mansion. It encompassed more than 40 acres, including a pine woods, an avenue of lime trees, a smaller house, and two ponds. Immediately Gurdjieff

★*Our Life with Mr. Gurdjieff* by Thomas and Olga de Hartmann.

began to make plans and alterations, envisioning a hall for Movements, and the very first day Gurdjieff's students set to removing earth and flattening the ground where the hall would be built.

The students were primarily English and Russian—the French themselves were withdrawn and skeptical at first—and later on there were quite a few Americans.

Physical work continued every day—especially for people who had little experience of it. The spindly, potbellied, fifty-year-old A. R. Orage experienced his first few weeks at the Prieure as chiefly hard physical labor. He literally wept in his room with exhaustion and aching muscles. And what was the point of it all? Here was one of England's literary icons, schooled also in philosophy, in history, set to *digging ditches*—only to fill them in again! Every day he told himself: just one more hour, just one more day.

Gurdjieff doubtless gave him a few directions for inner work along with giving him the shovel—directions for working at something physical with a new attention. And one day, working at digging, holding the shovel in newly callused hands, Orage found that a new energy arose in him, a new appreciation of his physical organism. He seemed more alive, more *in place,* more conscious.

Gurdjieff happened to stroll by and saw the change in Orage; Orage was now *happily* digging a ditch. Gurdjieff gave a short nod and said, "Enough. Now come, we go to café, have coffee."

Orage had crossed an interval. Now that Orage had restored a healthy contact with one of his centers—as well as finding a new humility, a truer perspective—it was time for him and Gurdjieff to talk about ideas. He was to understand the Work—and Gurdjieff—so well that Gurdjieff would call him "my brother."

As the Institute seasoned, the Movements were introduced, required for nearly everyone. There were also lectures; instruction—given singly and in groups—for inner work; and fourth way exercises of all kinds. The day began before dawn, for some, who had to prepare coffee and breakfast, and at 6:30 for the others. Intensive work was eventually begun, under Gurdjieff's direction, on the new Study House and Movements hall, which was constructed of a retrofitted airplane hangar. (Gurdjieff claimed it was a zeppelin hangar, though this seems unlikely, given the size of a zeppelin.) The hangar had been transported in sections and was rebuilt, sealed, and repainted and so altered that its origin was difficult to perceive. The work was exacting, even dangerous, when the supports and beams were lifted into place: perfect for the attenuation of attention, incorporating both physical "intelligence" and mental concentration.

Others worked in the kitchen; in gardens; at sewing: preparing hangings and decorations for the Movements house; and making improvements in the chateau itself. But such work was always ultimately "for the inner struggle": when they became deeply involved in gardening, Gurdjieff would notice and warn: "Identification! Identification!" They had become so absorbed in the task they had neglected to leave some attention for self-observation.

After a long day of hard physical work at le Prieure, one doubtless longed only for food and bed. There was indeed a simple, well-balanced meal—and never did vegetarianism simper at the Institute, for Gurdjieff provided meat for the wolf in man, so to speak, as well as green matter for the inner lamb. But after dinner the unstinting discipline of the Movements began, with Monsieur de Hartmann playing piano and Jeanne de Salzmann augmenting Gurdjieff's direction. The difficult Sacred Dances after such a long arduous day must have called for a supereffort on the part of some of the exhausted Brits, wondering exactly how they'd signed on for all this.

Many doubtless had had something in mind more along the

lines of an hour of soothing, incense-redolent Vedantic meditation, perhaps a lecture on the secrets of levitation or some similar
swami whimsy, a nice tea, a lecture on reincarnation over dinner,
and then, say, a stroll under the stars accompanied by the discar-
nate spirits of the Secret Masters. Even the Russians, Thomas de
Hartmann confided, had originally expected something of the
sort. But all found instead a rigor, a constant challenge: cryptic sacred dance, physical work simultaneously combined with mental
tasks, and a shrugging off of such ideas as reincarnation—for
Gurdjieff believed you can't reincarnate what you haven't developed. (He remarked that reincarnation had been so misunderstood and misrepresented that it was useless to speak of it.)

There was also "work for the emotional center" in the form of
Gurdjieff bellowing insults and staging assaults on the very concept of justice—so that many were driven to tears. At which,
once more, Gurdjieff would only shake his head and sigh. He had
been creating conditions in which they could observe their automatic reactions. They'd forgotten again . . .

But sometimes they didn't forget. Dr. Michel Conge, a physician who was a longtime student of Gurdjieff and an important
interpreter of his teachings, relates an occasion when Gurdjieff
"launched a stinging attack on one of my weak spots. I silenced
my emotions. He abruptly stopped baiting me and, turning to
Mme de Salzmann, simply remarked, 'Doctor understand!' And I
was gratified with that deep look which goes right into your soul,
after which he smiled and went onto something else."* Conge had
managed to be present enough to not identify with his automatic

---

*"Facing Mr. Gurdjieff" by Michel Conge in *Gurdjieff: Essays and Reflections on
the Man and His Teaching,* edited by Jacob Needleman and George Baker.

reactions to Gurdjieff's provocation—and thus the provocation was no longer needed.

Physical work at le Prieure was always demanding, and sometimes Gurdjieff spurred his pupils to new levels of intensity. "Throw yourself in with all your force," he would say in Russian. To the English: "Skorry!" That is, scurry. "Faster! Work very good! Skorry!"

On many levels, "superefforts" were clearly necessary. And supereffort looms large in the Gurdjieffian legend. In Russia, Gurdjieff had given the example of a man who was exhausted from walking all day through awful weather. All the man can think of is rest, when he totters home after walking 25 miles. But instead of sitting down to his warm, waiting supper, he forces himself to go out and walk *another 2 miles* before again returning home. The effort that counted was not the initial effort at a long, necessary walk, but the one that came purely out of an act of Will.

A more expedient way to summon a supereffort is to carry out ordinary work at a faster rate than would be normal, while bringing some active attention to it—a daily experience at the Prieure. And it was something imposed from without, by Gurdjieff. Normally we can't bring ourselves to superefforts without a push . . . and the push should come from someone qualified to know when too much is enough.

Gurdjieff watched his pupils carefully at their labor. When he saw that Thomas de Hartmann was physically overtaxed to the point where it might become dangerous, he told him to stop the hard work he was doing and sent him to rake and burn leaves for a while. (Only at le Prieure would this have been a break!) Both in the psychological and physical regard Gurdjieff was sensitive to limitations in others and knew just how far to push them past their normal limits. People who suppose themselves masters enough to direct someone had better be the real thing—for the whole course of the student's life is at stake.

ENCODED OUTINGS

Gurdjieff sometimes took select groups of students on excursions across France, occasionally to Vichy. These were invariably unsettling experiences, since Gurdjieff usually drove the lead car in the caravan—and when he was in the mood he could be a terrifying driver, rocketing along at speeds that made the car rollick onto two wheels at the curves. According to Gurdjieff's son Nicolas de Val, in his book *Daddy Gurdjieff: A Few Unedited Memories*, driving a car "literally intoxicated" Gurdjieff; he "drove abominably . . . caring little about distances between vehicles." No driver was ever more reminiscent of the automotively smitten Mr. Toad in *The Wind in the Willows*.

In Michel Conge's account, Gurdjieff would appoint someone to sit beside him and consult the map, but he refused to slow down at crossroads, so that signposts were a blur—they inevitably took the wrong road, and he refused to backtrack, heaping verbal abuse on the innocent map-reader. Sometimes he would deliberately lose the next car in the caravan, so that his hapless students would have to guess where he'd decided to fetch up for the night. If they managed to stay with him, he'd time things so that they came into some small town at two o'clock in the morning, when all the inns had closed, and then send someone—whoever disliked the task most—to pound on the door and wake up the grumpy, scowling innkeeper, demanding rooms for scores of Gurdjieff's followers.

Fritz Peters's memoir describes experiences as a boy going on some of these trips with Gurdjieff. Fritz was brought to the Institute at the age of eleven by Jane Heap—he had essentially been thrown over by his inept parents—along with his brother Tom. To one bemused innkeeper Gurdjieff insisted that young Fritz and Tom were the American sons of Henry Ford and thus important people who must be housed.

After a long trip, Gurdjieff would sometimes inaugurate a feast, when all anyone could think of was rest—and at three o'clock in the morning they yawningly submitted to toasts and elaborate picnics on hotel room floors. Again and again, with these apparently irrational, even perverse behaviors, he forced his students to come up against their habitual states of being. In the context of Gurdjieff's presence, these dismaying conditions forced his followers to see their anger and frustration, their embarrassment, as machinelike responses of their lower nature—and seeing this brought their higher selves to bear at the same time, creating an exquisite, productive tension between the two natures of mankind. And no real harm came to them—they were tired, frustrated, and embarrassed, but everyone got home safely, feeling they'd learned something.

Gurdjieff had appointed a prim, control-oriented woman, Miss Ethel Merston, as his administrator when he was away. On a trip, he and Miss Merston stopped at an inn where a large dog seemed to adopt Gurdjieff: he and the dog became instant friends. At their next stop, Gurdjieff asked Miss Merston if she would like to do something for him. All too eagerly, she said she would. Very well, Gurdjieff told her, that dog at the inn should belong to me. So go back to that inn and *steal that dog.*

Miss Merston was horrified. As Gurdjieff knew very well, this act of theft was utterly contrary to her nature. But he insisted—it must be done! Forcing herself every inch of the way, she returned alone to the inn. She immediately saw the dog wandering around, and—agonizing over it—she induced the animal to get into the car. Then the innkeeper popped up. She was busted! She began to babble some explanation about how the dog had jumped in the car on its own but the innkeeper only expressed puzzlement that they'd left the dog behind in the first place—because the gentleman with her earlier had already *bought* the dog.

Gurdjieff had never really put her at risk of being arrested—but, quite harmlessly, he'd forced her to go against the grain of her programming and confront her greatest fears.

In October 1922, Gurdjieff was not only feverishly working to direct the nascent Institute for the Harmonious Development of Man at Fontainebleau-Avon but also was engaged in multiple business deals for its support. He could not rely on donations alone. He opened restaurants, and sold them; he dealt in carpets; he plied hypnotherapy—something he was said to be quite good at, especially in the cure of addiction.

But quite unprofitably (in the conventional sense), that same month he accepted the dying Katherine Mansfield into the Institute.

Orage had pushed for her admission—but Gurdjieff's taking her in was an act of kindness, pure and simple. The brilliant Mansfield, one of the best writers of her age, was succumbing to tuberculosis. Her illness was far advanced long before she met Gurdjieff. She hoped that she might survive spiritually, at least, through Gurdjieff. And it's probable that she was drawn to him because she herself had observed that people are asleep—that they are tragically robotic.

Her husband did not approve; many of her literati friends did not approve. Various Mansfield hangers-on grumbled that this Svengali, Gurdjieff, was exploiting her in her illness.

But it was Gurdjieff who was being leaned on, here. Gurdjieff knew she was dying; he knew she probably could not be saved. He must also have known—he with his wariness of mankind—

that he would be blamed for her death if she died in his care. But he took her in anyway, perhaps because he saw something fine in her—some real spiritual willingness.

Gurdjieff was always deeply considerate toward Mansfield. He arranged a comfortable bedroom for her and a comfortable loft to rest in during the day: this was above the stables, as folk medicine held that the breath of horses and sheep and cows healed the lungs. (Probably this was more in the nature of psychological soothing than any kind of real treatment on Gurdjieff's part.) Alexandre de Salzmann painted a satirical and symbolic mural for her amusement there; various members of the Institute were caricatured in it as animals, each animal corresponding to some "chief feature."

Gurdjieff never shouted at Mansfield—she was too physically fragile for "work with emotional center"—and he did his best to heal her. He included her in activities that didn't physically tax her.

Mansfield wrote enthusiastic letters about everything she saw at le Prieure. Here, she said, were people who were really trying to awaken, the way it should be done: together, yet freely; ardently yet reverently. This is the truth, she said.

One night in January, descending the stairs, Katherine Mansfield collapsed, blood streaming from her mouth. She died shortly afterward in her bedroom.

And the aftermath came about exactly as Gurdjieff must have known it would: he was pilloried in the media as the man who "killed" Katherine Mansfield.

Ouspensky—who had come to le Prieure for a time—said it best: "Gurdjieff was very good to her and did not insist upon her going although it was clear that she could not live. For this in the course of time he received the due amount of lies and slanders."

A Foray into Ouspensky's Arc and Descent

Ouspensky's own visits to Fontainebleau were somewhat grudging and reserved. He felt that Gurdjieff allowed too many of the wrong sort in, and that in some way the Institute was primed for self-destruction—but he never specified just how. He soon turned his back on Gurdjieff entirely and created his own institute in England. He seemed to lose his way in the years that followed. He lived in Britain as an expatriot, never accepting it as home. And as the years wore on, Ouspensky sometimes bitterly claimed that he knew nothing at all.

Many of Ouspensky's students found his teaching valuable up to a point—but they would eventually go to Gurdjieff to get its real essence. According to C. S. Nott, with Ouspensky "the work was too theoretical, too one-centered, intellectual-centered; and often I would leave with a feeling of emptiness, of emotional hunger. . . . I get more from inner work with one lunch with Mr Gurdjieff than from a year of Ouspensky's groups."*

For some, Madame Ouspensky had something to offer that her husband didn't. Lord Pentland said: "She was regarded by all of us an independent source of the teaching. . . . For many of us, she was the senior teacher. Her instruction, tempered in the hard school of revolutionary Russia, at the kitchen of Gurdjieff's Institute, was direct, quite free from moralization."**

Gurdjieff had told Kenneth Walker that Ouspensky "stole the teaching." John Bennett, who studied under Ouspensky in England, broke with him to form his own group, prompting Ouspensky, in

---

turn, to say that Bennett was a "thief and a charlatan." From disintegration . . . comes disintegration.

Eventually Ouspensky understood this. His secretary, Marie Seton, quoted him as saying not long before his death: "I took over the leadership to save the System. But I took it over before I had gained enough control over myself. I was not ready. I have lost control over myself. . . . The System has become a profession with me."*

Still, that brilliant evocation of Gurdjieff's ideas, *In Search of the Miraculous: Fragments of an Unknown Teaching,* other philosophical and mystical writings, and the genuine wisdom that Ouspensky imparted to his loyal students (which they in turn impart to others) all stand the test of time as Ouspensky's legacy. Hearing *In Search of the Miraculous* read to him, Gurdjieff said, "Very exact is. Good memory. Truth, was so."

LIFE AND LE PRIEURE

Though the Institute for the Harmonious Development of Man could be a great challenge—in the best sense—it was not by any means unending Work and constant "intentional suffering." Gurdjieff believed in the value of a rest well earned. Also a believer in purging the pores, he caused a Turkish bathhouse to be designed and built—no small task—and it was used in chaste alternation by both men and women. Men sweating in the bathhouse were encouraged to tell stories, many of them bawdy; some witty or meaningful. Gurdjieff would encourage the multitalented Alexandre de Salzmann to perform his bathhouse stories, which he did like an expert standup comic, doing all the voices and faces—and Gurdjieff's laughter came in gales.

---

*Telos, special timeline issue.

Celebrations for every possible holiday, including "St. George's Day," were used as a pretense for Gurdjieff to host grand dinners, ritualistic meals that have become legendary. These great feasts of exotic Middle Eastern foods (one of his very favorite dishes, I blanch to say, was sheep's head) included many courses, many unusual appetizers and tidbits to try, and a great deal of vodka and armagnac drinking.

Gurdjieff hosted wonderful Christmas celebrations, and he saw to it that the children got a grand variety of presents. If some years he had the Christmas tree placed upside down, "roots symbolically turned to Heaven," what of that?

Gurdjieff collected a great deal of money that he spent somewhat lavishly, often buying armfuls of gifts to give away, almost randomly. He respected *payments*—but not money as a thing in itself. He traveled first class when he could afford to, but he was not truly extravagant. He quite cheerfully harvested "American dollars" from kneejerk enthusiasts whenever he could, and the wealthier a student was, the more harvest Gurdjieff expected; but he also gave money away, and took in students who had little money. And some he supported.

He sent for his family, from Russia, first his mother and sister and then his brother Dmitri, and he supported them too. How strange the Chateau must have seemed to them at first!

A Pause to Dare a Critique of Gurdjieff: A Cat May Look at a King

Gurdjieff was a spiritual master—but he was also a man taxed by extraordinary responsibility. Though he worked on a level ordinary men cannot understand, and though he doubtless had some abilities that people think of as "supernatural," he was not superhuman;

for example, he indicated that he was not as "free inwardly" as he wanted to be. He had flaws—who doesn't? He smoked, he drank more liquor and coffee than his doctors liked, and toward the end of his life he ate too much. (Though he was often reported to drink in the afternoon or evening, I have seen no accounts whatsoever of his being *actually drunk*.)

Here's Henry Miller, in his preface to Fritz Peters's memoir: "Much has been written about the scandalous behavior of Gurdjieff. And it is true that he seemed to care little for conventional behavior. In a sense, he was like a cross between the Gnostics of old and the latter day Dadaists."

Gurdjieff was a conductor for powerful energies; at times they may have been somewhat overwhelming; they certainly manifested sexually, for he left a fair handful of children born out of wedlock to his women followers. According to Nicolas de Val's book, even at sixty-five Gurdjieff kept de Val awake with the noise of his lovemaking in another room.

Though he was always kind to children, Gurdjieff does not seem to have taken all the responsibility that he should have for his own offspring, despite occasions of giving instruction and some financial help.

As a teacher, Gurdjieff had a tendency to rely on authoritarianism in a way that Americans, at least, react against—but it's all quite ironic, since ultimately he was interested in *freeing* people, even from himself. By his own account, Gurdjieff in some cases was intent on quickly learning things about people by deliberately "stepping on their corns," that is, provoking automatic negative responses from them that revealed their psychological mechanisms. In other instances he went out of his way to drive some students away, when they were becoming unhealthily dependent or simply needed to develop on their own. He did this to Fritz Peters on a train trip, making himself excruciatingly obnoxious, so that Peters was forced to cease being psychologically dependent on Gurdjieff—as Peters later acknowledged. It often happened that people realized Gurdjieff's real purpose, in the things he did, only long afterward.

I suspect—and others who knew him suggested as much—that he took a little too much delight in "stepping on people's corns," as he called it.

Though most of his teaching methods were drawn from tradition and sharpened by his expertise, he was willing to experiment, and he may have treated people, at times, like guinea pigs. Fritz Peters tells a story of Gurdjieff's hypnotic experiments with a Russian girl who was very susceptible to certain kinds of stimuli; when Gurdjieff played a special composition of his creation, she lapsed into a trance and on awakening was hysterical, to the dismay of her parents. She was not permanently harmed—still, using her thus, to demonstrate mankind's responsiveness to vibration, seems callous.

But he seemed ever ready to experiment. In 1936, he led Solita Solano into his room, where he

> told me to stand at the window with my back to him. He remained at the door. He said, "Relax all body. If head or any part wishes to move, let move. I wish make experiment and at same time give you something." In a few seconds, my head began to move from side to side and up and down, slowly. Then a wide hot ray or wave struck my neck with force and moved down, then up my spine. Startled, I said, "Oh, you're touching me!"
>
> "No," he replied from the door. A minute later he said, "Now enough." He left the room with no explanation and never referred to this again.*

*From "The Kanari Papers," *Telos,* vol. 4, no 3.

Note that his reply came from the door, which was some distance from her. He had not been touching her, physically. He had touched her psychically, though that term probably doesn't quite describe it either: Gurdjieff called it *hanbledzoin*. He could have abused that kind of power, to control people, to impress doubters—but he didn't. He remembered the oath he took at that spring in the desert.

Some apparent instances of his hypnotic effect on people were apparently an unintended result of his "hanbledzoin." In Gurdjieff's *Third Series: Life Is Real Only Then, When "I Am,"* he said, using the complex, precision-obsessed style he developed for his writing:

> there gradually formed within me, proceeding far beyond the control of my active consciousness, certain automatic influences upon people around me during their waking as well as their hypnotic state. On account of this, there soon began to become really perceptible to my waking consciousness various consequences, irreconcilable to my nature, of this automatic influence over people, which often evoked in me remorse of conscience.

Hence people were sometimes "hypnotized" by him without his intending it.

Was Gurdjieff right about everything? He gave us so many radical and challenging, even disturbing, ideas—I'm only looking at the tip of the iceberg in this book—that the question seems valid. His teaching is vast, and it seems unfair, even disrespectful, to expect him to have been right about every last little thing he ever said. To make such a demand on him (or any great teacher) fails to respect his struggle with his own humanity; it fails to recognize that a great teacher becomes great through monumentally persistent work that goes on despite his own human failings. To say he has no humanity, no capacity for error, is like saying a mountain climber didn't climb the mountain with sweat and toil and many slips and dogged persistence—instead he took a helicopter to the top. That, surely, is unfair to the climber.

Experimentation, self-observation, work on oneself, are there to demonstrate or repudiate the rightness of his ideas. One may follow the path and see for oneself—as he recommended.

Many people, writing and remembering Gurdjieff, used the same term: "he was an *enigma*." He seemed at pains to hide his true self—and his biographer James Moore speculates that he may have taken the oath of "the Way of Blame." This is the method of the Malamatis, a highly secretive esoteric order whose adherents hide their spiritual ascendancy and create conditions for inner struggle by deliberately provoking blame, aspersion, and calumny from others.

Student after student described their encounters with Gurdjieff as leaving them feeling that all their usual set of responses were meaningless. He sometimes gave them this feeling out of a powerful gaze or a long silence. Sometimes it was a simple refusal to respond mechanically to their questions. According to the introduction to *Gurdjieff: Essays and Reflections on the Man and His Teaching,* Gurdjieff had an "extraordinary ability to make use of all questions in order to evoke the inexpressible, to disarm the questioner, to block within him or her all recourse to standard modes of thinking, creating the necessary conditions for the direct transmission of a knowledge of being."

Mrs. A. L. Staveley wrote in *Memories of Gurdjieff*: "Somehow, when you were in his presence you were actually plunged into the present moment and that present moment could be really anything. In no way could one safeguard oneself, there was no formula, no pre-fabricated attitude such as served well in ordinary life—nothing."

Hence, with Gurdjieff, it's difficult to critique his behavior fairly without running afoul of any number of unknowns. For he was, as Margaret Anderson wrote, *The Unknowable Gurdjieff.*

The Study House was finished in December 1923, a work carried out by everyone but those assigned to the kitchen. The inner walls, screens, and windows were painted with oriental ornamentation. A canopy of white calico dressed the ceiling. The floors and some of the wall spaces were covered with gorgeous, intricate oriental carpets. Gurdjieff's aphorisms, in calligraphed ciphers designed by Alexandre de Salzmann, were hung at exactly placed intervals around the Study House. There was a stage at one end and to one side a sort of curtained, cushioned riser, for Gurdjieff himself, very like the throne where the magician sat to observe his pupils in *The Struggle of the Magicians.* There were electric lamps with translucent red shades and two fountains with changeable, prismatically multihued lighting, which were sometimes scented with spices and perfume. The place was constructed of simple materials and erected within a clunky military aircraft hangar—but with Gurdjieff's guidance, the overall effect was magically atmospheric, touching some mysterious part of people who saw it, especially when combined with a viewing of the Movements.

Weekend visitors to the Prieure included composers, English and American poets and writers, choreographers, and English lords. An experience of the Study House, for them, was like a visit to some place in Gurdjieff's heart and memory; they left impressed, at varying levels. Among the visitors were Diaghilev, Sinclair Lewis, and Algernon Blackwood.

The Study House aphorisms were there for the students, who had been trained to decrypt them.

Some of the aphorisms:

Like what "it" does not like.

The highest that man can attain is to be able to do.

The worse the conditions of life, the more productive the work, always provided you remember the work.

Remember you come here having already understood the necessity of struggling with yourself—only with yourself. Therefore thank everyone who gives you an opportunity.

Only conscious suffering has any sense.

Take the understanding of the East and the knowledge of the West and then seek.

If you have not by nature a critical mind your staying here is useless.

One of the best means for arousing the wish to work on yourself is to realize that you may die at any moment. But first you must learn how to keep it in mind.

The energy spent on active inner work is then and there transformed into a fresh supply, but that spent on passive work is lost forever.

Here there are neither Russians nor English, Jews nor Christians, but only those who pursue one aim—to be able to be.

INTERVAL IN AMERICA

America was the great fountain of cash flow, which was of interest in itself, but it also seemed potentially a refreshing spring of new students for the Work, since the Old World orthodoxies had a weaker grip there. Gurdjieff took a transatlantic steamer to New York in the spring of 1924, accompanied by thirty-five pupils who were to demonstrate the Movements to America.

Such luminaries as Theodore Dreiser, Christopher Morley, Walter Damrosch, John O'Hara, and Hart Crane took in the performances. Many of them had come thanks to Orage's involvement, and his spoken introductions framed the performances eloquently.

The centerpiece of the demonstrations were the Movements, but Gurdjieff would also demonstrate apparent "psychic phenomena" at some of these public events—*but he always announced that some of the phenomena they were to see were real and some unreal.* This announcement in itself is completely consonant with Gurdjieff's approach. It was a way of suggesting that his audience keep a critical (that is, skeptical) mind; and through this announcement he galvanized an additional level of attention on the part of the audience, as audience members poised themselves to discern the real from the unreal. As the mentalist tricks used in these entertainments required from the performers an extraordinary level of attention—for example, striking a tambourine in a rhythmic code mixed in with other music—the tricks were themselves demonstrations of a higher level of human activity than normal.

The demonstrations soon lost their novelty in overwrought New York, and attendance diminished. Money ran short, and Gurdjieff's followers were again obliged to find work. An invitation by an old musical friend of Thomas de Hartmann, Adolph Bolm, brought the troupe to Chicago, where there was some interest.

But the American audience that mattered, in several cities,

were seminal converts like Jean Toomer, author of the bestseller *Cane;* Stanley Nott, who was later to write several books on Gurdjieff; Jane Heap, editor of the influential "little literary magazine" *The Little Review,* which published the first excerpts of Joyce's *Ulysses* in America; and Heap's coeditor, Margaret Anderson, author of *The Fiery Fountains* and *The Unknowable Gurdjieff.*

Beelzebub, Offspring of Catastrophe

Back in France, Gurdjieff delayed in Paris while the others returned to le Prieure. When he arrived later, they were working in the courtyard, and Thomas de Hartmann relates: "He got out of his car and looked at us with a very serious expression—we did not know what awaited us."

Hartmann records this little moment as if he truly believed that it contained some omen of what was to come. And perhaps it foreshadowed what came on July 8, 1924.

All the morning of July 8, Olga de Hartmann had an unfocused feeling of dread. She went to Gurdjieff at his new Parisian apartment, an office and sometime domicile he used on those occasions when he had to stay overnight in Paris. Gurdjieff gravely told Olga to write to her parents in Leningrad, she was to tell them to sell everything and come to le Prieure, since there was soon to be a great famine in Russia. He had that day an appointment to look at some equipment he wished to buy—but he told Olga to cancel it. They went to a garage and he had her tell the mechanics to check his Citroën closely, "especially the steering-wheel." Normally they would have driven to le Prieure together, but that evening he sent her back to the apartment to do some inventory, to follow later in the train. This and the cancelled appointment surprised her. They seemed like anomalous arrangements, obscurely linked.

Later, as she napped in an armchair until it was time for her train, she heard Gurdjieff's voice calling her: "Olga Arkadievna! Are you there? Let us go!" She jumped up, sure she had not dreamed it—completely convinced she had heard him in person. But she could not find him. It was four-thirty, just time to get to the train.

One of the pupils met her at the Fontainebleau station—and told her that Gurdjieff had been in a car accident. She ran to the street, stopped the first vehicle she saw, and through sheer force of will induced the truck driver to take her to the hospital.

Gurdjieff was comatose and heavily bandaged. He was grievously concussed and bruised purple over much of his body, with a likelihood of severe internal injuries. Several doctors were in attendance. Olga learned that Gurdjieff had been found unconscious, muddy and bloody, beside his wrecked car in a copse near a country crossroads, with his head pillowed on a seat cushion pulled from the car.

They took him to the greater comfort of his room at le Prieure. There Gurdjieff was in a coma, or on the edge of it, for six days, responding only with slight motions of his hand or a mumbled word now and then. He had enough awareness, apparently, to refuse morphine—which alone, in his condition, must have taken a great act of will.

Then one morning he looked around and asked his wife: "Where am I?"

He improved thereafter, but his recovery was up and down for weeks to come. He would be some semblance of his old self in the morning and delirious in the afternoon. Later, recalling the aftermath of the accident, he described himself as feeling dead inside and physically like "a piece of meat between clean sheets."*

---

*Life Is Real Only Then, When "I Am."

Far too soon, he forced himself to get up, to get dressed, and to walk. He was bandaged and, for awhile, nearly blind and had to be helped by twelve-year-old Fritz Peters to hobble, in great pain, about le Prieure. He told his students to fell some pine trees from the chateau's property and caused great bonfires to be made. Night after night he would sit close in front of the bonfires, explaining once that he "drew force from them."*

Uncertainty ran high in le Prieure; fear ran deep. Olga and Gurdjieff's other followers felt that with Gurdjieff incapacitated a "mainspring" had been pulled from the mechanism of the Institute and it would now run down. Perhaps this is why, after some weeks had passed, Jeanne de Salzmann confided to Thomas de Hartmann that she suspected "Georgivanch" was "already acting"—that he had mostly recovered from his accident but was pretending to be more incapacitated than he was so that he could observe them having to act independently, as free-thinking conscious beings, without having to rely on him for every decision. And indeed he was soon to express his disappointment . . .

At one point in his car-accident recuperation, Gurdjieff sat across from Movement pupils and gave them a complicated sequence of Movements postures, which ended as they had begun, in perfect symmetrical closure. The exacting cognition required for this feat seemed to Olga and Thomas to be the work of a man with his wits quite intact, though he still pretended otherwise at times.

Gurdjieff remembered very little of the day of the accident. Revisiting the site of the crash, he pieced together what had happened.

There are various reports as to the quality of Gurdjieff's driving, but all agree that—perhaps due to his liking for intense

*Our Life with Mr. Gurdjieff.

experience—he was given to high speed. He had been hurtling along a country lane when another car came very suddenly from a crossroad, and he was unable to brake in time. Forced to swerve, he veered off the road, and the car went banging over rocks and hummocks—with Gurdjieff getting banged around himself inside the car. The steering wheel—which he had asked Olga to have examined—snapped off, causing a complete loss of control. He tried to control the car by using his hat to grip the stump of the steering column . . . saw a tree rushing toward him . . . and leaped from the car.

Ouspensky, on hearing of this awful accident, told the Christian esotericist Boris Mouravieff that it made him afraid. Dark forces were at work, Ouspensky muttered. And how could Gurdjieff let himself be brought down like a mere mortal by the Law of Accident?

But Gurdjieff had never said he was more than mortal; he never said he was above the Law of Accident, only that man might strive to become something that could transcend it, at times. Gurdjieff had shown a distinct facility for consciously guiding himself and his followers through life: surely in his perilous travels he almost miraculously averted any number of lethal accidents. But ultimately he was still a human being, under the oppressive weight of the forty-eight laws of our particular cosmos.

By late August, Gurdjieff was in many ways himself again. But he was not yet completely healed.

On August 26, Gurdjieff called his students together and formally—one might actually say *apparently*—closed the Institute. "First of all, there are very few people who understand. I gave all my life for my work, but the result from other people in general was not good and that is why I think it is not necessary for those few to sacrifice their lives here." He said that everyone should make preparations to go. He would, he claimed, liquidate the house. But he also said: "In two weeks I will begin a new work. The names of those who may stay will be posted."*

Gurdjieff had decided that if he was to fully recover he must give his organism everything it required in the way of food (and soothing armagnac) and get rid of anyone who was not carrying their fair share of the Institute's burden. He shed most of his followers, keeping only a core at le Prieure, though the number grew again in time. He tasked A. R. Orage to maintain American fourth way groups and to collect money from students, much of which was to be sent to maintain the Institute. The money-raising part of Orage's task became the bane of his life.

Gurdjieff had passed on some of what he himself had developed to certain of his followers, but he wasn't sure he had succeeded sufficiently as to be able to count on them to continue the current he had begun. He felt he must preserve his insights somehow. He therefore determined to write a book. But it wouldn't do to write a book that declared everything forthrightly. That was not the esoteric way—and for good reason. People had to work for knowledge, or they had insufficient respect for it, distorted it, and finally learned nothing. The bone, as he put it, must be buried deeply.

Gurdjieff buried much of his knowledge, over the next several years, in his great work: *All and Everything. First Series: "An Objectively Impartial Criticism of the Life of Man,"* or *Beelzebub's Tales to His Grandson.*

In *Beelzebub's Tales to His Grandson* Gurdjieff would create a "legominism": a work of art designed to transmit esoteric knowledge in symbology, for those willing to make the effort to unearth the meaning buried under its symbols.

Our Life with Mr. Gurdjieff.

This encoding of Gurdjieff's teaching was first written, in large part, in the mid- to late 1920s. The book was sometimes dictated to Olga de Hartmann and sometimes written out by Gurdjieff. It was composed in Russian and Armenian and then translated into English. It would not be published until 1950, a year after Gurdjieff's death.

Working with Gurdjieff, A. R. Orage had the unenviable chore of editing the book into something like readable English prose, without losing Gurdjieff's eye-poppingly idiosyncratic syntax and prosaic circumambulations. Orage was not permitted to edit the book into something more in line with modern English "bon ton" writing—to do that he would have had to cut a great deal of the book, removing its deliberately laid-down challenges. And Gurdjieff's intricate sentences are that way for a reason.

Some parts Gurdjieff rewrote ten and more times, constantly changing it to make it both more exact and, paradoxically, not too explicit: he "buried the bone" ever deeper. The "dog" was required to dig for the bone.

My edition of *Beelzebub's Tales* is one thousand, two hundred and thirty eight pages long.

"All and Everything," Here Described by Scarcely with Little

Before he was one of the chief devils of the Old Testament, identified with either Satan or his righthand man, Beelzebub was Baal-zebub, in Hebrew meaning Lord of the Flies—for *baal* simply means *lord*. But in Ugaritic, Baal-zebul means Lord of High Places, and with this in mind Beelzebub is thought by many scholars to be a pejorative of the original name for a god of the sky. Thus the Hebrews were, in effect, mockingly saying "the pagan's lord of the sky is but a Lord of the Flies." Other scholars believe that Baal-zebul was a god of healing, and *Lord of the Flies* (or *Lord of Filth*) thus meant that he had the power to remove sickness, which was represented by the flies accompanying decay. That is, he had power over the flies of sickness and could command them to withdraw.

It may be that Gurdjieff meant all of the above. In the intro ductory chapter (not an introduction in the usual sense) of *Beelzebub's Tales,* "The Arousing of Thought," Gurdjieff makes it clear that he intends to declaim in *contradiction to everything that mankind assumes to be true.* He will turn the world upside down. He will ruthlessly demonstrate that everything we know is wrong. That is sure to make people angry, to make them denounce him: he will seem to be speaking "Satanically," like a "Beelzebub," since he speaks against the status quo and all that is assumed to be true. Beelzebub, though, does not behave satanically; if anything, he's angelic. A world-weary sort of angel.

Though intricately thought out, "The Arousing of Thought" is a diatribe "offending every canon and personal taste," as Bennett put it. In this introductory chapter Gurdjieff warns that he is writing a book that will force us to conceptually start over from scratch.

And so he does—as the book goes on, he does Beelzebub's damnedest to destroy our preconceptions with ridicule, satire, anecdotes, historical revisionism, and outrageous opinionation. The acidic tone in chapter 1, while characteristic of Gurdjieff, might have become even more corrosive because his mother was dying at the time he wrote it and his wife was increasingly showing the symptoms of cancer.

In *Beelzebub's Tales* Gurdjieff is offering more than denunciation. Layered under ironic affect and an almost stage-magic misdirection is the secret of restoring mankind to its rightful place. He is offering the keys to the kingdom—that is, the kingdom of the sky. Beelzebub, the narrator of this vast, semiwilderness of a book, is the Lord of this understanding of the Sky. And he is a healer. Gurdjieff was always interested in healing, and in this work, with the reintroduction of truths known to the enlightened ancients, he hopes to heal all the world.

Beelzebub's Tales to His Grandson is stratified with parables, folk sayings, and satirical retellings of history—all in an inimitable language that resists any attempt at casual reading. Despite its fantastic surface, there are literal truths to be found in the book, from the Gurdjieffian point of view, especially in the chapter "The Holy Planet Purgatory" and in the general assessment of the condition of mankind. But the book is a vast allegorical fiction, perhaps something like *The Thousand and One Nights* in a way; it is similarly episodic and similarly crowded with characters.

As the story begins, the wise old more-than-human being Beelzebub is traveling through space on the starship Karnak . . .

Of course the name Karnak is meaningful; it is the name of a famous temple of ancient Egypt: for through ancient teachings that were crystallized, once upon a time, in Egypt, man can become liberated enough to "travel," to ascend, through the cosmos. Thus a temple is like a spaceship.

Beelzebub is traveling between star systems, with his grandson Hassein and his faithful servant Ahoon. There is a delay in the approach to their destination—a need to avoid the vexing radioactive tail of a comet called The Madcap—and Beelzebub says that one must accept obstacles and try to get some good out of them: another example of intentional suffering. He proposes to while away the time discussing, for the most part, a subject dear to his high-spirited grandson's heart, Hassein's "favorites" on the planet Earth, those "three-centered beings,"—that is, you and I—who fascinate and interest the youth more or less as an Earth boy is fascinated by an ant farm. Beelzebub had once been in sorrowful service-in-exile in that remote backwater, that nearly abandoned corner of the universe—namely, the Solar System, of which Earth is but a part—as punishment for rebelling against the established order. Rather like the Old Testament's Lucifer, he had fomented a widespread, impulsive questioning of the "logic" of the universe; like Lucifer, Gurdjieff's Beelzebub was, for a time, fallen—because of vanity, the egoism of having criticized without understanding. A true Gurdjieffian, Beelzebub used his sojourn in our solar system to improve himself—adversity became an opportunity for enrichment, and he was eventually welcomed back to his rightful place in the sphere of His Endlessness.

As the book wears episodically on, fascinating and internally logical but never exactly "plotted," Beelzebub answers his grandson's questions about the peculiarities of Earth, lambasting Russia, America, France, the Greek philosophers and their intellectual legacy, art, "religion" as it is understood today, science, and nearly any other large target in cultural sight. He speaks of Saint Jesus and Saint Moses and Saint Buddha, which handily sums up how he thought of them: he accords them a great deal of respect, but not exactly divinity, and this alone would induce apoplexy in the conventionally pious. He mourns the distortion of the original impulses from which religion arises; he refers, for example, to the "monsters" created by the lopsidedness of certain kinds of present-day Buddhist monasteries—people who have developed one side of themselves hugely to the detriment of other centers.

Gurdjieff liked to do difficult mental work in crowded, noisy cafés, alternating coffee and armagnac—and some part of *Beelzebub's Tales* was composed this way. There's a story that an acquaintance noticed Gurdjieff chuckling as he scribbled busily in one such Parisian café. Asked what was so funny, Gurdjieff explained that he was just imagining the deep etymological interpretations people would give to the ridiculous terms he had just made up.

For in *Beelzebub's Tales to His Grandson,* Gurdjieff employs endless tongue-wrenching neologisms (he invented more than six hundred for this book!), some with a noble ring and meaningful roots—e.g., Heptaparaparshinokh and Triamazikamno—many of them, unsurprisingly, having an Armenian sound to them. Others seem to be a deliberately ludicrous agglomeration of vowels or consonants.

Every spiritual tradition has its tiresome literalists, and there are Gurdjieffians who are quite pious and literal about much of the material in Beelzebub.

"It is absurd to attempt to arrive at a literal understanding of *Beelzebub;* it is a myth, and a myth is an allegorical monster to shock the mind."* So said A. R. Orage, who worked closely with Gurdjieff on *Beelzebub's Tales.*

Some people reverently intone such Beelzebubian tongue-twisters as "Aieioiuoa" and "Okidanokh" (perhaps not accidentally like "okey-dokey," in common usage at the time the book was written), "Hrhaharhtzha" and "Harhrinhrarh" forgetting that Gurdjieff himself wrote, in *Life Is Real Only Then, When "I Am,"* "Not having been able to restrain myself, and once again having bared one of my weaknesses, consisting in, as it is said, 'cracking a joke' at the most serious moments of my writings . . ." And notice that the last two terms, "Hrhaharhtzha" and "Harhrinhrarh" are largely constructed of the syllables associated with laughter. According to Nicholas de Val's book, while listening to *Beelzebub's Tales* being read aloud Gurdjieff sat smiling, sometimes inexplicably "guffawing."

It may be no accident that whimsical terms are used in *Beelzebub's Tales* as the nomenclature for serious—deadly serious—laws. Gurdjieff perhaps was hoping to forestall what had inexorably happened with the long-term interpretation of the Bible, which

---

A. R. Orage's Commentaries on G. I. Gurdjieff's All and Everything.

is so desiccatedly humorless. The veneration with which every word in the Bible is treated has led to foolish literalism and dogmatic recitation without real understanding. And a reminder to not take oneself too seriously, woven into the very text of *Beelzebub's Tales*, turns one's attention away from the self-important imaginings of strident dogmatism and to a real opening, a real humility toward the idea and the cosmic laws that are described.

Hence Gurdjieff's ironic tone in much of his writing, his peppering of *Beelzebub's Tales* with the ludicrous: the odd ancestral relationship of women to certain kinds of apes, for example; the chilly sun; the japing stories of Germans and Russians and Americans at their most bumbling and mindless and venal. Though Gurdjieff liked Americans for their energy and open-mindedness, *Beelzebub's Tales* subjects Americans to a vast, many-leveled sarcasm.

But I do not mean to suggest that *Beelzebub's Tales* is not energized with the sacred. It may be cloaked in humor, buried deeply in myth, layered in allegory—but the sacred is what gives the book life. And this book is uniquely alive.

THE SPACESHIP FLIES ON

As the ship Karnak rockets onward, Beelzebub presents Gurdjieff's personal Gnostic creation myth to explain allegorically how mankind came to be in the fine mess it's in . . .

A wayward comet called Kondoor obliquely struck the embryonic Earth, breaking from it two fragments, the moon and a smaller satellite, Anulios. An archangel was sent to straighten out the subsequent planetary imbalance. This esteemed archangel decided that in order to stabilize the moon and Anulios, the Earth must produce the right amount of Askokin, a particular sacred energy, to be drawn into the moon for its inner evolution. Since this vibratory material is harvested by the cosmos on the death of organisms,

organisms were in due course provided to the Earth. In time, Beelzebub tells his grandson, "three-brained beings" with the potential for developing objective reason arose: human beings. The Archangel was afraid that when their objective reason informed them that they were essentially sheep to be shorn, dying to feed the moon, they would despair and destroy themselves. In order to prevent this he introduced in them the "maleficent organ Kundabuffer." Planted at the base of the spine, this organ caused humanity to be subject to suggestibility, to be hypnotized by mass movements, to be caught up in pleasure-seeking and desire, and to see everything topsy-turvy. Buffers from that problematic organ prevent people from seeing themselves as they are, locking them in waking sleep.

By extension it induced third-force blindness, so that we could not see the enormous mechanism of creation of which we are a part—we see only "good" or "evil," and not the Tao flowing through positive and negative to generate the whole.

Thus human beings served the evolution of the moon so that the moon could take part in the Ray of Creation. Eventually the moon had soaked up enough of the necessary vibration so that the organ Kundabuffer was no longer needed, and it was duly removed. But humanity continued in sleep and third-force blindness, providing, through sheer bad habit and momentum, its own organ Kundabuffer, in effect; an organ growing from the habit of wanton insensibility and cultivated by faulty education. Through work on oneself a man can transcend this blind momentum and become whole again. . . . But every time someone, like Beelzebub's prophetic messenger the "esteemed Ashiata Shiemash" (possibly an idealization of Gurdjieff himself), tries to make it possible for people to awaken to their state, then some selfish, wrongheaded human being comes along and puts them back to sleep again. In *Beelzebub's Tales,* one nemesis is Lentrohamsanin, a Bolshevik-like antitraditionalist.

Gurdjieff also points the finger at "Hasnamusses," the kneejerk technocrats of our world, who make the higher—the spiritual— into the lower, and who make the lower, that is, scientism, mechanical thinking, into something they elevate. (Some have speculated that "hasnamuss" can be decoded as "has-no-must": that is, they have no conscience telling them what they must do, no overriding wish animated by contact with the higher.)

Gurdjieff seems to be trying to tell us that *some* cosmic accident caused the Earth to be fundamentally out of balance, fatally out of kilter. In Judeo-Christian mythology the fatal first cause of disharmony was the pride that went before the fall of Lucifer, which he then passed on to Adam and Eve. In Gnosticism the Demiurge allows our sparks to fall from the Pleroma so that he might have dominion over them. In Gurdjieff's mythos our Fall is initially caused by a mislaid comet and a well-meaning archangel— a kind of bureaucratic bungling. But it's all the same story: a tragic separation happened, and through sacrifice and right striving we heal that rift and restore harmony.

More specifically, Gurdjieff truly believed we're being "used" in some way by the universe, while being parasitical ourselves; yet we have a chance to be something more than parasites who are also fed on; a chance to serve the universe in a greater way . . .

But most of the fanciful imagery in *Beelzebub's Tales* is allegorical. The details of the working of the spaceship, described early on, undoubtedly have esoteric meaning:

The captain of the ship Karnak explains that one Saint Venoma founded space travel on his observation of the Law of Falling. He noted that it might be possible to move toward an object by putting oneself in relation to it so that one falls toward it; that is, one is caught up in its gravitational field. This system had its drawbacks, being very approximate and affected by every gravitational field and atmosphere it encountered.

The archangel Hariton developed a new system. Hariton contrived a device capable of more precise control, involving an inner cylinder into which the ship gathers the materials of space—the radioactive particles, nebulous gases, with which space, far from actually being empty, is filled—which then are constricted, rather like air in a jet's compressor. The regulated escape of these compressed energies forces the ship forward into the area of low pressure created by the engine's intake. I cannot resist mentioning that this sounds remarkably like what space engineers call a "ramscoop," a device first conceived, as far as I know, in the late 1950s—after Gurdjieff was dead—and now being used in unmanned spacecraft designs. The ramscoop scoops up free hydrogen, helium, and other particles thinly scattered through space and converts them into thrust energy.

While doubtless enjoying speculating about spacecraft, Gurdjieff's main purpose in sharing the captain's lecture with us was probably the staging of another allegory. One possible interpretation of the allegory might recall Gurdjieff's idea that we fall inevitably under "influences"—some lower, some higher. We can choose which influence we fall under by choosing a teaching; we choose an energy field when we choose a teaching. We then move in the direction determined by that influence's center of gravity. By taking in impressions, in a controlled inner world, where everything has its place in our overall function, everything that arises becomes fuel for us to move forward on our journey.

And according to Orage—this, too, is just his subjective interpretation—the smashing of the Earth by the errant comet into three fragments described in *Beelzebub's Tales* represents a kind of inner astronomical disaster: our three centers are fragmented by a psychological or social cataclysm, so that two centers "break off from us," falling into disharmony with the larger part of the system. So Gurdjieff's cosmogonic fable is ultimately the story of ourselves, our own tragedy acted out in our inner lives.

Perhaps because we are machines of a kind, Gurdjieff often used descriptions of machinery as allegory, as in one of the more difficult chapters of *Beelzebub's Tales,* "The Arch Preposterous." It comes relatively early in the book, as if Gurdjieff were hoping to use it to dissuade the unserious from proceeding further. Here he uses excruciatingly complex sentences and an abundance of painful neologisms—just try to say "Parijrahatnatioose"—to describe a machine created by the king of the planet Saturn. This "Hrhaharhtzha," described in a manner that may be a satire of Jules Verne, creates a special kind of vacuum so that those within its environs, protected by special suits, are no longer receiving baneful influences but are receiving a refinement of "the Omnipresent Okidanokh," inducing in them a state described by Beelzebub as follows:

> In all my three "being-centers"—namely, in the three centers localized in the presence of every three-centered being, and which exist under the names of "Thinking," "Feeling" and "Moving" centers—there began to be perceived separately and independently in each of them in a very strange and unusual way very definite impressions that there was taking place in the separate parts of my whole planetary body an independent process of the sacred "Rascooarno . . ."

On and on goes the description of the device, its capacity for revealing the background light that invisibly suffuses the universe, and its many applications. The machine seems to be an elaborate allegory for an esoteric, inner process of refining vibrations within man, and for the understanding of them in a kind of cosmic alchemical process, as they operate at various levels in the scale of the Ray of Creation. The vacuum may represent the receptivity, the nonegoic gnosis, with which we take impressions and receive the current from the Higher, which orders our inner being. The protective suits and shielding may symbolize the process of attaining nonidentification with negative or distracting influences coming from outside ourselves.

My "wiseacre" interpretation of Gurdjieff's meaning in these chapters may be mistaken, but my main point stands firm: what is not social satire and explicit teaching in *Beelzebub's Tales* is never just window dressing, though it may seem like it on first reading; the entire book is vibrant with meaning.

Despite his nearly steady-state irreverence, Gurdjieff spoke quite reverently of Our Common Father Endlessness, the intelligence of the totality of all things. This supremest of beings struggles to maintain a creative symmetry under pressure of the constant bleeding of energies through Heropass, the phenomenon of time. The Will of this god of totality sustains creation; if we first develop the necessary being-bodies and capabilities, especially objective reason, necessary to help sustain his Will, we might unite "with the Cause-of-Causes, i.e. with our Most Most Holy Sun Absolute, and begin to fulfill the purpose on which our ALL-EMBRACING ENDLESSNESS had placed HIS hope . . ." And through our work in the conscious transformation of energy we may thus diminish his endless suffering.

The chapter of *Beelzebub's Tales* entitled "The Holy Planet Purgatory," which I've just scantily quoted, is the beating heart of the great living organism of this book. Orage thought it the profoundest spiritual text he'd ever read—and as an old-time spiritual

seeker, he had read widely and far. The chapter describes the primordial state, how the arrival of time brought it out of balance,
and the process of creation that restores harmony; it goes on to
describe the laws that govern this creation and rebalancing, down
to the human level.

In many ways "The Holy Planet Purgatory" covers ground
that is familiar to readers of Plato, Plotinus, the Hermetica, and
certain Gnostics, but those sources are very general in their descriptions. They allude to an all-inclusive realm, the realm of
Ideas or the Pleroma, from which issues a creative energy that *de-
scends to us* with a current requiring our resistance to forces press-
ing us down, a dynamic struggle that is also an interaction that
enables us to rejoin the Higher and complete the cycle. Gurdjieff
is far more specific, describing stage by stage the levels of descent
and ascent, and the process of actualizing the Higher in the Lower.
He brings a murkily encoded ancient teaching to us and decrypts
it. Mystics and spiritual philosophers have spoken of the process
of creation as a flow from higher to lower, and of a circuit created
between the two for the completion of a whole; in "The Holy
Planet Purgatory" Gurdjieff shows us with startling clarity the
vital process of this "world creation."

Sometimes he is almost excruciatingly specific, as for example
in this extract from Beelzebub's treatment of the Law of Three:

> "A new arising from the previously arisen through the 'Harnel-
> miaznel,' the process of which is actualized thus: the higher
> blends with the lower in order to actualize the middle and thus
> becomes either higher for the preceding lower, or lower for
> the succeeding higher; and as I already told you, this Sacred-
> Triamazikamno consists of three independent forces . . . the first,
> the 'Affirming-force' or the 'Pushing-force' or simply the 'Force-
> plus'; the second, the 'Denying-force' or the 'Resisting-force' or

simply the 'Force-minus'; and the third, the 'Reconciling-force' or the Equilibrating-force' or the 'Neutralizing-force.'"

He describes quite definitely, too, the internally corresponding processes of the creation of the higher body through the combining of bodily and cosmic elements in "being-food."

In his interplanetary purgatory Gurdjieff creates a kind of blueprint in prose for the "reciprocal feeding of everything existing in the universe" along the Ray of Creation, and the laws of Three and Seven. He also gives us a vivid allegorical picture, on the "Planet Purgatory itself," of the inner conditions of a man committed to soul-creation and service to the Higher through conscious suffering; though the planet is an exquisite paradise, the "higher-being-bodies" that dwell there choose to suffer consciously, to continue the work in its highest form. God—His Endlessness— appears to them as a kind of living luminosity so as to comfort and encourage them. They live in a purgatorial state, in a kind of heaven, yet deliberately suffering materiality. They seem to represent, in the book, the inner state of a spiritual teacher poising himself in some halfway place between the Higher and the Lower, a permanent between-state generating the sublime tension, the awareness of the two sides of his being—a mysterious, transcendent suffering—that creates inner conditions for spiritual growth.

As Gurdjieff told Solita Solano: "You must now live in suffering between two worlds, the two worlds of man. You must die in first, be resurrected in second and only then live in both."

Much of *Beelzebub's Tales* seems designed simply to repudiate human assumptions—in "Religion," Gurdjieff dismisses conventional interpretations of sacred texts. Judas, for example, he calls a saint and Jesus' most cherished pupil, who seems to have deliberately provided the start of the "Holy Denying" for Jesus' Holy Affirming.

Some of that note of repudiation is found late in "The Holy Planet Purgatory," when Gurdjieff/Beelzebub tosses out the usual anthropomorphization of God—God as an "old Jew with a long beard"—as so much rubbish.

But on the whole, "The Holy Planet Purgatory" is Beelzebub's hopeful Holy Affirming to balance Gurdjieff's vituperative Holy Denying; it is the building-up that counterpoises the tearing-down that dominates elsewhere in the book.

SHAMELESS WISEACREING ON SENTENCE STRUCTURE IN BEELZEBUB'S TALES

Some parts of the book are more straightforward and linear than others, but as a motif the book resorts again and again to long, complex, self-referential sentences that seem to contain some secret in their very structural formulation.

Here is a comparatively short example from the chapter "Organization by Ashiata Shiemash," picked almost at random:

Meanwhile transubstantiate in yourself the following: when the mentioned particular psychic property of "egoism" had been completely formed in the common presences of these favorites of yours, and, later, there had also been formed in them various other secondary impulses already mentioned by me which ensued and now still continued to ensue from it—and furthermore, in consequence of the total absence of the participation of the impulse of sacred conscience in their waking-consciousness—then these three-brained beings arising and existing on the planet Earth, both before the period of the Very Saintly Activities of Ashiata Shiemash and also since, have always striven and still continue to strive to arrange their welfare during the process of their ordinary existence, exclusively for themselves.

Gurdjieff might simply have said, "people have always been selfish." But what seems a redundant repeating of circumstances is perhaps an ingenious medium for resonation; each sentence is somehow inclusive of a fuller dimensionality arising from point and counterpoint harmonized in what may be a kind of syntactical legominism of the Third Force.

The reader should remember that this passage is taken out of context. Once one gets used to the book, it is surprisingly readable.

The activities of Ashiata Shiemash in *Beelzebub's Tales* are another locus of meaning, a sort of vein of gold running through the echoing canyons of the book. We've mentioned that the discomforts and hypnotic suggestions that are woven into our lives lead us to suppress the awareness that is the stuff of which real conscience is made. We put our conscience to sleep. Some of the specific mechanism of this suppression of conscience is laid out in *Beelzebub's Tales:* the shattering of a shared, harmonious consciousness of the head brain with the consciousness of the feeling and sensing brains. And this schism comes from the way we educate our children: we train them to be insincere and deceitful so as not to disturb the general comfort zone of mass hypnosis. It's as if we're saying to them: "Stop asking such questions, child! You're keeping me awake!"

To restore conscience, Ashiata tells us, requires "conscious labors and intentional suffering," carried out through fearless self-observation, self-sensing, self-remembering, and genuine remorse. His umbrella term for this was "Being Partkdolg-duty."

. . .

Gurdjieff set out to find out the meaning and aim of existence, and he found what he sought, to his own satisfaction. He lays it out grandly it for us in *Beelzebub's Tales;* in a cosmic sense in "The Holy Planet Purgatory"; and in a more practical sense for humanity in Ashiata Shiemash's "Five Strivings of Objective Morality."

In order to create real conscience—the ultimate guide, the infallible compass, the light that will never go out within oneself—we must "transubstantiate within ourselves" what are called "the being-obligolnian strivings." The sound of the word "obligation" is possibly found in "obligolnian" for a reason, as Gurdjieff taught that we have an obligation to pay for our arising in the world. Life is a gift—but it is one we can choose to pay for, so as to receive a greater gift. Here are the five being-obligolnian strivings:

The first striving is to have in our ordinary being existence everything satisfying and really necessary for our planetary body.

This means to keep the body fed and tuned, in good health so it can be an instrument for our higher purpose. Fakir-like ascetic conquering of the body is not called for. The planetary body needs a certain degree of rest and enjoyment, when appropriate. According to Orage, one also needs to keep an "elasticity" in the planetary body; hence Gurdjieff had worked in forty different crafts. The body has bodily intelligence, its own brain in a sense, and that intelligence needs to be kept sharp and vigorous through challenging physical work. Crafts, carried out with as much self-remembering as possible, are a traditional means in the Gurdjieff work. The Movements also add to this quality.

This striving also incorporates providing a home for oneself and one's family.

The second striving is to have a constant and unflagging instinctive need for self-perfection in the sense of being.

We grow in authentic essence when we make "being-efforts." We voluntarily do work that is good for us and necessary but that the "it" that usually runs us doesn't want to do. We overcome our typical inertia and work meditatively and through efforts at self-remembering. We don't do this in self-defeating excess—but we do it persistently, making progress in conscious labor and intentional suffering as we move through life. We continue to cast our net in the stream of time . . .

The third is the conscious striving to know ever more and more concerning the laws of World-Creation and World-Maintenance.

To understand our place in the cosmos to the best of our ability—to reach for knowledge and to crystallize it as understanding, through acquiring the being that makes understanding possible. To keep enquiring as to who we are and where we are, and in what relation to the world we are. To know our place in the scale; to be humbled by that perspective and to accept its challenge. To accept that we really can't know any final answer—but must continue to ask the question.

The fourth is the striving from the beginning of our existence to pay for our arising and our individuality as quickly as possible, in order afterward to be free to lighten as much as possible the SORROW OF OUR COMMON FATHER.

Our existence implies an obligation. Death looms, and we have not much time to make the efforts that pay our way. A recent science magazine article said that there are more species of parasites than any other form of life. Any species can be seen as parasitical on some other—we feed off cattle and chickens, and ultimately the Earth itself. We rely on others to such an extent that we arguably feed off one another.

But we can become more than parasites if we recognize our obligation to help ease suffering wherever we find it; if we struggle to become more conscious; if we become "students of dancing," learning how to be in right relationship to the music of life.

The fifth striving is always to assist the most rapid perfecting of other beings, both those similar to oneself and those of other forms, up to the degree of the sacred Martfotai, that is, up to the degree of self-individuality.

This means teaching, and helping one another in work conditions. It means thinking enough of them to be honest with them, or—in the case of a Gurdjieff or a Milarepa—even harsh with them, though that strictness doesn't gratify the student's unconscious desire to be treated like an adorable child. The Fifth Striving is therefore to do what is needed to help others develop spiritually, even when it's a sacrifice on our part—and theirs.

The strivings constitute an octave, said Orage, and reading *Beelzebub's Tales to His Grandson* is certainly crossing an interval. Gurdjieff said the book must be read three times, at least, each time more deeply. Orage compared the process of understanding the book with learning to read hieroglyphics. The study of *Beelzebub's Tales* is a discipline in itself, but a rewarding one—for *All and Everything: Beelzebub's Tales to His Grandson,* while idiosyncratic, is a work of genius and profound inspiration.

A commentator on the book recently said: "If you judge a book by its capacity to frame itself according to its own terms and language, and to involve the reader not in a typical reading experience but a new kind of experience that requires the reader to shed his assumptions and enter into the writer's world, then *Beelzebub's Tales to His Grandson* can arguably be considered one of the greatest books ever written."

On "The Arch-Absurd" and Beelzebubbian Literalism in General

From that odd, marginal coterie who might be termed Gurdjieffian literalists comes the assertion that Gurdjieff was in earnest when his so-to-speak "beard," Beelzebub, in the chapter "The Arch-Absurd," says that "Our Sun Neither Lights nor Heats." Ignoring the implication of the chapter title, they insist that somehow it must be the case that the sun "is perhaps more covered with ice than the surface of what they call their 'North Pole.'"

In this chapter of *Beelzebub's Tales,* which works out to be a kind of preview of what is further developed in "The Holy Planet Purgatory," Beelzebub tells Hassein that he will explain how this can be the case, how daylight, darkness, heat and so on come about, given that the sun is "cold"—yet if he explains this, it is only obliquely.

The following paragraph contains a sort of intermittent sound poem, a polysyllabic flurry of terms. To approach real understanding of them, one must read *Beelzebub's Tales.*

In Gurdjieff's cosmology, the Absolute's being is diminished by Heropass—a.k.a. Time. Pondering "The Arch-Absurd," we infer that the Trogoautoegocrat, the system whereby the Absolute replenishes its being through Iraniranumange (the process of "reciprocal feeding"—energy fed to an individual and transformed to be used in turn by the Absolute) creates that mysterious substance Omnipresent-Okidanokh, utilizing the primordial element Theomertmalogos, through the Ray of Creation—which is a ladder for the descent and ascent of energies, its rungs arranged according to the Law of Seven, or Heptaparaparshinokh ("the line of the flow of forces constantly deflecting according to law and united again at its ends"), which in turn affects the ubiquitous creation-clay of the universe, Etherokrilno; here, the process of Djartklom takes place, and the law of Three, or Triamazikamno, conditions the crystallizations of (so I take it) planetary and solar bodies at this lower level, these crystallizations being embedded in a sea of energy. Their lawful interaction with this sea of energy produces radiations (not to be mistaken, says Beelzebub, for emanations), producing the heat and light that our world mistakenly assumes to be sourced in the sun.

Of course, the sun in real life is not "cold" in any literal sense: space probes have been sent close to the sun; they report that the sun's heat and radiation increase exactly as predicted.

Gurdjieff makes numerous references in this chapter and elsewhere to Mullah Nassr Eddin, the subject of absurd (but symbolic) tales, the spouter of inane-sounding (but significant) remarks—as if cluing us in that this Arch-Absurdity is a kind of Nassr Eddin story.

If Gurdjieff did not mean literally that the sun is cold—what did he mean? One can only hypothesize. First, we notice the chapter is early in the book, not long after the lengthy introduction in which he says he will turn all our conceptions upside down. If he says that what is hot is cold, he has immediately done what he promised to do—and this inversion possibly represents the necessity man must face, for in facing the truth he performs a *volte face,* he must turn suddenly to see himself; he must reverse, move away from the vanity of his usual condition, from identification with the ego, belief that he is in "control" of his life when he is mechanical, automatic. The sun then is the ego, the false self the planets the various "I"s that man becomes, identified with his false self. But the real self—the real emanator of heat—is something higher, is the emanation from the Absolute, found in turning to wholeness, sensing the whole of ourselves.

At another level, consider that for higher beings—angelic beings and the rare man who creates a body capable of living on the level of "all suns"—the sun is no longer "hot." At that level, one's body vibrates in a very fine, highly energetic reverberation. A being capable of living at the solar level may find our local sun rather cold, compared to the great suns, the galaxy, and so on.

Of course these are just two possible interpretations; they may be wrong or incomplete.

GURDJIEFF: THE CONCLUDING CHORDS?

The writing of *Beelzebub's Tales to His Grandson* entailed a long, torturous struggle with composition, translation, and revision that went on and on for years. It's interesting to note that when the prominent Gurdjieffian student Louise March proposed to translate the book into German, Gurdjieff told her that any translator of *Beelzebub's Tales* had to have a grasp of a number of key things, including scientific terms and procedures, liturgy and religious terms, and mythology. Gurdjieff went way out of his way to make the book's language precise, to redefine terms, so as to reach beyond the usual conventional kneejerk understanding of words.

Still, Orage at first found the book unintelligible. As he learned to read its symbols and helped bring them more into focus, however, its meaning unfolded for him. The book was like the sound of a river in the background for those who live on its banks: its long-term composition had its own life that flowed on, beside that of the Institute. While the book was formulated, life went on, and Gurdjieff's struggle to create something lasting continued at the Institute and elsewhere.

Gurdjieff's mother died in 1925, at le Prieure. A month later, Gurdjieff began a long period of collaborating with Thomas de

Hartmann; the two of them, bit by bit, created the mysterious piano music—now available on CD in various editions—that seemed to be a fusion of what Gurdjieff had heard in remote temples with his own sonic expressions of ideas. It has a classical ring, while also enjoining folk and spiritual forms, and expresses a sense of longing, mournfulness, and transcendence. Some hear it unmoved; others are transported. While listening to the music, one teacher of the work said to me, "This music gives energy."

Another milestone was approaching: the death of Gurdjieff's wife. As *Beelzebub's Tales* increased, she diminished, cancer gradually eroding her strength—but not for want of her husband's efforts to save her. Gurdjieff would sit beside her for hours; sometimes he would hold a glass of water between his hands, seeming to transfer some unknown healing quality to it; he would then hand it to her to drink.

He said that he kept her alive for two years longer than she would have lived otherwise, with this and other methods. It wasn't enough: she died in June 1926.

Gurdjieff taught that there were "three kinds of love." There was instinctive— that is, sensual—love; emotional love, which depended on type and was itself more or less automatic, and *conscious love,* the love of real significance, unselfish and deliberate. Gurdjieff may not have been conventionally "faithful" to Madame Ostrovsky, but he demonstrated conscious love for her, in his efforts to save her and in many other ways. After her death he went into his room and did not come out for two days.

· · ·

The Institute continued to be a draw for reporters, spiritual seekers both superficial and serious, and sensation-seekers—even for the man the newspapers liked to call "the evilest man in the world," Aleister Crowley. (Whoever made up that monicker for Crowley didn't get out much.)

Occultists of Crowley's ilk, even today, have tried to "plug into" the powerful current they sense in Gurdjieff's work, but they have had a two-prong plug, at best. Gurdjieff requires three.

Eyebrows were raised over Aleister Crowley's brief, touristy visit to le Prieure in July 1926. Crowley, a self-professed black magician, acknowledged to some of the others that Gurdjieff was "a great adept." According to James Moore's biography of Gurdjieff, and other sources, Crowley was heard to tell one of the boys at the chateau that he was "teaching his own son to be a devil." Getting wind of this, Gurdjieff called the boy over and spoke to him privately, and the boy thereafter pointedly ignored Crowley. When Crowley prepared to catch a train to Paris, Gurdjieff coolly confirmed his going—so that he was not obligated to be polite to him as a host anymore—and then raged at him: "You dirty inside! Go! Never come back!"

Crowley is said to have left white-faced and shaking.

In 1927 Gurdjieff found himself in crisis. That devil of a wrestling match, the composition of *Beelzebub's Tales,* was out-wrestling him. He would work through the night, fueled by armagnac and coffee, for days at a time, perhaps feeling like a single sculptor with small chisel trying to carve out the full-sized Sphinx. According to remarks he made later in his writing, he felt *Beelzebub's Tales to His Grandson* was going to defeat him—and he felt his teaching was not bearing fruit in his students, or less than he'd hoped. He lapsed into near despondency, perhaps feeling his

age for the first time. He was not making progress: he was tread-
ing water, somehow. He decided he must strike off, swim in a
definite direction.

To this end, he vowed to "banish" everyone who "made life
too easy" for him. This may seem paradoxical, but it is true Gurdjieffian logic. In order to cross this interval of resistance, he must
redouble his efforts and raise his struggle to a white-hot pitch.
That meant getting rid of people who kept him in a state of tem-
perate moderation. He began to encourage those who cosseted
him, who took care of everything for him, to set off on their own.
Madame Ouspensky—who had been coming to study with Gurdjieff, presumably against Piotr Ouspensky's wishes—he sent to
England to be with her husband. He sent the Salzmanns to Frank-
furt, and he laid the groundwork for sending the Hartmanns away.

But he still needed Orage. Gurdjieff had called A. R. Orage his
brother and friend. He was one of the few who understood. Orage
was also Gurdjieff's bridge to the "bon ton" world—to those who
could finance and help him spread his teaching—and Orage had a
gift for articulating what seemed beyond articulation.

But by degrees their rapport broke down. Orage requested a
"new initiation" that never quite came. On his shoulders was
much of the financial responsibility of the Institute; he was the
chief money raiser, and he obtained much of it in America by
selling visits to le Prieure as if they were timeshares, all the time
living in near poverty himself.

The Institute always needed more, and cash flow had a way of
drying up (especially after the great stock market crash). Then
Gurdjieff took to disliking Orage's choice in a mate; the woman
who was to become Jessie Orage seemed suspicious of Gurdjieff,
and never quite committed to the Work. Orage told Louise
Welch that he felt it was as if Gurdjieff regarded himself and
Orage as two aliens visiting the planet Earth—and Orage had had

the bad taste to marry one of the natives. An ongoing feud smoldered between Jessie and Gurdjieff and sometimes flared up. Gurdjieff regarded Jessie as pampered and domineering, and dominant women were something he regarded as a regrettable abbnormality typical of modern life.

Around this time Gurdjieff had finished a draft of Beelzebub and was beginning to write his *Second Series,* also known as *Meetings with Remarkable Men.*

In 1929 Gurdjieff made things more and more uncomfortable for the Hartmanns. They must learn to fly on their own. He deliberately alienated them—and pushed them out of the nest, sending them to live in another part of France.

On his third return to the United States in 1930, with a cryptic agenda that is still a matter for speculation, Gurdjieff entered the country like a barbarian invader. He seemed determined to offend everyone; he obnoxiously demanded money and then shruggingly gave it away; he shouted pointlessly and perpetually "stepped on corns"; he leered; and he made outrageous demands. Some have inferred that Gurdjieff was combining the Way of Blame with a test of the mettle of his American followers. He deliberately undermined his deal with Knopf to publish *Beelzebub's Tales to His Grandson*—he seemed unsure he definitely wanted it published, as opposed to simply circulated among followers. And when he sailed for France he left a disenchanted Orage behind.

It may help to understand this period if we turn to Margaret Anderson's memoir of the Work, *The Unknowable Gurdjieff.* She recorded these remarks by Gurdjieff: "Live a life of friction. Let yourself be disturbed as much as possible, but observe. . . . When there is no friction there is no development." He went on to say that if you remember to observe yourself when you're upset, then conditions are better than usual for seeing yourself as you really are—for taking in "the food of impressions."

Fritz Peters's memoir says that Gurdjieff *paid* a particularly irritating Russian, one Rachmilievitch, to stay on at le Prieure, when not only would the man have preferred to leave but *everyone else* wanted him to leave as well. Why did Gurdjieff do this? Gurdjieff told Peters he wanted the man around to provide friction for everyone's inner work. Gurdjieff valued this Rachmilievitch, who was given to bitching, doomsaying, and criticizing, *because* he was irritating!

Now, in America, Gurdjieff seemed to have made up his mind to create even more special conditions for work: to personally play "the Rachmilievitch," deliberately generating friction for himself. Again, this is a method that not just anyone should undertake—but then, few would want to.

Despite Gurdjieff's cultivation of conditions for intentional suffering, the next few years had their grace notes for the Work: the advent of both René Daumal, an important poet and essayist, and Kathryn Hulme. Daumal was to write the marvelous Gurdjieffian allegory *Mt. Analogue*—a masterpiece that, though not quite finished before he died of tuberculosis, continues to inspire seekers of all stripes. Hulme's *Undiscovered Country: The Search for Gurdjieff* is the touching true story of a woman coming of age in World War II and her spiritual growth through her work with Gurdjieff.

Gurdjieff made more visits to America—each one more disastrous than the last, at least outwardly. He alienated Jean Toomer by pretending to be madly venal, and then, with finality, he broke with Orage.

Gurdjieff then decided to take over Orage's New York groups and demanded that his students sign a paper repudiating Orage. Without hesitation, *Orage himself* signed the paper repudiating Orage; on learning this, Gurdjieff wept.

To Kathryn Hulme he said: "Which would you choose—all roses, roses, or all thorns, thorns? One for inner life, the other for outer? If both thorns you chose, an intentional contact can be made." Gurdjieff chose thorns, thorns for himself—and gave others a taste of the experience, often whether they wanted it or not.

LIFE OFFERS THORNS

In 1933, money ceased to flow steadily into the Institute, and the mortgage on the chateau was foreclosed. The Institute at Fontainebleau closed for good. Eventually Gurdjieff had to settle for an apartment in Paris.

Gurdjieff suffered another loss: tuberculosis claimed the cornerstone Gurdjieffian and innovative artist Alexandre de Salzmann. Perhaps this caused "remorse of feeling" in Gurdjieff: it's said by some that he was inexplicably cold to de Salzmann in the last year of his life.

The following year brought another epochal death: that of A. R. Orage, from heart disease. Later Gurdjieff wrote of the many people who came to him with spurious sentiments of sympathy over the loss of his famous disciple. It was another example, for Gurdjieff, of the automatic manifestations of sleeping man: endless displays of false feeling, false emotion.

Gurdjieff himself grieved deeply for Orage but privately. "This man . . . my brother."*

Despite his break with Gurdjieff, toward the end of his life Orage had said that he "thanked God every day" for G. I. Gurdjieff. And on Orage's gravestone is carved an enneagram.

In June 1934, Gurdjieff's student Olgivanna Hinzenburg married the great American architect Frank Lloyd Wright. Gurdjieff went to Taliesin, their home at Spring Green, Wisconsin, to visit

*Gurdjieff: Anatomy of a Myth.

them. During the visit, a peculiar salad Gurdjieff practically forced Wright to eat cured the architect's chronic gallbladder complaint; but, more important, Wright sensed in Gurdjieff a spiritual edifice of impressive proportions. Though Wright stopped short of discipleship, his wife had been Gurdjieff's devoted follower for ten years, and Wright's school for architecture students was organized in a style inspired by Gurdjieff and his Institute. James Moore suggests that Wright's teaching method, organized around "hand, heart and head," was inspired by Gurdjieff's moving, emotional, and intellectual centers.

Back in Paris, Gurdjieff experimented with a special group of students, all women, called The Rope, nearly all of them lesbians—this despite his having jeered at homosexuality. He did not try to change their sexual preference. Again, Consciousness triumphs over dogma.

The Rope included Solita Solano, Elizabeth Gordon, Kathryn Hulme, Margaret Anderson, Georgette Leblanc, and Jane Heap. Several of these women went on to write books about Gurdjieff and the Work. He would give them esoteric exercises—warning them to secrecy about the exercises, for if certain exercises were revealed the universe seemed to exact justice for the crime. In *Ladies of the Rope* Gurdjieff is quoted as saying that the exercises "let in fresh air in the rooms and drive out stink; for years apartments not aired; people use dining room for water-closet, leave there on the floor, have dirty banquets, break furniture. And in every room there are also many other compartments—all stink." This seems to refer to inharmonious development in the edifice of a human being: the wrong use of centers, the lack of conscious oversight and the subsequent decay of the possibilities of mankind. Gurdjieff delighted in referring to people as "merde"—perhaps because people reacted so strongly to such strong terms. It was part of "stepping on their corns" to say, as he said to Solita: "Your friends are all special *merde*. Seeing their *merdeness* will help you see your own." But Gurdjieff then put his harsh judgment in context: "Man has two mentations and you know what kind I wish for you. Only now is being-data being crystallized in you. In past everything rolled off like water from back of goose. All went in and out again . . . Look at those people in the street. You have something they not have."

Solita Solano, who once found Gurdjieff confusing and boorish, in time became his devoted secretary, while Jeanne de Salzmann, Alexandre's widow—with her brilliant understanding of the Movements and her stern determination to remember herself—became his star student and right hand.

In 1936, Gurdjieff moved to his final base of operations, 6 Rue des Colonels Renard, Paris. In 1937 his brother Dmitri died of cancer. The next year his faithful friend and follower Dr. Leonid Stjoernval died as well. It may be that Gurdjieff no longer felt the need to create obstacles to work with: death was creeping up on him, carving away his loved ones and followers; his Institute, at least at le Prieure, had died on the vine. Yet he soldiered on, pushing through the next interval in his own mysterious octave.

A Sketchy Sketch of the War Years

In 1939 a new case of mass psychosis broke out: World War II. Despite attempts by pupils to move him to safety, Gurdjieff insisted on staying in Paris. He had pupils who could not leave, after all. It was assumed by his followers in France and America that he was at best half-starved during the war years; no one outside

France was quite sure, once the Nazi occupation of Paris cut off communication. But in fact Gurdjieff did well enough to leave himself vulnerable to false accusations of "collaboration."

With characteristic resourcefulness, Gurdjieff kept his apartment relatively well stocked—he made cunning, harmless trades in the black market, and he also made some accommodation with the local shopkeepers, telling them that his "American oil well" would pay off after the war.

The war years brought particularly brutal winters—as if meteorologically reflecting the emotional iciness of the Nazis during the Holocaust. Heating fuel was hard to come by—*very* hard: students would sometimes bring Gurdjieff a single lump of coal as a gift. As the war ground on, Gurdjieff distributed gifts of food and money and comfort to those in need, as he saw fit. Gurdjieff had nothing but contempt for anti-Semites, and he helped his Jewish pupils to go underground, where they were protected by sympathetic Christians.

Somehow, Gurdjieff continued to teach during the war. Some have claimed that his groups included both members of the Vichy government and members of the Resistance. How could they be in the same room—let alone in the same groups? Somehow it makes sense, when we consider the atmosphere of transcendent nonidentification that was a fundamental condition of Gurdjieff's school.

Despite his corpulence and the aches of old age, Gurdjieff even taught the Movements.

His perplexing "toasts to the idiots"—constituting a whimsical, inexplicable sort of human typology—were introduced to his semiritualistic dinners. The floors of the little apartment groaned from the number of pupils who crowded in, some standing heron-like on one leg just to fit side by side against the walls.

. . .

Shortly after the liberation of Paris, Gurdjieff was accused by the French police of having undeclared foreign money—which he'd shruggingly hidden under his mattress. He was arrested—one can only imagine Jeanne de Salzmann's feelings as she watched the police take him away—and taken in for questioning. He later enjoyed telling the story of how he'd played the confused, kindly, half-witted old man who'd simply not understood about the various kinds of currency; this deception and many character references from grateful well-wishers secured his release: "external considering" at work, on two levels.

Others were not so fortunate. Thousands of "collaborateurs" were taken away, their heads shaved, to be executed—the innocent with the guilty. But Gurdjieff was not under the slightest suspicion, because of the help he'd given to Jewish students and their families.

Gurdjieff soon got back in touch with American pupils through visits from Kathryn Hulme, who had been working with authentic heroism in refugee camps, and others. He astonished the local shopkeepers by announcing that the "oil well" had paid off. He methodically paid his debts with money brought by students—especially American students. *They* were his "American oil well."

A postwar visit from Fritz Peters, now a war-haunted American soldier, demonstrates that even at the end of his life Gurdjieff was capable of superlative vitality, and something more. Peters describes the visit in the second book of *My Journey with a Mystic.*

Young Peters was suffering from an extreme battle fatigue—what we would now call posttraumatic stress syndrome—and in desperation he sought out Gurdjieff. Peters was emaciated, weak-

ened, and "half-mad." As they sat in Gurdjieff's kitchen, Gurdjieff, in Peters's account, seemed to focus on him and then to ra-
diate a mysterious energy, a "violent, electric blue light" that
entered into Peters as a new upwelling of life. Suddenly Peters
was fine again—full of energy and hope, almost completely restored. But Gurdjieff was visibly weakened. Peters became convinced that Gurdjieff was able to transfer energy from himself to
others through the air. And he had actually glimpsed the energy
in transit. The effort clearly had cost the aging Gurdjieff, as he
had known it would: a perfect example of his capacity for conscious love.

Dr. Michel Conge experienced another sort of transmission
from Gurdjieff. He recalled asking Gurdjieff a difficult, painful
question about a family member. Gurdjieff listened, "looking
straight ahead, into the distance and a little upward." But Gurdjieff did not reply in words. Instead, "he lowered his gaze toward
me and I understood. I was in contact with the invisible; everything was clear. But the inner shock caused by this sudden and intense light was so violent that I began silently weeping."

AND THE POSTWAR YEARS

P. D. Ouspensky's final years were not without accomplishment:
he had produced a series of Gurdjieff-inflected lectures, now collected in a book called *The Psychology of Man's Possible Evolution.*
But he had spent too much of his declining years brooding, ex-
tolling Russia with vodka-steeped nostalgia, unsuccessfully trying
to contact a hypothetical secret circle of conscious teachers, and
speaking by turns cryptically and cynically to his students.

In his final weeks, Ouspensky had himself chauffeured from
place to place, trying to memorize familiar settings from his past
so he would have a basis for remembering them on his next

recurrence—for he firmly believed that, instead of reincarnation, he had to be concerned with living the *same* life as P. D. Ouspensky over again, as the universe ran through a cycle of recurrence, each recurrence offering a new chance for consciousness and freedom.

Madame Ouspensky had never ceased to revere Gurdjieff, and at her husband's death in 1947, quite ill herself, she told his followers at Lyne, England, that they should go to Gurdjieff. On hearing of Ouspensky's death, Gurdjieff sent a telegram summoning Ouspensky's students: "You are sheep without shepherd." Many of them came, including John Bennett and—perhaps the most important—John Pentland, who would be an enormous influence on the Work in America, in after years. An English lord, John Pentland seemed to have a gift for understanding the Work, which Gurdjieff apparently recognized, for he made him one of the literary executors of his books and appointed him head of the Gurdjieff Work in America. (Interesting that the Work in America was not at first entrusted to mercurial Americans but to stolid Brits like Orage and Pentland.) With people crowded into his small apartment—and crowded around tables for his fantastic, ritualistic dinners—Gurdjieff continued to teach.

Dr. William Welch's memoir, *What Happened in Between,* described one such dinner. Gurdjieff was "a master cook in the preparation of his native dishes and exacting autocrat over his kitchen." He would oversee dinners for more than a hundred people, somehow crammed into his small apartment and cooked for in a small, crowded kitchen. (Gurdjieff would somehow prepare vast meals in hotels, too, when in New York, in rooms without any kitchen.) Guests sat "thigh to thigh, elbow to elbow"; some stood against the walls or perched on windowsills, managing their brimming plates and drinks as best they could. The rooms were usually close and too hot, the drinks too strong and too plentiful.

But Gurdjieff insisted on numerous toasts—often his "toasts to the idiots"—and keeping some self-possession despite the effects of many high-octane toasts was one of the exercises of the evening. Everyone was jocularly toasted as some kind of "idiot," according to a "science of idiotism." Gurdjieff was perfectly aware of the absurdity of the process, and he reveled in it. The term "idiot" retained its obvious mockery, but, as James Moore put it, Gurdjieff "reinvested it with the meaning of individuality (from a Greek root meaning 'I make my own.')" Each student was required to choose their own level of "idiocy": there was the ordinary idiot, the super idiot, the arch idiot, the hopeless idiot, the compassionate idiot, the squirming idiot, the square idiot, the round idiot, the zigzag idiot, the "enlightened" idiot, the doubting idiot, the swaggering idiot. Toasts were made to this or that kind of "idiot," each with its vile or benign characteristics—and Gurdjieff himself was the "arch idiot." The idiot toasts—which died with Gurdjieff, since they were distinctive to his sense of humor and fully understood only by him—reminded the toasters to be skeptical about themselves, to see themselves with an objectivity peculiar to this whimsical typology.

Gurdjieff's dinners consisted of great numbers of courses—far too many for most of his overheated, tipsy guests. Some courses were small—just tidbits to taste, in the Middle Eastern manner — and some challenging, like hot curries—or a calf's head, its boiled eyes supposedly a delicacy. Gurdjieff's place at the table was surrounded by "special dishes of avocado, sweet onions, clumps of tarragon, dill, sweet basil, sour cream, and thick mounds of tomato sauce, eggplant and grape leaves." But instead of eating these things himself he made small dishes of them, to send to people according to their (quite significant) nicknames: "for Crocodile," or "for Camel," and the tidbit would be passed to the designated person, who must eat it whether they wanted it or not. But Gurdjieff, with a look and a word or two, made a quiet connection, a moment of shared presence, with each one of them.

.   .   .

In 1948, Gurdjieff *again* had a serious car accident. This time he returned home ambulatory and conscious but horribly bruised and swollen. A dinner with students had been held up for him; fresh from the accident, he hobbled to the head of the table, took his place, nibbled a few bits of food, and, nearly fainting with pain, lifted his glass to make toasts. It was a demonstration of sheer Will, of intentional suffering at its most literal. Anyone else would have cancelled the dinner or said *Go on without me* and gone to hospital or to bed . . . and called for morphine. But Gurdjieff sacrificed all that he might have done for his comfort, in the immediate wake of his injury, for his students. He had taken what might have been the embarrassment of another car accident and transubstantiated it, so to speak, into a dramatic teaching.

He recovered rapidly on this occasion. Or did he? It's possible that his death a year later was related to deep-seated injuries resulting from this accident, conspiring with his age, for Gurdjieff was now well into his eighties.

Madame Ouspensky gave Gurdjieff something that her husband had been holding onto for years: the manuscript of *In Search of the Miraculous: Fragments of an Unknown Teaching*. It was her gift to Gurdjieff. As I've noted, Gurdjieff confirmed the accuracy of its account. Formerly, he said, he had hated Ouspensky. But now . . .

"Now I love him." And Gurdjieff authorized publication of the book.★

Work in the last years of Gurdjieff's life centered around the apartment on the Rue des Colonels Renard, and consisted of exercises

★*Gurdjieff: Anatomy of a Myth.*

given to groups, rare personal interviews given to students, work on the Movements—now often supervised by Madame de Salzmann, though Gurdjieff was involved—and readings from *Beelzebub's Tales* or *Meetings with Remarkable Men*. Dinners and toasts continued, with Gurdjieff playing his mournful improvisations afterward on the concertina; there were occasional forays in the Citroën, though it was increasingly difficult for Gurdjieff to drive.

One morning A. L. Staveley and a few others arrived at the apartment "in the, by then, familiar state between fear and almost aching anticipation." According to Mrs. Staveley's *Memories of Gurdjieff*, they found that the door of the room they were to foregather in was locked. They milled about, uncertain, "each hoping someone else would take the initiative. . . . Mr Gurdjieff appeared. . . . You could say his regard rested upon us . . . and in that regard was the merciless compassion that never missed anything. Stroking his mustache, he said in a tone of distress, 'Oh, is scandal! Such important people to be kept waiting!'" Gurdjieff left, came back with "an absolutely gigantic screwdriver and a miniature tack hammer." He proceeded to pretend to be taking off the hinges of the door, with exaggerated, clown-like gestures, a comical miming, muttering about the scandal of it all. Deliberately using a tiny hammer with a huge screwdriver, knowingly having no effect. Then the woman who knew where the key was entered, chided by Gurdjieff for keeping these "important" people waiting, took the key off the lintel where it had been all along and unlocked the door. "She unlocked the door in silence and in silence we sheepishly filed into the room . . ."

Gurdjieff made tentative plans to buy a new chateau for his Institute and to publish *Beelzebub's Tales to his Grandson* at last. He sailed to New York in the winter to try to raise money for the Institute and to renew contact with students.

Returning to France, Gurdjieff was physically drained. Yet he soon went on what was to be the final expedition of his life. He had often taken students on car trips around France and Switzerland; these were teaching opportunities disguised as apparent holidays. This trip to the Lascaux cave paintings seemed to have a grim, almost ritualistic purpose. Gurdjieff was already ill and was finding it difficult to walk at times. He had to be helped to hobble up to the caves. He suggested that the elegant Lascaux paintings, which depict primitive scenes with a panache that seems redolent of more sophisticated men than Cro-Magnon cave-dwellers, originated with travelers from the lost continent of Atlantis.

Despite his obviously growing illness, Gurdjieff continued to force work on himself. He was in a Movements class in September 1949 and was giving the choreography of Movement 39 to the class when he collapsed. As we say in the American West, he went down "with his boots on."

A little over a week before his death, Gurdjieff was handed the proofs for his book *All and Everything: Beelzebub's Tales to His Grandson*. The symbolism of closure on his magnum opus must have hung heavy in the air for him; he had to have known death was near.

He grew sicker: ever more dropsical and wracked with coughing. At last the doctors insisted on the hospital and would not be denied. Many of his Parisian students saw him for the last time alive sitting up on a stretcher, a lit cigarette in one hand, as the attendants lifted him into the ambulance. His fez was set jauntily on his head, and he made a little wave goodbye and said: "Au revoir, tout le monde!"

Until we meet again, all the world! Said lightly—in a nonidentified sort of way.

For he knew he was dying. According to Solita Solano, he had cancer (he was a heavy smoker). She wrote in an open letter to friends: "Besides the tumor, his heart was dilated and his lungs were 'raddled' from the bouts of coughing, bronchitis, from which he had suffered for thirty years. Only to Gabo did he speak of his pain; made him bend down one day so the others could not hear, and said, 'Very, very bad pain' in Russian (Ochen, ochen)."*

In the hospital the doctors decided to drain him of dropsical fluid. He sat up in bed and, accepting only a local anesthetic, smoked a cigarette and drank coffee while they made the puncture and drained 12 liters of fluid from him. And all the while he wore his old red fez at a jaunty angle.

The Hartmanns had not seen Gurdjieff for years—but they had remained deeply grateful to him. Now informed that he was dying they rushed to be with him—though Thomas was sick with his own cardiac ailment. They arrived too late.

Dr. Welch, a prominent student of Gurdjieff, said that he had seen many men die, and Gurdjieff met death "like a Man without quotation marks." Another time Welch said, "I have seen many men die. He died like a king."

There was a period of convulsiveness, at the end . . . and then it was over. Dr. Welch also recorded that Gurdjieff's head and neck were quite anomalously warm for hours after his death.

First a convulsiveness—like a woman in birth pangs, almost— and then this strange, impossibly prolonged localized warmth. In the East the mystics say that the soul leaves the body through the head. Had Welch seen peripheral evidence of the birth of the body Kesdjan?

Hundreds packed the Orthodox church where Gurdjieff's solemnities were performed. The priest was amazed by the silent,

*Letter by Solito Solano, Library of Congress; October 29, 1949.

reverent atmosphere. The undertaker, *who didn't know Gurdjieff,* burst into tears when he saw the body.

Two menhir-like standing stones, modeled after ancient monuments, were erected at either end of Gurdjieff's grave. Do they represent Holy Affirming and Holy Denying? There's an inscription informing the visitor that this was "A Teacher of Dancing."

But let us conclude this pencil-sketch of Gurdjieff's life with his last recorded words, spoken with difficulty to Jeanne de Salzmann—whom he appointed to a leadership role in carrying on his Work: "The essential thing, the first thing, is to prepare a nucleus of people capable of responding to the demand which will arise. . . . So long as there is no responsible nucleus, the action of the ideas will not go beyond a certain threshold. That will take time . . . a lot of time even."*

JEANNE DE SALZMANN

The *Gurdjieff International Review* sums up: "For more than forty years thereafter, she worked tirelessly to transmit his teaching and to preserve the inner content and meaning of the Movements."**

According to Gurdjieff, she was one of the few who had Worked enough to create something "real." Something lasting. It was Jeanne de Salzmann who provided the "shock" that was to carry the Gurdjieff teaching across the interval created by his death. She was the mother—and presumably the teacher, too—of the late Michel de Salzmann, himself a very important figure in the Gurdjieff Work.

A great many people in the Gurdjieff Work knew her, as she lived, quite actively, until 1990. Those who knew her speak of

---

*From the foreword to *Life Is Real Only Then, When "I Am."*
**Gurdjieff International Review,* Vol. V, No. 1, Spring 2002.

Jeanne de Salzmann with something like quiet awe. The awe is understandable when one has seen the film *Sacred Dances,* a cinematic record of many of the key Gurdjieff Movements, in which she appears in person, narrating, explaining; here, it is immediately apparent, is an extraordinary person. The attention she brings to the moment is like a kind of magnifying glass—one sees her and all that is happening around her with a startling clarity. Without pretension or pomp she comes across, quite effortlessly, as an enlightened being.

I've selected a few of her remarks, collected by pupils (taken from the article "Behind the Visible Movement: Quotations as Recollected by Her Pupils," which appeared in that same issue of the *Gurdjieff International Review*.) Mme. de Salzmann emphasized the Movements, and most of these statements relate to the Movements, which in turn relate to the Work:

> *Behind the visible movement there is another movement, one which cannot be seen, which is very strong, on which the outer movement depends. If this inner movement were not so strong, the outer one would not have any action.*

> *You must constantly divide your attention between something which is higher than yourself and your movement. You always lose yourself in one or the other. As soon as you stop making this effort, you become identified with the movement.*

> *You must consider these Movements as a condition, an exceptional one given to you to work on your attention.*

> *In so dividing your attention, you are filling the place that you can fill. One day you may be capable of more, but today, this is your place.*

The thought must have its own center of gravity; it cannot just be either here or there. We must find this center of gravity. It is the same for the body; if it is not centered, no movement will be possible. It is the same for the feeling.

Usually you think about your movement, but you do not do it. You maintain your thought on the movement, and then when it is the time to do it you give up, and the movement is done, no matter how, without you.

You do not realize enough that your attention is your only chance. Without it you can do nothing.

EIGHT

"GURDJIEFF, *NOT WILL DIE!*"

It's said that in Gurdjieff's last years a student approached him and asked what they would do if he should, God forbid, die on them. Gurdjieff rounded furiously on the student and said sharply: "I, Gurdjieff, NOT will die!"

He didn't mean he would live on in the physical sense. He would live on in the higher realms, having created for himself something that can survive independently there: independent but in service to God, all at once.

And of course his work lives on. It is quite vital. Pains have been taken to keep it authentic and alive.

Gurdjieff said that disappointment is a preliminary to entering his work. People are disappointed in their lives, in their religion, in science, in themselves, in their abilities, in everything they've tried till now. Then, thoroughly disappointed, they are ready to try something really challenging—something genuinely extraordinary.

Gurdjieff's teaching seems negative to some people—seems too austere. Just consider some of these iron-fisted negatives: Humanity is asleep and lies to itself when it thinks it's awake. We are machines, all the time. We cannot *do*. We may build an empire, and still we are not doing, we are but elaborately reacting. We feel emotions, but authentic, honest feelings of love and compassion and hope and faith in the higher sense are usually beyond us. Yes, we experience feelings of love—but there is an active love, a love that obtains only from a certain high level of consciousness, that we usually never experience. We have no inner unity; no *real I*. Most Christians cannot be Christians, are incapable of it. And real Christianity started before Christ. . . . We never tell the truth, even when we are sure we are telling the truth.

What a series of outrageous statements! But let's consider humanity's condition. People seem puzzled by the inability of the human race to learn that violence is a stupid way to deal with our problems. We seem puzzled that wars continue; we're baffled that we have the means to feed the starving but we don't; that we *can* produce goods without polluting the planet but we *don't;* that we can live without addictions but we *don't;* that we *know* what kindness is and all the benefits of it but rarely practice it.

We're aware of our weaknesses. Our literature, our movies, are full of morals about how we should behave; how we should be responsible, caring, unselfish, patient, nonviolent. We tell ourselves this in our fiction and poetry and art and philosophy, again and again. But most of us never change, not significantly. *Why?*

What would keep us in this vicious circle, this dilemma? It would have to be some form of blindness. Something in us—self-love, vanity, our defenses—prevents our seeing what traps us in the vicious circle. What if what we're not seeing is exactly Gurdjieff's hard, bitter truths, which may seem to us so outrageous?

When we look at life, we see it's red of tooth and claw; we see it involves a painful birth and the necessity of work and the hard facts of old age and death. These conditions are undeniable truths. By extension, it makes sense that the real truth of spiritual evolution would be equally stark, equally demanding. So for me, Gurdjieff's austerity, his indifference to the comforting trappings of New Age spirituality or lace-edged religion, is reassuring: it means his teaching has the ring of truth. And of what use is anything but the truth? What good is comfort, in a spiritual teaching, if we can't feel a real connection with truth? Of what use are hope and faith if they are not real hope and real faith?

Most people, thinking they want to take up a course of spiritual improvement, are dismayed by the schools where something real is taught. What's the joke? "There's a seeker born every minute." Superficial seekers are not seeking the truth, they're seeking comfort.

Perhaps they read a book—say, *The Chicken Soup of Zen*—and, inspired by the book, they show up at an authentic Zen center. Then they find they're required to get up, in that particular tradition, at, say, four o'clock in the morning (if they sleep late around there), and sit in a painful zazen posture for a seemingly infinite time before a rather austere breakfast that leaves them still hungry; and then comes a full day of conscious physical work. In many Zen schools the master might actually give you a pretty sharp smack with a stick if you're not sitting up straight in the practice of zazen. When does enlightenment come? Only after years of zazen, if at all.

The student faced with this reality suddenly remembers that he has to visit his ailing mother, and he leaves the center and heads for the nearest International House of Pancakes and, later, a channeler who channels the Angel Gabriel—who says to chant his name while you're getting a tan at the beach.

The Gurdjieff Work does not usually demand the same *kind* of discipline found in an authentic Zen center (I keep saying *authentic* because there's a fair amount of fake tourist-"Zen" out there), but it does require that the practitioner make serious demands on himself or herself. It may require just as much or more—in terms of Inner Work. One very good teacher of the Work recently said that he was originally drawn to the Gurdjieff ideas because they seemed "uncompromising, and had an overall quality of being *adult.*"

The benefits of the Gurdjieff Work are quite real, even if I were to doubt the creation of spiritual bodies, or doubt that I, at any rate, could work hard enough to create one. People Working on themselves are not as likely to blow their house in Las Vegas or to marry a brute. It doesn't make them mistake proof, but if they're really Working, chances are they're not going to do anything *really* stupid. More to the point, their lives are freer. They keep things more in perspective in times of crisis—like the boy Gurdjieff on that artillery range—and they don't identify so easily with every apparent insult or emotional upset that comes along. Objective about themselves, they're likely to be more compassionate to other people, and that benefits everyone. Living in the present moment, life is more vivid, more meaningful. And Gurdjieff suggested in *All and Everything* that people who conserve their experiences through self-remembering actually stand a better chance of living longer (he also said there were many other factors, including the inherited ones). All that is reason enough for either the Gurdjieff teaching or work on oneself in some similar tradition of mindfulness, like Vipassana Buddhism or Sufism or Father Thomas Keating's Christian methodology, or Zen . . . that is, authentic Zen.

Despite his skepticism of the full value of some Ways—and his recognition of the limits of institutional religion—Gurdjieff accredited other paths:

There do exist enquiring minds, which long for the truth of the heart, seek it, strive to solve the problems set by life, try to penetrate to the essence of things and to penetrate into themselves. If a man reasons and thinks soundly, no matter what path he follows in solving these problems, he must inevitably arrive back at himself, and begin with the problem of what he is himself and what his place is in the world around him. Socrates' words "Know thyself" remain for all those who seek true knowledge and being.*

It makes sense that we could not hope to change until we could see ourselves—and thus see the causes of our problems. But if we're in denial about our state, if we insist, in our blindness—blindness induced by giving in to what Gurdjieff called "buffers"—that we are not asleep, that we are not machines, that we know how to be honest and how to *fully* love, then we can have no hope of changing. And change we must. Gurdjieff warned that a certain number of evolved, conscious people are necessary. If there are not enough evolved people, the world does not fulfill its function; it becomes an obstacle to the great agenda of cosmic evolution, and humanity is allowed to destroy itself.

Yet Gurdjieff's message is one of real hope—it resonates authentically, partly because it comes from someone capable of authentic, conscious hope. It is not the usual hope, the hope of an automatic response to anxiety. It is *hope of consciousness*. And consciousness is our only hope.

* *Views from the Real World* by Gurdjieff.

FARTHER UP THE OCTAVE: BIBLIOGRAPHICAL SUGGESTIONS

Gurdjieff wrote only a few books—though *Beelzebub's Tales* itself is a monumental literary edifice. Many books have been written about him and his teaching. I haven't read every last word on Gurdjieff, but of the numerous books I've read, it's fair to say that they are not all of equal value.

I wrote this little book not as a person well schooled in Gurdjieff's ideas but as a student trying to understand them by researching the book and by writing about them. As this book is only a preliminary introduction to the subject, I recommend here some further reading. I encourage readers to explore further with much additional reading and, most important, by contacting reliable groups.

For a comprehensive reading guide, see *Gurdjieff: An Annotated Bibliography* compiled and with annotations by J. Walter Driscoll and the Gurdjieff Foundation of California, with an introductory essay by Michel de Salzmann, the son of Jeanne de Salzmann. My edition is from Garland Publishing. Used copies turn up online and elsewhere. There are updates available for it. Driscoll issued "Gurdjieff: A Reading Guide" in 1999 as an interim bibliography, and he is well along with an exhaustive update of the annotated bibliography. Driscoll is also the co-editor of the *Gurdjieff International Review,* the best publication about Gurdjieff and his ideas. For information on it, see www.gurdjieff.org.

Meanwhile, here are my recommendations. Publishing details are only for editions I consulted.

All and Everything: Beelzebub's Tales to His Grandson by G. I. Gurdjieff. The Dutton edition (New York, 1964) can still be found. Two Rivers Press of Aurora, Oregon (founded by A. L. Staveley), put out an excellent edition in 1993.

Meetings with Remarkable Men by G. I. Gurdjieff. New York and London: Arkana, 1985. Somewhat autobiographical, somewhat allegorical. Sometimes reads like an adventure story.

In Search of the Miraculous: Fragments of an Unknown Teaching by P. D. Ouspensky. New York: Harcourt, Brace and World, 1949. An indispensable book. Gurdjieff approved of it. "This what I say!" It is unsettling, fascinating, hope-giving.

The Psychology of Man's Possible Evolution by P. D. Ouspensky. New York: Knopf, 1954. A collection of lectures summarizing some of Gurdjieff's key psychological ideas. Brief, precise, and immensely powerful.

Gurdjieff: Essays and Reflections on the Man and His Teaching, edited by Jacob Needleman and George Baker. New York: Continuum, 1996. Gives an insightful overall picture, from many perspectives.

J. B. Priestley once said you "won't have to do any intellectual slumming" in Gurdjieff's world: this book is proof.

Views from the Real World—from talks by Gurdjieff. New York: Viking Arkana, 1984. You hear his voice, in this book, and it is so direct and no-nonsense as to be almost unbearably refreshing.

A. R. Orage's Commentaries on G. I. Gurdjieff's All and Everything, edited by C. S. Nott. Aurora, Oregon: Two Rivers Press, 1985. Illuminates the great book.

Life Is Real Only Then, When "I Am" by G. I. Gurdjieff. New York: Viking Arkana, 1991. This is a short, abortive book—unfinished, though one confused commentator claims Gurdjieff "meant it that way"—and should probably be read after one has grasped many of the other books. But it is of interest, and the title of the book itself teaches.

EXCELLENT FURTHER READING:

Our Life with Mr. Gurdjieff by Thomas and Olga de Hartmann. New York: Penguin Arkana, 1972. Flat, unembroidered prose, yet sometimes startling. Reads with real narrative power—some of which obtains from their humility. Their affection for Gurdjieff the man shows.

Exchanges Within by Lord Pentland. New York: Continuum, 1997. Transcriptions of insightful talks by one of the greatest teachers of the Gurdjieff Foundation, speaking to fourth way work groups. An insider glimpse of one side of the Work. Best after reading the books already listed; hugely valuable.

Gurdjieff: Anatomy of a Myth: A Biography by James Moore. U.K.: HarperCollins, 1993. Sometimes prolix, sometimes like reading a good novel, not without a welcome, refined humor; has the ring of truth. The most definitive biographical material to be found in one book.

The American Soul by Jacob Needleman. New York: Tarcher/Penguin, 2002. Professor Needleman shows the hidden dimension of spirituality and conscience animating American history; much emphasis on the Founders. A message of real, living hope.

Time and the Soul by Jacob Needleman, San Francisco: Berrett-Koehler, 2003. Most, perhaps all, of Needleman's books are Gurdjieff-influenced works on spirituality and philosophy, and all are deeply meaningful. He has made a grand lifelong study of the wisdom traditions and the great philosophers, and takes value from the full spectrum and not just Gurdjieff. *Time and the Soul* is an especially effective, short book that summarizes some of Gurdjieff's ideas—in the terminology of the wisdom traditions—and in a lively, invigorating way. Needleman's *Money and the Meaning of Life* is also recommended.

Lost Christianity by Jacob Needleman, New York: Tarcher/Penguin, 2003. A new edition of this spiritual classic illuminating Christian mysticism from a (subtle) fourth way perspective.

Inner Christianity by Richard Smoley. Boston and London: Shambhala, 2002. This lucid explanation of mystical Christianity shows how it interfaces with other forms of western mysticism, including Gurdjieff's teaching. A triumph of bold clarity where clarity is usually not permitted. The most *helpful* book on Christian mysticism I've come across.

The Breathing Cathedral by Martha Heynemann. San Francisco: Sierra Club, 1993. She collates Gurdjieff, Dante, Stephen Hawking, and her own experiences, weaving it all seamlessly and poetically together. Powerful stuff.

Undiscovered Country by Kathryn Hulme. Boston: Little, Brown, 1972. Gripping, touching book about her life and encounters with Gurdjieff.

Opening by William Segal. New York: Continuum, 1998. He was a Gurdjieffian and a Zen scholar and a great teacher of the Work. A provocative book.

The Unknowable Gurdjieff by Margaret Anderson. New York: Penguin Arkana, 1991. She should know how unknowable he was, she was there. In the form of memoirs and notes; very revealing and compactly explanatory.

Toward Awakening: An Approach to the Teaching Left by Gurdjieff, by Jean Vaysse. New York: Harper and Row, 1979. A bit dry, but fascinating and very accurate, if limited—it only approaches certain areas of his teaching.

My Journey with a Mystic, by Fritz Peters. Laguna Niguel California: Tale Weaver, 1986. Incorporates two books in one volume—*Boyhood with Gurdjieff* and *Gurdjieff Remembered,* together with a preface by Henry Miller. Peters grew up around Gurdjieff and stayed in touch till near the end. There's humor here, and Gurdjieff's human side. Good reading.

Teachings of Gurdjieff: The Journal of a Pupil by C. S. Nott. New York: Routledge and Kegan Paul, 1961. He was there and he learned something.

Memories of Gurdjieff by A. L. Staveley. Aurora, Oregon: Two Rivers Press, 1978. A rather slight little book but touching, meaningful, and sometimes charming.

Psychological Commentaries on the Teaching of Gurdjieff & Ouspensky, by Maurice Nicoll. New York: Weiser, 1977. Very practical, insightful, detailed series of books. He became a major teacher of the Work in England.

Living Time by Maurice Nicoll. London: Watkins, 1952. This book was epochal, an epiphany for many people. Go with him, in his straightforward, intelligent, terse presentation, and you will find your ideas of time radically altered, with new hope as the result. It can be found.

Mount Analogue: An Authentic Narrative by René Daumal. Translated with an introduction by Roger Shattuck, postface by Vera Daumal. London: Vincent Stuart, 1959. Subsequent editions issued with the variant subtitle, *A Novel of Symbolically Authentic Non-Euclidian Adventures in Mountain Climbing.* New York: Pantheon, 1960. *Unabridged,* Boston: Shambhala Pocket Classics, 1992. I strongly recommend this allegorical novel. J. Walter Driscoll comments: "The way Daumal developed the metaphor of the magic mountain and described its symbolic scaling in this novel is deeply inspired by his practice of Gurdjieff s teaching."

Voices in the Dark: Esoteric, Occult & Secular Voices in Nazi-Occupied Paris, 1940–44 by William Patrick Patterson. Fairfax, California: Arete Communications, 2001. Including transcripts from 31 of Gurdjieff's wartime meetings. Those transcripts came from the Library of Congress and make fascinating, sometimes unnerving reading. Much about the Parisian wartime milieu in general.

Here are some additional works recommended and noted by J. Walter Driscoll; the remarks quoted here are from his interim bibliography "Gurdjieff: a Reading Guide" (1999), and are included with his permission.

On Attention: Talks, Essays and Letters Based on the Ideas of G. I. Gurdjieff by Christopher Freemantle, edited by Lillian Firestone Boal. Denville, New Jersey: Indications Press, 1993. "Still available on the Internet. Freemantle was a student of Ouspensky's, went on to work with Gurdjieff, and served as a senior group leader for many years. This posthumous anthology gathers ten intensely focused contemplative essays on the immanent struggle with attention. Includes 98 pages of excerpts from letters to his students."

Asking for the Earth: Waking up to the Spiritual/Ecological Crisis by James George. Shaftsbury, Dorset, England: Element, 1995. "He attempts to link Gurdjieff's cosmological ideas with James Lovelock's Gaia hypothesis and documents the crisis caused by human degradation of the environment; attributing it to our alienation from a sense of spiritual presence and conscience."

A Wish to Be by Cecil Lewis. Shaftsbury, Dorset: Element, 1994. "Originally broadcast as a series of Reflections for the BBC World Service, these 29 brief talks are each introduced by one of Gurdjieff's aphorisms. By examining such themes as self-discovery, human nature and our inner potential, Lewis describes simply and sincerely, the struggle involved in applying Gurdjieff's aphorisms and teachings in daily life."

Gurdjieff: An Approach to His Ideas by Michel Waldberg. Translated and abridged from the French by Steve Cox. London/Boston: Routledge & Kegan Paul, 1981. "Based on a 1966 lecture, this book provides an accurate and sympathetic introduction to Gurdjieff's ideas. Waldberg devotes particular attention to the form and content of *Beelzebub's Tales* and to Gurdjieff's psychological ideas as presented in Ouspensky's *In Search of the Miraculous*."

Venture with Ideas by Kenneth Walker. London: Luzac Oriental, 1995. "Bound for almost thirty years by a promise to Ouspensky to not speak publicly or publish anything learned at his meetings, the author was freed to write about his experiences with Ouspensky and Gurdjieff by the death of both men and the publication of *Beelzebub's Tales* and *In Search of the Miraculous*. Walker describes the impact of Gurdjieff's system 'on a man who had received an orthodox scientific education' as a physician. Offering autobiographical vignettes as well as explication of core ideas and practices, Walker also describes the strong impact Gurdjieff made on him during their brief encounters."

Who Are You Monsieur Gurdjieff? by René Zuber. Translated by Jenny Koralek, with a forward by P. L. Travers. London: Routledge & Kegan Paul, 1980; New York: Penguin Arkana, 1990. "Zuber's compact memoir draws on Christian aspects of Gurdjieff's ideas, thoughtfully considers the impact of his teaching and offers richly observed anecdotes about him between 1943 and 1949. Zuber emphasizes 'that Gurdjieff's teaching was purely oral, and that it sprang spontaneously out of life circumstances or from dialogues with his pupils. I never heard him lecture. The very idea seems absurd to me.'"

There are other worthwhile books on the subject. I commend you to J. Walter Driscoll's bibliography and reading guide.

Other Works Quoted
in This Volume

Cosmic Trigger, Vol. I, by Robert Anton Wilson. Berkeley: And/
Or Books, 1977.

Ladies of the Rope: Gurdjieff's Special Left Bank Women's Group by
William Patrick Patterson. Fairfax, California: Arete Communications, 1998.

Powers of the Word by René Daumal. Edited and Translated by
Mark Polizzotti. San Francisco: City Lights, 1991.

The Story of Philosophy by Will Durant. New York: Time Incorporated, 1962.

The Struggle of the Magicians by G. I. Gurdjieff. Cape Town, South
Africa: The Stourton Press, 1957.

The Varieties of Religious Experience by William James. New York:
Penguin Classics, 1982.

*The Way of Hermes: New Translations of The Corpus Hermeticum and
The Definitions of Hermes Trismegistus to Asclepius.* Translated by
Clement Salaman, Dorine van Oyen, William D. Wharton, and
Jean-Pierre Mahé. Rochester, Vermont: Inner Traditions, Bear
and Company, 2000.

What Happened in Between: A Doctor's Study by Dr. William J.
Welch. New York: Braziller, 1972.

Witness: The Story of a Search by John G. Bennett. Sante Fe: Bennett Books, 1997.

ARE WE
"FOOD FOR THE MOON"?

Some people are stopped dead in their reading of Gurdjieffian "Work books" when they come upon the idea, usually as it was repeated by Ouspensky, about humanity being "food for the moon." (A prominent teacher of the Work once insisted to me that Gurdjieff "never taught that idea after 1917 or so" and had basically abandoned it. Perhaps Gurdjieff let it slide because people were taking it too literally.) The idea is that unevolved humanity exists merely to create emanations that are consumed by the moon to be used to promote the moon's physical evolution into a future state when it will be something "like the Earth." This sounds absurd and improbable—but only if you suppose he meant the moon per se. My personal—I emphasize *personal*—interpretation of this teaching is that the moon in this teaching represents the inert, more-or-less lifeless part of the cosmos. It stands for all of the lower cosmos. The moon is the first stop in a kind of "energy sink" where our life energies will go if we don't work on ourselves. Our crude energies are then absorbed by the cosmos for the general encouragement of life, and the moon is *the nearest example* of a "lower" planet where these energies could be used. It's not likely to ever become like the Earth—but *some* lower planetary state somewhere will receive these and other energies, and will be encouraged, on some quantum level perhaps, to evolve . . .

There does seem to be a tendency—the anthropic principle, it's called in some physics circles—for life to develop, almost on its own initiative, in "dead" matter, setting the stage for the arising of life in general and humankind in particular. Matter seems frontloaded to generate life. The energies harvested from people, from beings everywhere, might help create that "frontloading," that priming of the evolutionary pump. But of course this interpretation of Gurdjieff's teaching is very speculative indeed—which is why it's in this appendix.

THE OCTAVE AND
THE RAY OF CREATION—
AND THEORETICAL PHYSICS

As the ancient Hermetic formulation has it, *as above, so below*: the lawful patterns of the cosmos are reproduced in man, who is a microcosmic mirror of the macrocosmos, and the same patterns can be studied within man.

Organized along the Ray of Creation, each lower world is *within* the next higher world, like Chinese boxes, every self-contained unit fitting exactly within a larger—so everything is here, yet paradoxically the higher universe is in some respects out of reach. All the types of matter in the universe are found in man—solar, astral, gross, and so on—but some are of such a relatively fine quality, vibrating at such an exquisitely attenuated frequency, that they are inaccessible to us as we ordinarily are. Yet there are times we can get help from those highly refined levels.

Energies are transferred up and down the Ray of Creation. Influences pass from the Absolute, down through the concatenation of energetic transactions to the planets. The Will of the Absolute helps this influence pass down across the barrier of the first interval; after this, the Will of the Absolute is in effect diluted, so that once it passes through All Planets it would then be stymied by the interval of discontinuity between All Planets and the Earth were it not for the organic life on Earth, a kind of biological substrate that acts as an "accumulator" and transmitting station for forces, "bootstrapping" the energy over the "abyss" of the interval . . .

Emanations of a certain quality are needed by the *re* level and lower levels; other kinds are needed for the evolution of the planets, the sun, and beyond. Events on Earth, Gurdjieff averred, are affected by the cosmic need for particular energies. When certain kinds of energies are needed, certain organic events—often dire, perhaps even great wars—are elicited through planetary influences, generating the needed wavelengths through the Earth's organ of perception and transmission, organic life, in a manner capable of passing the intervals.

Is this yet another cold, grim idea? These effects happen lawfully, according to the innate mechanism of the cosmic structure. Nature, again, has always been quite evidently rigorous, unforgiving, and impersonal. Consider, for example, natural selection, and the relentless replacement of the old with the young.

Yet God does what can be done for us, within the rules and necessities of cosmic balance: great possibilities are always on offer for those willing to pay the price in attention, and work.

Gurdjieff moves from this simple scale to a computationally perfect elaboration of a Law of Octaves beyond the scope of this book; the reader is referred to *In Search of the Miraculous* for his marvel of cosmic mapping.

Gurdjieff's lectures on the role of the octave in the cosmos, as recorded by Ouspensky, seem to parallel some of the arcane formulations of quantum physics. Basarab Nicolescu, a theoretical physicist at the Centre Nationale de Recherches Scientifique, relates Gurdjieff's teaching to the work of the quantum pioneer Max Planck. Planck expressed this as a universal constant, the Planck Constant, and in finding a constant he also found an "inconstant," that is, a repeating discontinuity in the overall structure of energy. Gurdjieff, in *Beelzebub's Tales*, called this the "obligatory-gap-aspects-of-the-unbroken-flowing-of-one-whole." As Nicolescu puts it,★ "it is discontinuity which permits unity to exist in diversity and diversity in unity." Gurdjieff perceived in the vibratory spectra a cosmic ladder of seven-leveled octaves, each expressing a discontinuity of vibrations that gives shape to the Ray of Creation and, by extension, to our spiritual efforts. It is not known for sure whether Gurdjieff knew much about Planck— Gurdjieff seems to have found the same truth in different sources.

> *I wonder what I'd see*
> *if I could walk away from me?*
> —Lou Reed

★"Gurdjieff's Philosophy of Nature" by Basarab Nicolescu. In *Gurdjieff: Essays and Reflections on the Man and His Teaching.*

INDEX

Note: Italic numbers indicate illustrations.

Absolute, 150, 152, 157–58, 160,
    289–90
    reunion with, 16
    See also God
Abyss, symbolism of, 92
Action, 116–17, 160–61
Affirming, holy, 154, 242–43
Age, and time, 22
Air, 99, 103
Aisors, 72
*All and Everything, First Series. See
    Beelzebub's Tales to His Grandson,*
    Gurdjieff
Allegory, *Beelzebub's Tales* as, 232, 234,
    235, 237–40
America, visits to, 224–25, 254–57, 263
American Beauty (film), 37
Ancients, secret knowledge of, 50–51
Anderson, Margaret, 222, 225, 257
    The Unknowable Gurdjieff, 254
Animal sacrifice, Gurdjieff and, 76
Ani ruins, discovery of texts, 71–72
Antediluvian civilization, 71–72
Aphorisms, 222–23
Art, 36–39
Artillery-range duel, 54–56
Ashokhs (reciters of verse), 45, 49–50
Astrology, 79–80

Attention, 129–30, 154, 168, 173, 178
    divided, 26–28, 128, 131
Augustine, Saint, 17
"Automatic pilot" state, 21–22
Automatic responses, 5, 22–24, 34, 79,
    128, 188–89, 209–10, 218
Automobile accidents, 226–28, 264
Awakening, 2, 12–14, 29, 34, 35, 169
Awareness, 244

Babylon, 76
Bahauddin (Naqshbandi Sufi teacher),
    107
Balance, universal, 142
Ball, Alan, *American Beauty*, 37
Bar Daisan, 107
Bathhouse, at Institute, 216
Beckett, Samuel, 36
Beelzebub, 230–32
Beelzebub's Tales to His Grandson, Gurdjieff,
    58, 59, 76, 81, 85, 87, 148, 192,
    193, 229–50, 268, 277
Behavior, 30–31, 61
    See also Automatic responses
Being, 31, 117–18, 130, 136–38, 179,
    188
    creation of, 93, 103, 129, 133, 134, 135
    of Gurdjieff, 174
Being-obligolnian strivings, 245–47

Bennett, John Godolphin, 81, 98, 107, 201, 215–16, 231, 262
   Witness, 42–43
Bible, Old Testament, 15, 50–51
Bodies, 119–20, 130, 245
Body of light, Buddhist idea, 57
Bogachesky (Evlissi, tutor), 58–59, 78
Bogga-Eddin (dervish), 88, 107
Bolm, Adolph, 224
Borsh (Dean of Kars cathedral), 51–53, 59
Britain, Gurdjieff in, 202–203
Brook, Peter, 5, 7, 49–50
Buddha, 16–17, 19–20, 56, 233
Buddhism, 85, 93
Buffers, 28, 133–34, 236
Bullet wounds, 83–84, 99–100, 104, 105–106

Catastrophe, Beckett, 36
Celibacy, monastic, 146
Centers of self. *See* Three-centered beings
Charlatanism, 162
Chief feature, 135–36
Childhood of Gurdjieff, 45–46, 49–53
Children, education of, 244
Christian churches, 92–93
Christianity, 17, 58–59
   as Gurdjieff's source, 107
Civilization, 140
Clairvoyants, 59–60, 162
Collectedness of the self, 188
Conge, Michel, 80, 209–10, 211, 261
   A Study of the Ideas of G. I. Gurdjieff, 152–53
Conscience, 58, 73, 132, 135, 244–45
Conscious love, 251
Consciousness, 12–14, 19–29, 31, 127, 275
   collected, 101
   conscience and, 58
   evolution of, 143
   objective, 26–27, 161
Conscious suffering. *See* Suffering, intentional
Contradictions, 53–54, 59–60, 65, 81, 133
Control of life, lack of, 15
Corpus Hermeticum, 17, 121–22, 153
Cosmic laws, 228

Law of Seven, 91, 157–59, 162, 164–65
Law of Three, 148–52, 154, 156, 164, 241–42
Ray of Creation, 150–53, 156–58, 236, 240, 289–91
Cosmos, 86, 102
   and evolution, 142
Crazy Wisdom: The Life and Legend of Gurdjieff, Taylor, 6
Creation, process of, 241–42
Creation myth, *Beelzebub's Tales*, 235–37
Cronenberg, David, *eXistenZ*, 38
Crowe, Cameron, *Vanilla Sky*, 38
Crowley, Aleister, 252
Current, creative, 151–54

Daddy Gurdjieff: A Few Unedited Memories, de Val, 211
Dance, 185
   Dalcroze system, 197–98
   Sarmoungian, 90–91
   See also Gurdjieff Movements
Dark City (film), 38
Daumal, René, 5, 185–86, 255
Death, 96–97
   defeat of, 125
   existence after, 12, 56–58, 271
Decision-making, self and, 33–34
Denying, holy, 154, 242–43
Dervishes, 70, 84–88, 98
   Gurdjieff disguised as, 97
Desert spring epiphany, 99–103
Desire, and human suffering, 16–17
Detachment, balanced, 96
Devil, need for, 102
Dhammapada, 19–20, 56
Dinners, ritualistic, 259, 262–64
Disappointment, 271
Disguises, 74, 76, 88, 97, 190
Divided attention, 26–28, 128, 131
Doing, 116–17, 126, 206
Dolmens, 195
Dordjieff, Aghwan, 88, 98–99
Dreams, 36
Drugs, Gurdjieff and, 6
Duel between teenage rivals, 54–55
Dukes, Paul, 109

Earth, life on, 69–70, 141
Education system, Gurdjieff's views, 63
Efforts, human, 159–61
Egypt, 76
  ancient map, 75
Ekim Bey, 70–71
Emotional center, 35, 52, 69, 125–26,
  134, 144, 145, 146–47, 209
  higher, 172
Emptiness, 93, 122–23
Energy, 35, 80, 133–34, 157–58, 241
  cosmic, 141, 142, 287–88
  in Gurdjieff's teaching, 143
  transfer of, 261, 289–90
Enlightenment, 26–27
Enneagram, 107, 162–65, 163
Esoteric ideas, 7–8, 87
  teachers of, 5
Essence, 49, 120–23, 144, 192
Essene Brotherhood, 59
Essentuki, Gurdjieff in, 176–78, 182–83
Eternity, 127
Ethniki Hetairia, 83
Evlissi (Bogachevsky), 58–59, 78
Evolution, spiritual, 141–44, 147–48, 158,
  272–73
eXistenZ, Cronenberg, 38
Expeditions, 76, 83, 84–86, 211–13, 266
  Gobi Desert, 93–98
  to "Persia," 178–81
  to Sarmoung monastery, 88–93
Experiments, 62, 78, 122–23, 219–20
External considering, 121, 133, 168, 260

Faith, 97, 192
Fakir, way of, 125
Family of Gurdjieff, 44–51, 98, 217
  children, 98, 218
  deaths in, 250, 258
  grandmother, advice from, 46–47
  mother, 44, 250
  in Russian Revolution, 189–90
  wife, 108–109, 173, 251
Fasting, 168
Fear, 56, 145
Fight Club (film), 37–38
Films, 36, 37–39
Fincher, David, Fight Club, 37–38

Finland, miraculous events, 168–71
"First Initiation," de Salzmann, 67
Fontainebleau-Avon. See Gurdjieff
  Institute
Food, 28–29, 43–44, 95, 99, 164
Fourth Dimension, idea of, 112
Fourth state, 27
Fourth way, 4, 126–29, 148, 229
France, Gurdjieff in, 203
Free association, 128
Freedom, 28
Friction, 103, 132, 134, 254–55
"From Hermes Trismegistus to Asclepius:
  Definitions," 119–20
Fund-raising, 64, 72–74, 108, 229, 253
Fusion, 135

Gautama. See Buddha
Georgian Theological Seminary, 67–68
Germany, Gurdjieff in, 201–202
Gilgamesh, 50–51
Giorgiades, Anna Ivanovna (sister), 44
Giorgiades, Dmitri (brother), 44, 258
Giorgiades, Ioannas (father of Gurdjieff),
  44–52, 62–63, 67, 189
  and life after death, 57–58
Giorgiades, Sophie Ivanovna (sister), 44
Giovanni (former priest), 97–98
Glimpses of Truth, Gurdjieff, 109, 115
Gnosticism, 15–16, 26, 237
Gobi Desert expedition, 93–96
God, 15–18, 31–32, 53–54, 63, 101–102,
  117, 240, 242
  Gurdjieff's views
  Ray of Creation, 289–90
  See also Absolute
Gordon, Elizabeth, 257
Gospel of Thomas (Gnostic), 16, 26, 29,
  120
Grades of man, 69
Groundhog Day (movie), 6
Growth, 19
  spiritual, 153, 154
Gurdjieff, Georgei Ivanovich, 2–9, 19,
  41–59, 68–109, 264–68
  automobile accidents, 226–28, 264
  behavior of, 217–18, 221–22
  children of, 98, 218

Gurdjieff, Georgei Ivanovich (*continued*)
and Ouspensky, 109, 113–23, 167–71, 264
personal crisis, 252–56
and Russian Revolution, 189–97, 200
search for truth, 18, 61–65, 70–109
teaching methods, 4–5, 43, 123–25, 130–38, 155–57, 168–71, 176–89, 207–13, 218–21
World War II, 258–60
writings of, 277–78
Beelzebub's Tales to His Grandson, 58, 59, 76, 81, 85, 87, 192, 193, 229–50, 268, 277
Life Is Real Only Then, When "I Am," 81, 99–102, 104, 234
Meetings with Remarkable Men, 7, 41, 43, 44, 45–49, 54–57, 62, 71–72, 74, 87, 94, 106, 254
Gurdjieff: Anatomy of Myth, Moore, 44–45, 80–81
Gurdjieff Foundation, 7, 91
Gurdjieff Institute, 155, 182, 198–99, 201, 203, 205–17, 228–29, 252, 256
finances of, 213, 229, 253–54
Study House, 222–23
Gurdjieff Movements, 91, 184–88, 198, 207, 208, 245, 265, 266, 269–70
New York demonstration, 224
Gurdjieff Work, 8, 70, 77, 121, 124–25, 129–30, 155–57, 180, 271, 273–74
in America, 262
Jeanne de Salzmann and, 268–70
Orage and, 207
Gymnastics, sacred, 184–88, 198
See also Gurdjieff Movements

Habit, struggle with, 177
Hanbledzoin, 101, 220
Hartmann, Olga de, 174–75, 178, 179, 180, 183, 202, 206, 225–26, 230, 254
Our Life with Mr. Gurdjieff, 113
and Russian Revolution, 191–95, 197
Hartmann, Thomas de, 5, 44, 114, 174–75, 179, 181–84, 196, 198, 201, 208–209, 210, 225, 250–51, 254, 267

Our Life with Mr. Gurdjieff, 113
and Russian Revolution, 191–94, 197
Hasnamusses, 237
Heap, Jane, 205, 211, 226, 257
Hermetica, 17
Hesychasm, 53
Higher centers, 146–47
Hinton, C. H., 112
Hinzenburg, Olgivanna, 177–78, 256–57
History, 30
Holiday celebrations at le Prieure, 217
Holy Trinity, 149
Hope, 192, 275
Hulme, Kathryn, 5, 205, 255–56, 257, 260
Undiscovered Country, 42
Humanity, 1–2, 36–39, 63, 141–42, 272–75
as food for the moon, 287–88
Humanization, 137
Humor, Gurdjieff and, 43
Hurrying way, 126–29
Hvareno (kingliness), 174
Hypnotism, 219–20
Hysteria, 60–61

Ialdabaoth, 15–16
Ideas, 7–8, 241
Identification, 28, 56, 133, 161, 208
Immortality, 119, 120, 126, 158
Impressions, 28–29, 87–88, 131
Incompleteness, sense of, 14–15, 21–22
India, travels in, 83, 98
Individuality, 34, 48–49, 118, 148
Influences, 79–80, 238, 289–90
Inherency, 101–102
Inner considering, 121
Inner truth, desire for, 79
Inner work, 27, 127–28, 134, 146, 207–208
Inner world, aspects of, 144–47
In Search of the Miraculous: Fragments of an Unknown Teaching, Ouspensky, 2–3, 4, 25, 26, 30, 41, 112, 113, 140, 162, 216, 264
Insight, 171–72
Instinctive function, 145–46
Instinctive-moving center, 35, 52, 125

Institute for the Harmonious
  Development of Man. *See*
  Gurdjieff Institute
Institutions, spiritual, 92–93
Intellectual center, 35, 52, 68–69, 126,
  136, 144–47, 181, 187
Intelligence:
  divine, and laws, 87
  physical, 145
Intention, 70, 93
Intolerance, 145
Involution, 149
Islam, 93
Ismatun brotherhood, search for, 83

Jacques-Dalcroze, Emile, 197–98, 201
James, William, 24
Jesus Christ, 17, 59, 161, 188, 233, 242
Job (Old Testament), 15
Judeo-Christian mythology, 237
Jung, Carl, 12

Karma, 116–17
Karnak, 232
Karpenko (Russian youth), 54–55, 71, 94
Khaida Yoga, 126–29, 188–89
Knowledge, 50–51, 136–38
Krishnamurti, 44
Kundabuffer organ, 236

Ladies of the Rope, Patterson, 42, 107, 219,
  257
Language of *Beelzebub's Tales*, 233–35, 250
Lascaux cave expedition, 266
Law of Accident, 228
Law of Seven, 91, 157–59, 162, 164–65
Law of Three, 148–53, 154, 156, 164,
  241–42
Laws, 152
  cosmic, 86–87
Leblanc, Georgette, 257
Legominisms, 62, 229–30, 244
Lewis, C. S., 127
  Screwtape Letters, 121
Lies, recognition of, 173
Life, 29, 288
  after death, questions of, 56–58
  meaning in, 2, 14–15, 54, 245

Life Is Real Only Then, When "I Am,"
  Gurdjieff, 81, 99–102, 104, 220,
  234
Linklater, Richard, *Waking Life*, 39
Love, 55, 192, 251, 261
Lubovedsky, Yuri, Prince, 76–77, 79, 90,
  91, 93
Lynch, David, *Mulholland Drive*, 38

Machines, 2
  man as, 29–35, 61, 86, 116, 140
Magnetic center, 79
Maimonides, Moses, 32, 57
Malamatis, 221
Man, 29–35, 61, 69, 86, 116, 140
Mansfield, Katherine, 5, 109, 205, 213–14
March, Louise, 250
Mardiross, Eoung-Ashokh, 59
Mark, Saint, 111
"The Material Question," 62, 64
The Matrix (film), 37
Meetings with Remarkable Men, Gurdjieff, 7,
  41, 43, 44, 45–49, 54–57, 62,
  71–72, 74, 87, 94, 106, 254
Meetings with Remarkable Men (film), 91
Memories, 12, 146
Memories of Gurdjieff, Staveley, 42, 221, 265
Mental exercises, 168
Mercourov, Sergei, 108
Merston, Ethel, 212–13
Mesmerism, 101
Mether, Thomas, 107
Miller, Henry, 5, 6, 218
Mind, powers of, 102–103
Miracles, 60, 111–38, 158, 167–68
Money, Gurdjieff and, 64, 217
Monks, way of, 125–26
Moon, food for, 287–88
Moore, James, 105, 221, 252, 257, 263
  Gurdjieff: Anatomy of Myth, 44–45,
  80–81
Morality, 58–59, 245–47
Moses (Biblical), 233
Moses of Cordova, 32
Mottl, Felix, 175
Mount Analogue, Daumal, 255
Mouravieff, Boris, 107, 112, 228
Movements. *See* Gurdjieff Movements

Moving-instinctive center, 144, 145, 181
  Movements and, 187
Mulholland Drive (film), 38
Music, 78, 251
My Journey with a Mystic, Peters, 6, 109, 260–61
Mysticism, 17, 53

Naqshbandi Sufis, 107
Narrow-mindedness, 145
Nature, humanity and, 141–42
Needleman, Jacob, 134
  Time and the Soul, 2, 142
Neologisms, 233–34, 239
New Model of the Universe, Ouspensky, 112
New York City, Gurdjieff in, 62, 224
Niccol, Andrew, *Simone*, 39
Nicholas II, Tsar, 47, 81, 98, 175–76
Nicolescu, Basarab, 290–91
Nicoll, Maurice, 202
Nietzsche, Friedrich Wilhelm, 112
Nonviolence, 172
Nothingness, 147
Nott, C. Stanley, 98, 215, 225

Objectivity, 56
Obstacles, inevitability of, 96
Octaves, law of, 157–58, 290–91
Opening, Segal, 157
Orage, Alfred R., 5, 82–83, 92, 202–203, 205, 207, 213, 224, 229, 245, 253–54, 255, 256
  and *Beelzebub's Tales*, 230, 234, 238–41, 247, 250
Orage, Jessie, 253–54
Ostrovsky, Julia (wife of Gurdjieff), 108–109, 173, 251
Our Life with Mr. Gurdjieff, de Hartmanns, 113, 175
Ouspensky, Piotr Demianovich, 4, 5, 8, 20, 65, 107, 111–13, 149, 167–73, 195, 197, 202, 213–16, 261–62
  and Gurdjieff, 109, 112, 113–23, 148, 190, 200, 228
  In Search of the Miraculous, 2–3, 4, 25, 26, 30, 41, 81, 162, 216

The Psychology of Man's Possible Evolution, 36
  Tertium Organum, 109
  and war, 139–40
Ouspensky, Madame, 215, 253, 262, 264

Patterson, W. P., *Ladies of the Rope*, 42, 107, 219, 257
Paul, Saint, 15
Peace, social reform and, 82
Pentland, John, Lord, 147, 215, 262
Pentland, Lady, 125
Personality, 120–23, 145, 146
Peters, Fritz, 211–12, 218–19, 227, 255, 260–61
  My Journey with a Mystic, 6, 109
Peters, Tom, 212
Petrov (student of Gurdjieff), 194, 197
Philokalia, 107
Physical center, 68–69
Planck, Max, 291
Planetary influences, 79–80
Pogossian, Sarkis, 68–69, 71–72, 73–75
Pohl, Vladimir, 108
Politics, Gurdjieff and, 80–83
Prayer of the mind, 168
Predetermination, 116–17
Present moment, 127
Priesthood, Borsh and, 52
Prieure, 203, 205–17, 222, 227, 229
  See also Gurdjieff Institute
Problem-solving, Gurdjieff and, 45
Progress, 2, 139–40
Proyas, Alex, *Dark City*, 38
Psychic phenomena, 224
The Psychology of Man's Possible Evolution, Ouspensky, 36, 261
Psychotherapy, 19
Pythagoras, 158

Quantum physics, octaves and, 290–91
Questions, 61–65, 70

Rachmilievitch, 255
Radko-Dmitriev (Russian general), 192
Ram Das, 5, 127

Ray of Creation, 150–53, 156, 157–58, 236, 240, 289–91
Reactions, 30, 32–33, 61, 145, 168–69
Real I, 11, 31, 104, 145, 147
Reason, 31, 56, 147
Reconciling, holy, 149–50
Reed, Lou, 291
Reincarnation, 209
Religions, 53–54, 63, 85–86, 233, 242–43, 274–75
Renunciation, 126
Repudiation, 242–43
Responsibility, 31
Reynard, Paul, 125
Role-playing, 4–5, 113–14, 180, 188–89
The Rope, 257
Russian Revolution, 174–76, 189–97, 200

Sacred Dance (film), 269
Sacred dances, 90–91, 208
See also Gurdjieff Movements
Sacrifice, 104, 143, 183–84
Salzmann, Alexander de, 5, 197–99, 214, 216, 222, 253, 256
Salzmann, Jeanne de, 7, 125, 186–87, 197–99, 208, 227, 253, 258, 260, 265, 268–70
"First Initiation," 67
Salzmann, Michel de, 8, 268–69
Sanaine monastery, 68
Sari-Ogli, Dr. (Seeker of Truth), 94
Sarmoung Brotherhood, 71–72, 88–93
The Scarlet Flower, de Hartmann, 175
Schools, spiritual, 65, 92
Schumacher, Olga Arkadievna de, 174–75
See also Hartmann, Olga de
Science, 62, 69, 86–87
Screwtape Letters, Lewis, 121
Second Series, Gurdjieff. See Meetings with Remarkable Men
Secret of the Golden Flower, 185
Seekers of Truth, 48, 65, 68, 77, 83, 84
expeditions, 88–98
Segal, William, 172
Opening, 157
Self, 32–33, 69, 188

mastery of, 100–101
Self-consciousness, 25–26
See also Self-remembering
Self-destructive people, 14–15
Self-knowledge, 19, 87–88, 117
Self-observation, 27, 28, 32–33, 35, 87, 128, 131, 133, 143–44, 154, 181, 208, 254
Self-perfection, 246
Self-reasoning, 100–101
Self-remembering, 25–26, 102, 104, 127–29, 173, 245, 274
Self-study, 147
Self-transformation, 28
Seton, Marie, 216
Sex function, 145
Shandarovsky (student), 191
Shocks, 101, 103, 158, 159–61, 188
Silence, 172–73
Simone (film), 39
Sincerity, 9, 173
Skridlov (professor), 76, 93, 97
Sleep, 20–29, 34–36, 116, 120, 171–72
Social reform, Gurdjieff and, 82
Solano, Solita, 42, 219–20, 242, 257, 258, 267
Soloviev (Seeker of Truth), 77, 88–90
death of, 94, 96
Sophia (feminine principle), 15–16
Soul, 4, 17, 28–29, 57–58, 120, 125
Space travel systems, 237–38
Spinoza, Baruch, 31–32, 57
Spiral patterns, 150
Spiritual elite, 112
Spiritual master, Gurdjieff as, 217–18
Spiritual seeking, 64–65
Spiritual self, 69
Spiritual teachers, 18–19, 73, 85, 87
Spiritual ways, 125–29
Spy, Gurdjieff as, 81, 82, 88
Staveley, A. L., 7, 265
Memories of Gurdjieff, 42, 221
Stillness, 152–53
Stjoernval, Leonid, 109, 169, 182, 192, 258
"Stop!" exercise, 178
The Struggle of the Magicians (ballet), Gurdjieff, 109, 187, 199–200

Students:
  of fourth way, 128
  of Gurdjieff, 5, 108, 113–25, 168–69,
    172–74, 176–82, 207, 259–60
    Russian Revolution and, 189–97
    The Rope, 257
  of Gurdjieff Work, 155–57
  of Ouspensky, 262
Study House, 222–23
A Study of the Ideas of G. I. Gurdjieff, Conge,
    152–53
Suffering, 16–17, 124, 131
  intentional (conscious), 124, 132, 135,
    168, 177–79, 183–84, 232, 242,
    244, 246, 255, 264
Superefforts, 180, 188, 210
Supernormal states, 101–103
Symbolism, 97, 162–65
  in Beelzebub's Tales, 232
  of desert spring epiphany, 103
  of Gobi Desert expedition, 95–96
  of Sarmoung monastery tale, 92
Synthesis, Gurdjieff's teaching as,
    106–108

Taylor, John Maxwell, Crazy Wisdom: The
    Life and Legend of Gurdjieff, 6

Teachings:
  of Gurdjieff, 4–8, 16, 19–29, 271–73
    source of, 106–109
    war years, 259
    writing of, 230
  of Ouspensky, 215–16
Telepathy, 169–71, 206
Terrorism, 137–38
Tertium Organum, Ouspensky, 109, 112,
    115, 202
Texts, Ani ruins discovery, 71–72
Theater, 36
Third Force, 149–50
Third Series. See Life Is Real Only Then,
    When "I Am," Gurdjieff
Thought, instruments of, 112
Three-centered beings, 35, 52, 69, 144,
    232, 239
Tibet, Gurdjieff in, 98–106
Time, relationship to, 22

Time and the Soul, Needleman, 2, 142
Toomer, Jean, 5, 205, 225
Toward Awakening: An Approach to
    the Teaching Left by Gurdjieff,
    Vaysse, 11
Transfiguration of Gurdjieff, 174
Transmutation, 120, 132–33, 145–46
Transubstantiation, 245
Triamazikamno. See Law of Three
The Truman Show (film), 38
Truth, 18, 29, 64–65, 273
Tuskegee syphilis experiments, 137

Understanding, 1, 18–19, 97, 138, 147
Undiscovered Country: The Search for
    Gurdjieff, Hulme, 42, 255
Unity, 20, 31, 147–48
"The Universal Traveling Workshop," 64
The Unknowable Gurdjieff, Anderson,
    254

Val, Nicolas de, 218, 234
  Daddy Gurdjieff: A Few Unedited
    Memories, 145, 211
Vanilla Sky (film), 38
Vanity, shattering of, 183–84
Vaysse, Jean, Toward Awakening: An
    Approach to the Teaching Left by
    Gurdjieff, 11
Vibrational influences, 80
Views from the Real World, Gurdjieff, 187
Vitvitskaia, 76–79

Waking Life (film), 39
Walker, Kenneth, 215
War, 35, 45, 79, 105–106, 139–40
Ways, spiritual, 4, 125–29, 143, 274–75
Welch, Louise, 253
Welch, William, 267
  What Happened in Between, 262
Will, 118–19, 125, 134, 188, 210, 264
  divine, 150, 152, 240, 290
  evolution of, 143
Wilson, Robert Anton, 6
Witness, Bennett, 42–43, 201
Wolfe, Edwin, 104
Women, Gurdjieff and, 218, 254, 257
  Vitvitskaia, 76–79

Work:
    physical, 155–57, 176, 178, 207–10
    on self, 77
    See also Gurdjieff Work
World Brotherhood monastery, 97–98
World War I, 139–40
World War II, 258–60
Wounds, 83–84, 99–100, 104, 105–106
Wright, Frank Lloyd, 5, 256–57

Yelov, Abram, 68–69, 71
Yevlampios (Orthodox teacher), 68
Yezidi people, 60–61
Yogic traditions, 84–85, 126
Younghusband, F. E., 104–105

Zakharoff, Andrei, 175, 177, 178, 181,
    190, 197
Zen schools, 273